# THE SKELETON CREW

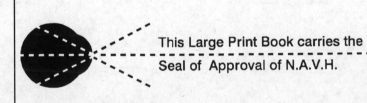

This Large Print Book carries the
Seal of Approval of N.A.V.H.

# THE SKELETON CREW

## HOW AMATEUR SLEUTHS ARE SOLVING AMERICA'S COLDEST CASES

## DEBORAH HALBER

**THORNDIKE PRESS**

*A part of Gale, Cengage Learning*

Farmington Hills, Mich • San Francisco • New York • Waterville, Maine
Meriden, Conn • Mason, Ohio • Chicago

GALE
CENGAGE Learning®

**LIBRARY OF CONGRESS CATALOGING-IN-PUBLICATION DATA**

Halber, Deborah.
  The skeleton crew : how amateur sleuths are solving America's coldest cases / by Deborah Halber.
    pages cm — (Thorndike press large print crime scene)
  Includes bibliographical references.
  ISBN 978-1-4104-7177-2 (hardback) — ISBN 1-4104-7177-2 (hardcover)
  1. Cold cases (Criminal investigation)—United States. 2. Criminal investigation—United States—Citizen participation 3. Large type books. I. Title.
  HV8073.H2175 2014
  363.250973—dc23
                                   2014019789

Published in 2014 by arrangement with Simon & Schuster, Inc.

Printed in Mexico
1 2 3 4 5 6 7 18 17 16 15 14

*To Bill, Brett, and Claudia,*
*with all my love forever*
*And to those brave enough*
*to seek what's missing*

# CONTENTS

# PROLOGUE:
## THE WELL DRILLER

I'm looking around a Cracker Barrel in Georgetown, Kentucky, wondering if I'll recognize him. The only photos I've seen of Wilbur J. Riddle were taken four decades ago, when he stumbled on the corpse wrapped in the carnival tent.

He was forty years old then; with his tousled dark hair and strong jaw, he resembled Joaquin Phoenix with sideburns. Even in black-and-white, Riddle looked tanned, a shadow accentuating the taut plane of his cheek. His short-sleeved shirt unbuttoned jauntily at the neck, he stood slightly apart from three pasty, grim, steely men with buzz cuts, dark suits, and narrow ties. They seemed preoccupied, dealing with a body where a body had no right to be.

Throwing the photographer a sidelong glance and a faint smirk, Riddle alone seemed cocksure and unfazed. In time, he would end up just as invested as the Scott

County sheriff and state police, if not more so. He would become the father of sixteen and grandfather of forty and would still be escorting people out to the shoulder of Route 25 — X marks the spot — where he found her. Somebody might have been tempted to charge admission.

He's thought about asking the state of Kentucky to put up a marker along the guardrail: the Tent Girl memorial plaque. She's a local legend. Parents invoke her — an unidentified murder victim whose face is carved onto her gravestone — as the fear factor that has hurried two generations of children to bed on time.

But she's more than that.

Tent Girl drew me in. As I delved into the world of the missing and the unidentified, her story would transform the shopworn whodunit into something altogether different — the whowuzit, I'll call it — in which the identity of the victim, not the culprit, is the conundrum. Her story supplanted the tweedy private eye or world-weary gumshoe of my expectations with a quirky crew of armchair sleuths who frequented the Web's inner sanctums instead of smoke-filled cigar bars. Her story was rags to (relative) riches, triumph of the underdog, and revenge of the nerds all rolled into one. Tent Girl, by becoming separated from her name, also invoked a murky psychological morass of death and identity where — judging from my companions' faces whenever I brought it up — most people would rather not go, but that I felt perversely compelled to explore.

There are a dozen versions of the story of Wilbur Riddle stumbling upon Tent Girl. Some newspapers had him trip over the body instead of merely notice it. The victim's age was sixteen or twenty; she was five-one or five-eleven; she had a white towel draped over her shoulder or wrapped around her head or there was no towel at all; Riddle tore open the bag and looked at her before the police arrived or he stopped what he was doing as soon as the odor hit him. The pulp classic *Master Detective* magazine told Riddle's story, calling him "Bart Cranston" throughout.

I go to Kentucky in 2011, forty-three years after Tent Girl's discovery, and scan the Cracker Barrel customers milling around the sock monkeys and dishtowels and handmade soap. The place smells like lilac and frying bacon.

Finally, I spot someone with a receding hairline and doughy cheeks whose mouth, I imagine, reflects that younger man's smirk. The man I have figured for Riddle nods at me; maybe he's been interviewed so many times he can easily pick out the writer in a room full of nostalgic kitsch. He's wearing a crisp blue windbreaker, button-down shirt, khakis cinched tight with a brown leather belt, and running shoes. He's trim, his gait stiff but quick.

We're seated at a booth and Riddle orders the country breakfast, scrambled eggs and a biscuit smothered in pasty white gravy. Coffee mugs are refilled and people go about their business apparently unaware of Riddle's fame, even though this particular Cracker Barrel is less than ten miles from where he found her. He peers at me over the plates and scowls when I mention a documentary being made about the case. "I wish they'd get it over with and let the girl go. They done enough," he says, and I think maybe he's sick and tired of the whole sordid affair. But then he starts to tell me what happened on May 17, 1968.

Riddle drilled water wells for a living. He arrived at a work site — a new Gulf station near a minuscule town called Sadieville — on a pleasantly sunny Friday morning to find a note plastered to the windshield of his Chevy truck. The towering scaffolding of Riddle's drill rig was stowed, its hydraulics, levers, spindles, and winches idle after Riddle drilled "way down pretty deep" the day before, as he recalls, without hitting much water. The note instructed Riddle to hold off on any more drilling until the boss arrived.

The planned gas station was situated at the off-ramp for exit 136 of the brand-new four-lane Interstate 75 running from Kentucky's southern border to its northernmost tip. The interstate would link the county to one of the busiest highways in America, supplanting nearby US 25 as the major thoroughfare heading east to Cincinnati and west to Georgetown, the county seat, with its ornate General Grant–style courthouse. US 25, two narrow lanes that still meander past limestone ledges and hug a tributary of Eagle Creek in Sadieville, spans a literal shift, between Kentucky and Ohio, and a figurative shift, from the South to north of the Mason-Dixon Line.

Around a month before Riddle showed up for work that day in May, four hundred miles away in Memphis, James Earl Ray had gunned down Dr. Martin Luther King Jr. as King stood on a balcony of the Lorraine Motel. In the days and weeks following the assassination, fires and riots erupted in more than a hundred cities, killing forty and injuring thousands. A light-infantry brigade from Fort Benning, Georgia, was called out to Baltimore the day after the shooting to help quell looting mobs. Among the army recruits on high alert at the base was slight, dark-haired nineteen-year-old James William "Billy" Matthews, whose son would one day compete with Riddle over Tent Girl like knights jousting over a maiden.

In Scott County, the bucolic countryside was dotted with sleekly muscled Kentucky Derby contenders munching unnaturally green turf behind fences so white they hurt your eyes. The creatures' placidly whisking tails could lull you into believing that most bad news originated very far away.

Riddle, Kentucky born and bred, inherited his bad-boy looks and blue-collar profession from his father, who could find water during even the driest stretch of summer, when local streams were nothing more than dusty furrows. Riddle's father taught him the secrets of the divining rod. You held on to a slender, pale switch from a beech tree, and when you went over a vein, the tip — the base of a letter $Y$ — dipped straight down toward the earth as if something powerful had grabbed hold of the other end.

Riddle also learned where to collect jugs of pure clear spring water that bubbled up from the ground year-round. In 1789, one such spring had provided the water for a Baptist minister's new concoction called Kentucky bourbon whiskey. It was this fabled system of underground springs that Riddle intended to tap at the construction site.

The note on Riddle's rig bought him some free time. As he drove up that morning, he had spotted linemen working on utility poles around a quarter mile from where the gas station was being built. He left his red Ford pickup — his shop truck that rattled with tools — parked beside the rig and ambled a few hundred yards toward Route 25.

At the intersection with Porter Road, workmen were stringing cable. Even tiny Sadieville, consisting of a train station and not much else, was getting connected to the modern world. Maybe, Riddle thought, he could score some of those old hunks of glass his buddy was so fond of. First made in the 1850s for telegraph lines, by the 1960s glass insulators were outmoded, regularly discarded from utility poles and snapped up by collectors. Roughly the size of a diner sugar dispenser, mushroom-shaped or with protrusions like Mickey Mouse ears, they came in brilliant blues, greens, and reds, and collectors had rude and fanciful names — snotties, globbies, comets, boulders, hockers, fizzies — for the objects and air bubbles frozen inside the glass.

The mercury was edging up, portending a glorious spring day. Riddle wore his standard work uniform, a short-sleeved, greenish-gray collared work shirt, chinos, and a zippered jacket. After collecting his shop truck to cover more ground and searching pole to pole along the creek, he was juggling an armful of insulators when he spotted a bundle tucked partly under a big rock next to a dead redbud tree.

Something lumpy was wrapped up in a dark green tarp, the ends secured with rope tied in square knots threaded through round brass eyelets, on the creek side of a sagging waist-high fence around twenty paces from the roadway. The fence, strung with a single strand of barbed wire, skirted the edge of the gravel pull-off where Riddle had left his truck.

The hot, muggy spring had spawned weeds and wildflowers that gave off an acrid aroma, and the air was abuzz with all manner of flying and crawling insects — woodland ground beetles; gawky, long-legged as-

16

sassin bugs; iridescent blue cuckoo wasps — and a dozen kinds of flies. Something about the shape of the bundle struck Riddle. He approached the dark green bundle, put down the hunks of glass on the rock slab, and looked more closely. It was around four feet long, lumpy, wrinkled, and V-shaped, as wide around as a small tree trunk. Later, some would surmise that the bag had been first set down on the rock and then hoisted over the fence, a snag on the barbed wire leaving a slit in the fabric.

Riddle saw something inside. An animal of some kind? He nudged it with his foot, then tugged on a corner of the tarp. It teetered on the edge of the embankment and then rolled around thirty feet into a gully, and he followed it. He stepped on the tent. Something inside felt hard through the sole of his work shoe. Then he noticed a slit, maybe a foot long. A stench wafted through the torn fabric. The odor was overwhelmingly bad, knock-back-your-head bad, like fishing bait left too long in Tupperware.

The smell helped Riddle guess the worst; in any case he was in it now, too late to continue on his way back to his truck and prepare his drill rig as though it was just another day on the job. He was alone at the

17

bottom of a steep embankment, trapped on one side by a creek too wide to pick his way across, with only birds and bugs for company. Had he called out, no one would have heard him.

As the bundle rolled, the tarp had come away. He took a step closer.

Riddle didn't want to admit it, but the odor and the hairless, blotchy, parched veneer he could see inside the tarp didn't leave much room for doubt. It looked, he told me over biscuits and gravy, "like a body in there."

For a few minutes that must have felt longer, Riddle stood next to the bundle considering his predicament. A thousand flies flitted about. Unseen by Riddle, the squirming larvae of thousands more were at work within the bag at his feet. It was quiet. The utility workers were gone. No cars passed on Route 25. He stood down where she was for a while, thinking what to do. "If I was to leave and someone was to come in there and see a body in there, they might have thought I had put it there," he reasoned.

He wasn't a criminal but his past wasn't lily-white. He had seven kids and a third, young wife at home. Riddle was a ladies' man and a maverick — defiant, as some put it — and there were those who might wish him ill. He had no idea who was dead at his feet. If he raised the alarm, would he change from Wilbur Riddle, onetime bartender, known rogue, and womanizer, into Wilbur Riddle, Scott County good citizen, or Wilbur Riddle, murder suspect? He had to think this thing through.

Finally, abandoning the glass insulators on the flat stone, Riddle scrambled up the embankment to the pull-off where he'd left his shop truck, climbed behind the wheel, and screeched off for Sadieville's nearest operating filling station, a Chevron. He slid coins into a pay phone.

"Bobby, this is Wilbur. Wilbur Riddle," he said when the Scott County sheriff picked up. "I think I found a dead body."

Cruising in my rented Toyota along Route 25, Riddle and I retrace the path the sheriff, deputy sheriff, and coroner took from the Georgetown courthouse that day.

Over in the passenger seat, Riddle seems complacent. He's pushing eighty-five, yet despite his many missing teeth making him sound like he's got a mouthful of marshmallows, his remaining hair is slicked back neatly and his shirt is ironed. The whiff of cologne drifting toward me reminds me of

Riddle's reputation as a ladies' man. I sense him eyeing me. "You from Ohio?" he asks after a bit. "Boston," I remind him.

Riddle points out houses for which he dug the wells, the rock quarry where his cousin was killed in a car wreck, a sign for a place called Stamping Grounds, named for the buffalo that used to roam Kentucky. Riddle clearly likes the spotlight, relishes acting as tour guide. "I'll tell you a good story, the story of my life," he offers. "It'd really be something. It'd be worth listening to."

We pass a church. It's Sunday and Riddle gazes out at the packed parking lot. "That church is the kind of church I belong to. Church of Christ," he informs me. "I read the Bible every day. I believe in church. I really believe in it. And a Christian life's not a bad life. One of the best lives you can live."

I say something noncommittal and keep my eyes on the road. But Riddle isn't ready to drop the subject. "What church you belong to?"

"I don't go to church," I tell him. Riddle suddenly sits up a bit straighter in his seat. "You never been baptized?"

"No." I think uneasily about the signs I had spotted on the highway: JESUS IS COMING. ARE YOU READY? and HELL IS REAL. An enormous billboard challenges in three-foot-high letters: IF YOU DIED TODAY, WHERE WOULD YOU SPEND ETERNITY? The nearby Creation Museum, with its display of animatronic dinosaurs playing with children in the Garden of Eden, comes to mind.

"That's something I believe in," Riddle continues. "What the Bible is trying to say is, you must repent and be baptized to enter into heaven. And I don't know you very well, but I know that you don't want to go to hell."

There's something we can agree on. "I don't want to go to hell," I say cheerfully, and luckily we have to confer on which direction to turn at the next traffic light.

We arrive at the Gulf station, now an empty lot with a faded remnant of the old orange sign, where he had shown up for work that day. A minute later he directs me to pull over near a guardrail that wasn't there in 1968. The shoulder is a weedy patch of grass. The fact that the former clearing was once the first pull-off available to northbound drivers exiting the highway at the Sadieville interchange was not lost on investigators.

Riddle climbs out of the Toyota and lumbers through the underbrush. He squints toward the creek.

It's April, but it snowed last night. Hints of green poke through white patches on the brown leaves. I follow a few steps behind Riddle, who is zigzagging through the brush. "Here it is," he says, pointing to the flat rock where he first saw the bundle. He knows it's the right one because he's taken to leaving a rusted old knife blade on it for occasions like this one, when someone asks to be shown, once again, exactly where he found her.

That day in 1968, after reliving the morning's events for the state police and watching the body disappear into the ambulance, encased in something like a carnival tent (within days, *The Cincinnati Post* would dub her Tent Girl), Riddle sped twenty-five miles to the dilapidated farmhouse where he lived in Monterey, in Owen County. As he talked about it decades later, he seemed to have suspected that something life-changing had happened to him that day.

Two months later, in July 1968, Billy Matthews, the young Tennessean undergoing basic training at the United States Army Infantry Center at Fort Benning, was deployed to Vietnam. A year later he returned home with a Purple Heart, and he and his wife conceived a child. Tied, perhaps, to Bil-

22

ly's exposure to Agent Orange in the Vietnamese jungle, the infant they named James Todd Matthews was not robust. But unlike two of his siblings who would succumb to congenital defects within hours of birth, Todd, dark-haired and dark-eyed like his father, survived, and surgeons later patched up his damaged heart.

Todd wouldn't encounter Wilbur Riddle or Tent Girl until two decades after Riddle had stumbled on the body. The well driller was still dining out on the story, carrying a well-worn copy of *Master Detective* featuring Tent Girl as "the most baffling case in Kentucky's criminal history" and himself as the heroic "Bart Cranston." Todd — single-minded and sensitive, artistic and shy, a bit of an oddity among his teenaged Tennessee peers — started dating Riddle's daughter and, to the Kentuckian's consternation, ended up stealing away — to Wilbur's mind — seventeen-year-old Lori *and* Tent Girl.

By the time his son-in-law got hold of the case, I remind Riddle as we drive away from the roadside gully, the mystery of her identity was decades old — frosbitten, as cold cases go. Riddle doesn't seem to hear me.

"I found her," he insists stubbornly in the car, his watery eyes staring straight ahead at

23

the Kentucky landscape, his calloused right hand gripping the grab handle above the passenger door. "She'd probably still be laying there on that rock if it weren't for me."

# 1
# THE ULTIMATE
# IDENTITY CRISIS

Chances are good that you or someone you know has at one point stumbled over a dead body. There are shockingly large numbers of them out there. According to the National Institute of Justice, America is home to tens of thousands of unidentified human remains, with four thousand more turning up every year: intrepid adventurers or athletes who left their IDs at home; victims of accidents and mass disasters; suicides; undocumented immigrants; the homeless; runaway teenagers; victims of serial killers; and those who cast off a former identity, changed names, and left no forwarding address.

From the sheer number of unidentified individuals, you'd think that American roadways, bodies of water, vacant lots, and woodlands are littered with nameless bodies quietly decomposing, infested with maggots, swelling up like balloons, drying out like jerky, poked at and gnawed by animals. There are men and women, young and old, black, white, Asian — or, as a forensic anthropologist would classify the victims' skulls, in dated-sounding terms: Negroid, Caucasoid, Mongoloid. Some are discovered within hours or days; some are skeletons or a single bone by the time somebody happens upon them.

These anonymous dead become law enforcement's version of wards of the state — an onerous responsibility, a major pain in the ass. Unidentified corpses are like obtuse, financially strapped houseguests: they turn up uninvited, take up space reserved for more obliging visitors, require care and attention, and then when you're ready for them to move on, they don't have anywhere to go.

Like infants abandoned on doorsteps, their fates are determined largely by who finds them. One corpse might get a thorough going-over: measured and weighed; gender, race, and approximate age determined; hair and eye color, if hair or eyes remain, noted; scars, tattoos, and old injuries inventoried. Just over a state or county line, another set of remains might be butchered, misplaced, or rushed to the crematorium, sending potential clues literally up in smoke.

In the normal scheme of things, after a person dies, he or she is remembered, revered, commemorated. The lucky or the wealthy get a bridge or building named after them. But when bodies are divorced from their personal identities, the living are left in the lurch. The unidentified dead don't yield up any of the soothing coping rituals — dedications, obituaries, memorials, eulogies, reminiscences — we rely on in the wake of a death.

What's left are mournful monikers such as Tent Girl, Somerton Man, Princess Doe, Saltair Sally, the Boy in the Box, the Belle in the Well, the Lady Who Danced Herself to Death: celebrities of sorts in their hometowns, but generally unknown and unacknowledged elsewhere.

The stories of Tent Girl and other fabled, unidentified corpses such as the Lady of the Dunes, murdered in my home state of Massachusetts, reveal uncomfortable truths about our law enforcement and medicolegal systems. They also expose the transience of personal identity. Driver's license? Photo ID? Passport? It turns out we maintain our day-to-day identities superficially. We're easily separated from the paper and plastic that

27

proves we are who we say we are. Unlike pets and sharks, we're not microchipped — not yet, anyway — and even medical alert bracelets don't always include names. Despite the common belief that DNA is a tell-all human barcode, DNA is useless as an identification tool without a sample to compare it to.

If you've been unlucky enough to suffer the ultimate identity crisis, more permanent, unique identifiers — the tattoo of Cold Play lyrics on your left shoulder blade, the diamond drilled into your front tooth, the fillings in your molars — might match up with a notation on a missing-person report. The data — a picture of the tattoo, an estimated height and age, the postmortem photos, and usually the remains themselves — are stored away on the chance that a name will miraculously find its way into the system, or that new information will surface within weeks, months, years, or decades. But too often, it doesn't surface at all.

We don't like to think that public agencies would abandon cases that prove too challenging, but — confronted with more immediate concerns than a quietly decomposing body — they often do.

What would it be like, I wondered, when so much revolves around identity, to have none? The Latin root of identity, *identitas,* comes from idem — the same. We automatically sort our fellow beings into categories: like us or unlike us, same or different. Sociologists say this sorting is fundamental to our world: identity lets us know who's who and what's what. Our primitive selves survived by discerning friend from foe. Yet identity is fleeting. The "you" known to others can disappear, leaving behind a nameless body that people find perplexing, frustrating, pitiable . . . and, for me and many others, an irresistible mystery.

Thanks to famous criminal cases — O.J. Simpson, Laci Peterson, Anna Nicole Smith, Michael Jackson, and Caylee Anthony among them — the language of forensics and the notion that experts "read" clues from remains and skeletons has infiltrated our public consciousness. Powerful computers have given the art and science of facial reconstruction a boost. *CSI, NCIS, Dexter, The X-Files, Cold Case, Fringe,* and *Bones* have made the tools famous — and misleadingly effortless.

The real world of the unidentified is complicated and, until recently, almost entirely undocumented and unquantified. It wasn't until 2004 that the Department of Justice set out to tally exactly how many

29

unidentified bodies had been stowed in freezers and evidence rooms, cremated, or buried in potter's fields for the past century.

With a far-from-comprehensive response to this first-of-its-kind national census, the Justice Department's Bureau of Justice Statistics tallied more than thirteen thousand sets of unidentified remains. Because record keeping was so uneven — some coroners working on the questionnaire turned up long-forgotten skeletons stowed in Bankers Boxes in back rooms — the National Institute of Justice estimates the real figure is closer to forty thousand: the population of Wilkes-Barre, Pennsylvania; North Miami Beach, Florida; or San Gabriel, California.

In researching and writing this book, I found that many people are unaware of the extent of the problem. Even those who have heard figures tossed around, such as eighty thousand people reported missing in the United States on any given day, don't imagine that Jane and John Does make up a significant subset of that number. A longtime forensics specialist told me most people are flabbergasted when she cites the number of unidentified remains in America. In any other realm, so many neglected deaths would lead to a public outcry, she observed ruefully. Not so for the unidentified, although there's no shortage of justice waiting to be served on their behalf.

"I don't know how the police and the city morgue didn't realize that the body they had for 7 months in the refrigerator was my brother's body," wrote the sibling of thirty-two-year-old Andrea Zabini, a native of Italy who had been in the United States only ten months when he disappeared in North Miami in 2001. "Our angel Dafne," Alessandro Zabini addressed a letter in halting English to Daphne Owings of South Carolina, who noted similarities between Andrea's description and that of a John Doe who had been discovered dead in an open field frequented by the homeless. "You from far away did it . . . [Y]ou gave us the serenity, because now we can give him a grave and we'll have a stone, where we can cry [for] our relative."

Most relatives of the nameless dead don't get that closure. Around half of the unidentified die natural, accidental, or self-inflicted deaths. The rest have been murdered. (For a small number, the official cause is "undetermined.") If you watch detective shows, you know how law enforcement feels about a cold case homicide. When investigators don't even know the victim's name, the odds of finding — let alone convicting — the killer round to zero.

An unidentified corpse is the Blanche DuBois of the forensic world: completely dependent on the kindness of strangers like Daphne Owings, Todd Matthews in Tennessee, Ellen Leach in Mississippi, Betty Brown in North Carolina, and Bobby Lingoes in Massachusetts. The web sleuths labor to reunite the unidentified dead with their names, provide answers to families, and help law enforcement reopen long-dormant cold cases. This book is the story of the men and women whose macabre hobby of trolling Internet bulletin boards and gory law enforcement websites in an attempt to match names of the missing with the remains of the unidentified dead has propelled a remarkable shift in the number of cases that are solved, and in the relationship between the public and law enforcement.

As I met the web sleuths and delved into the world of missing persons, the unidentified, crowdsourcing, and cold cases, I found out what a crucial role a kind and curious stranger can play in bringing closure to families whose loved ones have disappeared.

In May 2010, I saw a photo in *The Boston Globe* of a woman with well-shaped eyebrows and a sensitive mouth. She had deep-set eyes and luxurious auburn hair swept back off her high forehead in a ponytail.

She looked familiar, like someone I might see running along the shoulder of my suburban street or waiting in line at Starbucks, but the colors in the picture struck me as garish and her expression eerily bland, as if she were posing for a Disneyesque mug shot. Then I realized what I was looking at wasn't a photograph at all.

It was a digitally constructed approximation of what a murder victim looked like before her face decomposed.

In 1974, the story said, a woman had been found dead on a beach in Provincetown, Massachusetts, her hands chopped off at the wrists, her skull bashed in. She was nude, lying on a thick beach blanket, a pair of Wrangler jeans neatly folded under her almost-severed head. Her toenails were painted a bubble-gum pink. She had been dead for days, maybe weeks. The local police chief called the murder horrific, brutal for any time and any place, but particularly shocking for Provincetown.

I knew Provincetown as an artsy community at the end of the stunning Cape Cod National Seashore, a great place to spend a summer weekend but an unlikely setting for the lurid, the sensational, the sinister. Amazingly, despite years of effort by investigators, thousands of tips, two exhumations, DNA tests, and directives from psychics, no one had ever identified the redhead. Now a new, go-getter police chief was reopening the case on the chance that state-of-the-art forensic techniques would provide a name and a history for the woman who was known only as the Lady of the Dunes.

Considering its subject had been dead for more than thirty years, the reconstruction in the *Globe* was startlingly lifelike. Even the new chief, a tough-guy Vin Diesel look-alike with a shaved head, noted kind of wistfully that she had beautiful hair. She had also had thousands of dollars' worth of dental work, yet no dentist had ever stepped forward with records that matched her teeth.

The Lady of the Dunes belongs to a certain category of unidentified victim — young, attractive, female — that communities tend to fetishize. She was buried under a flat stone the size of a sheet of loose-leaf paper at the edge of a grassy field adjacent to austere gray-shingled St. Peter the Apostle church in Provincetown, the marker engraved "Unidentified Female Body Found Race Point Dunes" along with the date she was discovered: July 26, 1974. Flowers still appear regularly at her grave, and people make pilgrimages to hers and other unidentified victims' resting places as if to sacred sites.

Over the next few days I kept thinking that the Provincetown murder victim must have been someone's daughter, maybe someone's mother, sister, aunt, or cousin. How could no one miss her? How could she have ended up in a quaint Cape Cod town one hot summer day, never to be heard from again, and how could her disappearance have raised not the slightest alarm among her relatives, friends, coworkers? Why did no one ever report her missing? And if someone had, how had no one made the connection to the Lady of the Dunes?

At least three Provincetown police chiefs consumed with her case swore to solve it; all retired, defeated, as the years passed. Incredibly, a new suspect in her murder would be identified in 2012 as I wrapped up research on this book.

I'm not particularly spiritual, but I felt sad for the Lady of the Dunes, a young woman robbed of her history, her future, and something we all take for granted: a name. Everyone I talked to agreed that it seemed impossible. If by a random stroke of bad luck I became a victim of a fatal accident or a deadly attack far from home, I was pretty confident word would make it back to someone who cared about me. And yet the thought nagged at me.

I closed the newspaper and went to my computer, where Googling "Lady of the Dunes" generated websites populated with small cities of dead people who, like her, had never been identified. They are unsettling, these sites: a Facebook for the dead. Some warn viewers that the photos within are disturbing and graphic. But nothing prepares you for the seemingly endless collection of heads: artists' reconstructions, vivid color portraits that capture an inquisitive look in the eyes or a stubborn set to the mouth, crude pencil sketches, cartoon-like illustrations, and distorted clay dummies sporting wigs, like something out of a beautician's academy for the hopeless. Then there are the postmortem photos: waxen faces with unseeing eyes, some individuals sporting grievous, barely disguised injuries.

I scrolled past image after image. It was like walking into a morgue, pulling out drawers, and yanking the sheets off body after body. What if you logged onto a site like this and came across the face of someone that you knew?

Who, I wondered, would go out of their way to create or peruse an Internet morgue?

James Todd Matthews's cause of choice is dumped, unclaimed, unidentified, and otherwise abandoned dead people.

Identifying the unidentified dead is not a celebrated cause like saving the whales. As one cold case investigator put it, unidentified corpses are the bottom of the food chain, and citizens like Todd taking up these cases only serves to exacerbate the already uneasy relationship between cops and civilians. Even the word "civilians," which the police commonly use to refer to citizens, smacks of the military and emphasizes the divide between those among us who wear uniforms and carry guns and everybody else.

The police occupy a lonely rung of society where they band together for self-preservation. Their tough exterior projects distrust: "Cynicism, clannishness, secrecy, insulating themselves from others — the so-called blue curtain," write criminologists Larry J. Siegel and John L. Worrall. Many cops believe — understandably — that lawyers, academics, politicians, and the public have little concept of what it means to be a police officer. So it's not surprising that when self-proclaimed web sleuths started seeking information about cold cases around 1999 — when the Internet came of age — their phone calls and e-mails weren't universally welcomed by law enforcement.

Working my way through the names of administrators listed on the Doe Network, a site that logged thousands of details on hundreds of missing and unidentified people, I connected with Todd Matthews and soon arranged to meet him in Virginia Beach, home to beachside motels, honky-tonk bars, and pizza joints, at a conference for cops and forensics personnel who routinely confronted bodies: the newly dead, the decomposed, the dismembered.

In contrast to Todd's childhood in a bucolic region of Tennessee, I'd grown up in a gritty neighborhood in a borough of New York City. With as many as two thousand murders a year — one every four hours — crime was a fact of life in the 1970s. This was the FORD TO CITY: DROP DEAD era; the age of the sensational headline, of over-inked black type on gray pulp newsprint unrelieved by color. There was, of course, *The New York Times,* but on the subways and buses everyone's head was buried in the tabloids — the *New York Post* and my family's favorite, the *New York Daily*

*News.* I'd get home from school to thirty-point type screaming terrifying gems like HEADLESS BODY IN TOPLESS BAR, about a robber shooting and decapitating the owner of a Brooklyn strip joint.

A few years later, serial killer Son of Sam gave New York City a collective nervous breakdown, generating a run on locks and Mace. David Berkowitz started a yearlong killing spree the summer I graduated from high school, picking off his victims — among them young women with long hair, the way I wore mine at the time — with a .44 double-action revolver. One of his victims was slain only a mile from my apartment building.

More than two decades after I'd left daily newspaper reporting to write about academic research, I became acquainted with the existence of the Lady of the Dunes and jumped at the opportunity to reenter the gritty world outside the ivory tower. I'd come to learn that many who spend their days among the unidentified also end up reinventing themselves.

Todd Matthews refers to himself, with only a hint of irony, as a hillbilly. Imagining himself some Southern version of Kojak, he'd set out as a teenager to crack Kentucky's biggest unsolved mystery: the identity of a murder victim known as Tent Girl. Now in his forties, a minor celebrity of sorts who played an active role in early grassroots efforts such as the Doe Network, he shares podiums regularly with FBI agents and forensic experts. On the day of the Virginia Beach event, Todd walked into the linoleum-and-cinder-block lobby of an almost win-dowless police academy with his laptop under his arm. Our fellow attendees were, by definition, a pretty hardened bunch. Gentle, soft-spoken, almost effeminate, Todd stuck out in this crowd like a canary among raptors.

He smiled at a Sofía Vergara look-alike detective behind the desk who, like almost everyone in the building, had a service revolver strapped to one hip. She checked our names on a list and pointed us toward an urn of black coffee, Styrofoam cups, and sticky, cinnamon-scented pastries. I watched Todd mill around, greeting people he recognized from the crime conference circuit.

I thought Todd's aquiline nose, thick chevron mustache, ragged soul patch, chestnut-brown eyes, and white teeth made him good-looking in an early-'80s sort of way. Around five-seven, his shaggy dark brown mane gained him a couple of inches. He exuded a Zen-like calm — until he started to speak. His middle Tennessee dialect — Tommy Lee Jones with a dash of Jed Clampett — was so rapid-fire, I had trouble recognizing it as English. "Dead" became "day-ud," "well" was "way-eel."

Besides losing the flip-flops and baseball cap I would come to recognize as integral parts of his look, Todd hadn't dressed for the part of speaker. In a short-sleeved golf shirt and jeans, he angled down the microphone; the previous presenter was a head taller. "I wore a suit in Vegas and everyone thought I was Tony Orlando," he told a sea of unsmiling cops. "I don't wear a mic because it wears down the chest hair."

After twenty minutes of leading the audience through the various ins and outs of using an online database to compare the details of the missing and the unidentified, Todd relinquished the podium to a forensic pathologist whose PowerPoint was a parade of gore: a corpse's face and neck striped from sternum to forehead with perfectly even, vertical tire treads; skulls bashed in by hammers or riddled with bullet holes; severed limbs, bloodied and mangled or denuded of skin. No one in the audience blinked.

Maybe Todd logged a couple of converts among law enforcement that day. He knew what he was up against. He'd spent years during his one-man investigation of Tent Girl trying to gain the confidence of cops who didn't hide the fact that they considered him a time-sucking, death-obsessed wacko. He'd lost track of the number of times he'd been turned away, ridiculed, dismissed, hung up on.

No one was actively investigating Tent Girl back then, almost no one was keeping track of the thousands of other unidentified bodies, and no one was effectively trying to match them to the tens of thousands of people still listed as missing. Incredibly, it would take thirty years from the time the issue was first raised for a universally accessible system dedicated to this purpose to materialize. One of the first people to advocate for such a thing was a dumpling-shaped woman in wire-rimmed spectacles who took the stage shortly after Todd: Dr. Marcella Fierro. Fierro started her career as an ambitious young medical student in upstate New York. Only the ninth woman in the country certified in forensic pathology, Fierro joined Richmond's Medical College of Virginia Hospitals and the office of the Virginia medical examiner, where she would one day meet author Patricia Cornwell. As a technical writer for the medical examiner in Richmond, Cornwell gained intimate knowledge of forensic science — material that would later surface in her wildly popular crime novels. And Fierro became the model for Kay Scarpetta, the unassailable expert pathologist featured in more than a dozen of Cornwell's best-selling books. (Fierro points out that she is not the *physical* model for Scarpetta: "Kay is blond, blue-eyed, and a hundred and fifteen pounds. I've never been blond, I have brown eyes, and I haven't weighed a hundred and fifteen pounds since I was twelve.")

In the 1970s, more than a decade before her friendship with Cornwell began and when Todd Matthews was still in kindergarten, Fierro heard a speaker at an American Academy of Forensic Sciences meeting call for a national registry for the unidentified. The subject resonated with her. Fierro had noticed that if a nameless but potentially recognizable body — an unidentified, or UID in law enforcement lingo — turned up on her autopsy table, the police took photos and issued a missing-person report or an APB. But if the body had decomposed or lacked fingerprints, "forget it," Fierro said. "There was really nothing."

It was obvious — to Fierro, at least — that this was a problem. It turned out to be a bigger problem than she could have imagined, involving law enforcement agencies, police departments, coroners, and medical examiners across fifty states with overlapping responsibilities for the unidentified and a communication breakdown that rivaled that of Apollo missions on the far side of the moon.

Big urban police departments considered their smaller, more rural counterparts hicks and rubes; professionally trained medical examiners with advanced degrees looked down on locally elected coroners. Consequently, if a missing person became an unidentified body several states away, or even in the next county, the case might remain unsolved because public service officials in one location didn't deign to share information or confer with their counterparts elsewhere.

They did all agree on one thing: no one wanted to talk to the public.

Theories abound on why law enforcement entities are so fiercely autonomous. Major urban police forces as we know them have been around since the mid- to late nineteenth century, state police forces evolved independently at the end of the nineteenth century, and the Federal Bureau of Investigation came into existence even later. Within a single municipality, police power can be divided among dozens of separate organizations, creating legions of fiefdoms. It was unclear whether a stray human body "belonged" to the medical examiner or to law enforcement. The fact was, no one entity owned the problem of UIDs, and early on, no one seemed to know how to go about identifying them.

Yet seeds were being sown. Around the time that Fierro was performing her first autopsies in Richmond in the mid-1970s, a police artist and an anthropologist from the Smithsonian Institution joined forces to attempt to elicit the "personality" of a skeleton found in woods adjacent to a Maryland industrial park. Science had not yet enabled investigators to reconstruct personality based solely upon the fragmentary remains of an individual, the pair wrote. But they decided to try to give one victim a presence that others might recognize.

The anthropologist determined that the victim was a seventeen- to twenty-two-year-old female, shorter than average, with a skewed right hip and a once-broken collarbone. Digging through evidence boxes, the police artist pulled out jewelry and a sweater found with the remains. He fingered strands of her long hair, traced and measured the skull, and started to sketch, conferring with the anthropologist on the shape and placement of her eyes, ears, and mouth.

Within days of the finished sketch's appearing in a local newspaper, police had identified Roseanne Michele Sturtz, who had not been seen since the previous year. People who knew her said that the twenty-year-old nightclub dancer favored one leg and had broken her collarbone when she was six.

A few years later, a father devastated by his son's brutal murder funneled his considerable energy and intensity into shaking up what he perceived as a deeply flawed system. After the disappearance and horrific 1981 murder of six-year-old Adam, Florida hotel developer John Walsh became an impassioned advocate for the missing. He joined forces in 1984 with the then-new nonprofit National Center for Missing & Exploited Children (its acronym, NCMEC, is pronounced "nick-mick") in Alexandria, Virginia, which Congress would later sanction as the official national resource center and information clearinghouse for missing and exploited children. Walsh went on to host *America's Most Wanted,* among the first TV shows to enlist the public's help in solving

46

crimes, paving the way for a growing movement: ordinary citizens working on cold cases. A decade later, the web sleuth phenomenon would force law enforcement's hand in ways Walsh likely never anticipated.

Fierro continued to forge her own connections within forensics and with the unidentified. When she had treated living patients, asking probing questions always gave her insight into what might be ailing them. So when confronted with UIDs — whom she saw as patients who happened to be dead — she talked to them as well. She asked them to tell her their stories, and she found that when she examined them the right way, they responded as eloquently as if they could speak, telling her whether they were right- or left-handed, if they had ever been seriously injured or undergone surgery, their age and race, whether they took care of their teeth, if they had ever borne a child. No detail was insignificant. "You have a genius for minutiae," Watson once chided Sherlock Holmes, who routinely made mental notes of esoteric facts. Holmes countered that recognizing distinctive calluses and scars on the hands of cork cutters, weavers, diamond polishers, and other tradesmen might help him identify an unclaimed body.

In the late 1980s, Fierro wrote a handbook for pathologists on tricks of the trade for conducting postmortem examinations of unidentified remains. She approached FBI officials, who, years after the American Academy of Forensic Sciences speaker had called for a registry of the unidentified, were still not the least bit interested in setting up such a thing. Considering that the FBI wouldn't have a working computer system that allowed its thirteen thousand agents to track case files electronically for almost another three decades, she shouldn't have been surprised.

Around the time Fierro was learning the silent language of the unidentified, Todd Matthews was a twenty-year-old factory worker in Livingston, Tennessee, who possessed an odd sense of kinship with the deceased. The fact that there were many like Tent Girl, nameless and forgotten, wouldn't reach the public consciousness for more than another decade. The way one longtime forensic anthropologist saw it, when Todd managed to identify Tent Girl, he triggered a gold rush. The case details of long-forgotten UIDs started to find their way out of dusty filing cabinets and onto websites, becoming an untapped mother lode of potentially useful crowdsourcing data.

*CSI,* with its gee-whiz forensics, premiered in 2000. The following year, 9/11 struck, and the desperate need to identify thousands of victims of the World Trade Center attacks helped advance DNA as a forensic tool. Some of the pieces for a new approach to UIDs had started to fall into place.

At the Virginia Beach conference, I met Betty Dalton Brown, an amateur sleuth living in North Carolina who spoke to Todd Matthews almost daily but had never met him in person. "I think he's around sixty, very distinguished, gray hair, goes to the opera," she said. "He's the one with the mullet," a Pennsylvania man informed her. (Todd insisted later that he was going for long-haired country boy, *not* a mullet.)

I recognized Betty as one of the scheduled speakers who, just before the conference, had grimly taken in the sea of seats in the empty auditorium and muttered, "Anybody have any Scotch?" Betty, petite, with shoulder-length dirty-blond hair, looked tough *and* feminine that day in black Western boots, black jeans, and a frilly checked blouse. Despite her attack of nerves, she pulled off her first-ever public talk about her search for a missing half brother, and I learned later that Betty has an uncanny knack for finding almost anything and anyone on the Internet. She'd blow away in a strong wind and she can be prickly, to put it mildly, but I decided that, in a showdown, I'd want Betty Brown on my side.

After the official program in Virginia Beach ended, a small group that included Betty, Todd, and me reconvened in a Holiday Inn lounge. I gazed at Todd's Hawaiian shirt, baseball cap, flip-flops, and ebullient hair. Knowing Todd only a matter of hours, I was a little worried that any minute he was going to confess that he believed the unidentified dead had been abducted by aliens or would be resurrected as vampires, and then I was going to have to stop myself from saying what I was thinking, which was something along the lines of *What a weirdo hillbilly fanatic.* I didn't tell him it wasn't considered normal in most circles to keep human skulls in your basement, as he mentioned he did, or to wear a soul patch.

I didn't have to say those things. Todd seemed resigned to the disdain with which some Yankees viewed him, and viewed the South as a setting for surreal fantasies and historical romances, Disney movies, and gothic nightmares of descents into madness. Hans Christian Andersen meets William Faulkner.

Sitting over blue drinks that night with the web sleuths and a jovial forensic expert from a Texas university, listening to stories laced with details of decomposition as we ate rare burgers, I was wondering what kind of hideously ghoulish subculture I had gotten myself mixed up with. But as the night wore on, the waves crashed along the far side of the Virginia Beach boardwalk, the gory anecdotes became funnier, the blue drinks kept coming, and my companions were turning out to be excellent company.

In the wake of Todd Matthews's successful identification of Tent Girl in 1998, many civilian sleuths took to the Internet to search out potential matches between the unidentified and the missing. By 2001, the same unidentified corpses that were once almost universally ignored had evolved into tantalizing clues in a massive, global version of Concentration played around the clock by a hodgepodge of self-styled amateur sleuths, a dedicated skeleton crew that shared a desire to match faces to names — and names to dead bodies. Anybody with an idealistic bent, a lot of time, and a strong stomach could sign on: a stay-at-home mom in New York, a chain store cashier in Mississippi, a nurse in Nebraska, a retired cop and his exotic-dancer girlfriend in Houston.

Venturing into the web sleuths' demimonde of aliases and screen names and pseudonyms, I came across SheWhoMustNotBeNamed and Yoda and abcman and Texaskowgirl. They were an underground society whose members wouldn't recognize one another if they passed on the street; their real-world personas were unknown to the kindred souls they encountered online.

On Websleuths Crime Sleuthing Community, users commented on celebrity fiascos such as Lindsay Lohan's latest woes, reports of serial pedophiles, Oscar Pistorius's arrest in the shooting death of Reeva Steenkamp. Among the many topics being tossed around at any given moment was the unidentified. The last time I checked, Websleuths contained almost 85,000 separate posts in more than 3,500 topic threads dedicated to the unidentified. Far fewer, admittedly, than the one-million-plus posts about Caylee Anthony, but at least some of those who spent their time in the realm of the unidentified were actively trying to match faces with names rather than simply rubbernecking at human train wrecks. When new users described how they found their way to the forum, their words made them seem benevolent, socially conscious — and a tad fanatical.

I've been fascinated with true crime
stories for years . . . If I ever find a match
[for] just one [unidentified corpse], I'll
know I made a difference in the world.
— FLMom

i have been surfing cold cases on the
internet for a few years now . . . it
started when i read about a jane doe in
upstate new york. I couldn't believe that
one so young was still not identified after
all that time — on one site i saw the
photos from the morgue and they just
burned in my brain — i keep checking
sites for young girls missing from the
1970s to see if i can find a match —
nothing yet. but her case haunts me.
— Jeanne

Then there's Paul, who works for a medical examiner and wants to provide identities
to the "many unfortunate subjects who have
as yet no name." Scott, another budding
addict, wrote a paper for a college English
class about Princess Doe, an unidentified
young girl found in 1982 at Cedar Ridge
Cemetery in Blairstown, New Jersey, and
kept coming back to the websites. I'd always

thought of the dead, as, well, dead, yet I had come across a community that embraced deceased strangers like long-lost loved ones who happened to be more likely to get in touch via Ouija board than cell phone.

By solving Tent Girl, Todd Matthews had unwittingly tapped into a like-minded posse who began to call, text, or e-mail one another almost daily, across time zones and often late at night when their families were asleep. They compared notes on cases, dug through archives, posted on true-crime forums and online bulletin boards. Websleuths.com, Can You Identify Me?, the Charley Project, JusticeQuest, and Porchlight International for the Missing and Unidentified joined the earlier sites such as the Doe Network and the Missing Persons Cold Case Network. They forged a growing commonality while keeping a low profile among the uninitiated, because it's hard to work human remains into cocktail conversation.

Over the years, as the posse grew, outside his trusted inner circle Todd found himself negotiating a minefield of politics, not always successfully. Unleashing the web sleuths, Todd had created a monster: an army of gung-ho volunteers demanding sensitive information from police and clamoring to pass along their proposed solutions. Police investigators dismissed the early amateur sleuths as busybodies, hung up on them, refused their calls, ignored their messages, and generally disparaged the people they called the Doe Nuts.

At first, it seemed to me that the cause attracted a stalwart band of do-gooders, impervious to the gruesome nature of the work like macabre Robin Hoods. I was unaware back then that this subculture was no more immune from backstabbing and vindictiveness than Wall Street. In the web sleuth world, achievement could be measured by posting the most information, say, or by attracting hundreds of members, but everyone agreed that matching a missing person with unidentified remains was the Holy Grail. In pursuit of the grail, web sleuths of vastly different backgrounds, worldviews, and political leanings, drawn to the quest for highly personal reasons, found themselves camped out in a corner of cyberspace with individuals they would likely never have otherwise met or chosen to bunk with.

Strung up like dirty laundry was evidence of their clashes: forum members banned for perceived or real infractions, users vilifying one another via fake online identities.

Faceless, behind screen names, separated by time and space, web sleuths baited their perceived enemies with insinuations and wisecracks. Some were capable of elevating philosophical rifts and personality clashes into out-and-out turf wars. "Websleuths is SUPPOSED to be [a] TRUE CRIME forum," posted someone who variously called herself JaneInOz and Pepper. "However there are now so many rules about what can and can't be said, that no meaningful discussion can take place without someone taking offense . . . Every discussion seems to turn into a bash fest." I felt JaneInOz hit the problem squarely on the head when, at the end of a diatribe directed at Utah-based Websleuths.com co-owner Tricia Griffith, she concluded, seemingly without a trace of irony, "I don't dislike you. Heck, I don't even really know you."

"Many of these groups suffer from a healthy dose of egomania," complained one anonymous poster. "They feel they are being 'attacked' or 'stalked' — I assume as a way of exaggerating their own self-importance."

I agreed with what came next: "I often wonder how any serious volunteer could put up with all this and find it remarkable that, not only do they put up with it, but they keep joining groups such as this for even more senseless heartache and extracurricular bullshit. Perhaps masochism is a prerequisite for membership in online groups."

Cyberbullying aside, some web sleuths struck me as purposeful and committed. Despite Wilbur Riddle's possessiveness of the body he found, it was obvious to me why Todd Matthews, not Riddle, became associated in people's minds with the legendary Tent Girl. To Riddle, the fact that a girl had been killed and dumped was a shame, for sure. It was also a good yarn, an attention-getter. Riddle clearly believed Tent Girl was his, a prize he had stumbled upon and collected that day in 1968, whereas Todd, not a churchgoer but a firm believer in a higher power, felt a soul-wrenching connection with the girl wrapped in the carnival tent. From the moment Riddle showed him *Master Detective*'s hyperbolic headline, Todd felt he had always known her. He identified with her. He, too, could have died young. He, too, lacked an unambiguous identity in a world that everyone else seemed to navigate with ease. He was convinced that a divine force impelled him to search for her name — a search that would both obsess him and sorely try him for ten long years.

In 2010, after more than two decades as a factory worker in the small town where he grew up, Todd landed a position with an agency overseen by the U.S. Department of Justice, rallying law enforcement and volunteers to use new Internet-based tools that help match up missing persons with unidentified bodies.

You might think this would validate Todd's commitment and the volunteers' efforts, but the fact that Todd was suddenly being paid to facilitate matches on the Internet — something a growing cadre of amateur sleuths did with significant investments of their own time and money — caused dissension in the ranks. While trying to enlist the beast's strength — crowd-sourcing all those neglected cases — Todd incurred its wrath.

It had taken Todd Matthews years to accrue the power and respect that placed him at a podium in front of a sea of uniforms and gun holsters, and the journey had cost him personally. To some, Todd was a hero, a pioneer. Others considered him a traitor, a sellout, and a contemptible publicity hound. Some web sleuths accused Todd of selfish motives, pointing to his appearances on

*Good Morning America,* his onetime radio show, his consulting gig for a TV pilot based partly on his life, his ongoing quest to launch a dramatic TV series based on web sleuthing. Todd is the subject of, or quoted within, a slew of newspaper and magazine stories, and a Memphis filmmaker is working on a documentary about him.

"You look for things to fill that hole in your heart that you cannot ignore," Todd once wrote to me, referring to the deaths of two of his siblings. "Others being eased from suffering does hold Rx for the soul — it does. But you have to keep going. It's a temporary fix. There's no real cure, you see. It's about managing the cycle like a recovering addict."

I couldn't have imagined when I met Todd that, less than two years later, he would be voted off his own island. But nothing changed the fact that Todd Matthews was at the center of a revolutionary era for law enforcement and the Internet. And there were others like him, obsessed with a nameless body.

# 2
# YOU CAN DISAPPEAR HERE

For decades, Provincetown police chief James J. Meads kept the skull of the Lady of the Dunes on his desk, vowing he wouldn't retire until he uncovered her real name.

I met Jimmy Meads in June 2010. He had retired reluctantly eighteen years earlier, the woman's identity still unknown, but he had cemented his reputation as the gutsy, strong-willed chief who continued to champion her case. Third-generation Provincetown, Meads descended from Portuguese fishermen. He lived in a traditional Cape on a narrow lane off Commercial Street's leather shops, art galleries, and restaurants, a short walk from the harbor where his father used to launch his boat before dawn.

Opposite Meads's house was one of the most chic and popular guesthouses in town. The then owner, Park Davis, with close-cropped graying hair and an engaging smile, told me a man once shot a woman execution-style in a public parking lot not far away. One of Davis's poodles, perched at a window, was the only witness. Police eventually located that assailant, but no witnesses, not even canine ones, saw the murder of the Lady of the Dunes.

At seventy-seven, Meads, in jeans and a navy blue T-shirt with a fire department insignia, still had an iron jaw and the physique of a bodybuilder. If I had broken the law I wouldn't want to meet his ice-blue gaze, but retirement seemed to agree with him. Mild-mannered, he showed me his collection of antique blue glass lining the shelves along his kitchen ceiling and the birdhouses he'd built and mounted in the backyard. He'd bought and renovated the house around 1974, the year of the infamous case.

That year, on July twenty-sixth, a couple and their daughter visited a local artist at her primitive shack nestled among the dunes. The dune shacks had been thrown together more than a century earlier, shelters for crews who kept watch for ships running aground in storms and fog. By the 1970s the shacks had been turned into artist studios and rustic beach getaways.

Isolated, with no electricity, indoor plumbing, or telephone, they promised uninterrupted solitude and refuge.

Tooling along featureless Route 6, the Cape's only divided highway, you'd have to have faith that the endless roadside scrub oaks and crabgrass hid something worthwhile. Even the Pilgrims had ditched Provincetown for Plymouth. But the dunes, spooky and wild and tall after all the flatness, make this tiny place alluring.

You can disappear here, a longtime resident told me. Those seeking to distance themselves from the world make their way to Provincetown.

That Friday, as afternoon slipped into evening, the couple's thirteen-year-old daughter set off for a walk with her beagle. They wandered toward the Coast Guard station on Race Point, named for the fierce riptides that tear around the outermost tip of Cape Cod. On the deserted beach they would have heard crashing waves and chittering seabirds.

Jeep tracks, bike paths, and nature trails crisscross Provincetown's thirty miles of beach. By day, families with children play in the surf, and by night, gay men cruise Herring Cove for hookups in the tall grass, secret spaces like this one among the dunes.

Shadows lengthening, the girl — and the dozens of others who likely tromped down that stretch of beach that day — didn't immediately spot the woman hidden in a pine grove that formed a small private room with scrub brush walls and a pine-needle floor. The sea breeze might have masked the odor of the blanket's sole occupant. But up close it would have sat heavy in the air, thick and sweet. The beagle picked up the scent.

The dog bounded past clumps of stunted oak and beach plums into the outdoor alcove where a woven green beach blanket big enough for two had sat undisturbed, the coroner estimated later, for a week, perhaps as long as three weeks. After days in the heat and sun, putrefaction must have been in full swing, sulfurous intestinal gas and disintegrating red blood cells generating a greenish skin discoloration on the woman's lower abdomen, chest, and upper thighs. In a week, most of the body would have turned aquamarine.

Girl and dog ran back to the shack, where the adults, with no landline and twenty years too early for cell phones, set off on foot for the National Seashore park ranger station. Chief ranger James D. Hankins was the first official to make his way to the crime scene.

■ ■ ■ ■

By 1974, Jim Hankins had spent sixteen years with the U.S. National Park Service, the last two as head ranger for the northern section of the Cape Cod National Seashore. I tracked down Hankins in his home state of Tennessee, where he had retired. Growing up there in the foothills of the Great Smoky Mountains, he'd always wanted a career outdoors. He'd worked in stunning spots: Cape Hatteras, the Blue Ridge Parkway, the Chesapeake and Ohio Canal. At the Cape Cod National Seashore, Hankins supervised round-the-clock patrols of the miles of woodlands and beaches that made up twenty-two thousand acres of the sublime vistas found only at land's end. Park rangers in those days acted as police officers, firefighters, and maintenance crews rolled into one, he said. The worst troublemakers Hankins encountered were pretty harmless, like the exhibitionist who paraded nude on the upper deck of his shack just as dune buggies loaded down with unsuspecting tourists rolled by.

Hankins seemed more peeved about the transformation of the shacks into residences. In his view the shack owners were squatters on public land who over the years accrued more privileges that, in his opinion, they didn't earn and never should have had. He also didn't care for the sleeping bag set — young people crashing for the night on sandy beaches or in roadside rest areas. But he conceded that if someone slipped into the dunes toting a sleeping bag and without a vehicle, he or she might evade the night patrol and get away with sleeping under the stars.

A few weeks before the body was found, the Cape had celebrated the Fourth of July with parades and fireworks. Tens of thousands of visitors had streamed in for the holiday weekend, stretching the limits of the police force and park rangers, but things had quieted down again — Hankins had thought — when the beagle walker's parents alerted a ranger at Race Point, who called Hankins at home. He jumped into his jeep and drove deep into the dunes, following dune buggy trails.

He saw what the girl had found, and his earlier casual remark about slipping past the ranger station took on a sinister truth. Two people apparently had entered the dunes; one had gotten out undetected, even though every vehicle entering national parkland had to stop and buy a permit.

Hankins made his way back to the ranger station and called Jimmy Meads at home. The two were friends; Meads trusted Hankins and had given him a bit of law enforcement authority that park rangers didn't ordinarily have.

Meads drove from his tidy Cape several blocks to what served as the police station those days: a dank, mold-infested labyrinth of offices and holding cells in the basement of Town Hall. He collected two detectives and drove with them to Race Point. They transferred to a jeep — a police sedan would have sunk in the sand — and drove on to the clump of scrub pines.

Meads saw the mutilated body and immediately thought of drug dealer and former police informant Antone "Tony" Costa, although he knew that Costa couldn't have had a hand in this murder.

Jimmy Meads was a sergeant in March 1969 when two young women went missing. One cold day, his boss, Chief Francis "Cheney" Marshall, was combing the woods not far from the Truro Old North Cemetery with a couple of Massachusetts police detectives and a state trooper. They were searching for the women from nearby Providence, Rhode Island, who had gone to Provincetown for a winter weekend getaway and never returned home.

The three men left their vehicles near the road and followed a rutted dirt track three hundred yards into the woods to a clearing on the edge of a knoll. Marshall noticed a large pine tree at the edge of the mossy clearing. Six feet off the ground on the tree's trunk, a knob and the remnant of a broken limb protruded.

Strands of rope stuck to the bark of the knob; there were rope fibers on the trunk, and bits of stained rope on the bed of pine needles. Near the base of the tree the trooper saw something glitter in the dirt. He picked it up and brushed it off: a single gold earring with a dangling square of black onyx.

He cleared leaves and turf, revealing the outline of a recently dug hole, then grabbed one of the shovels the men had brought. Three feet down, the cold earth softened, but the roots of the tree made for rough going. He knelt, scooping out dirt with his hands. One of the detectives knelt beside him; the others walked over. Seeing nothing but soil, a detective was about to tell the men to stop digging when suddenly the trooper yanked his hand out of the dirt as if he'd been bitten. "There's something down there," he said.

Something white was visible under a layer of sandy soil. "Jesus Christ," Marshall said. An arm protruded from the hole. A ring decorated with alternating turquoise and orange beads circled the little finger of the hand. A detective pawed the dirt aside, revealing a mat of brown hair. It came away in his hand like a Halloween fright wig. He carefully loosened the dirt around the hair and cupped his hands around the head. He lifted it from the ground.

As author Leo J. Damore related in this scene from his 1981 book, *In His Garden,* the detective "cradled the head in his arm. He brushed sand and gravel clinging to the open eyes and took dirt from the gaping mouth. The face was a mask of terror, lips drawn back in a grimace of surprise and pain. The face was bluish, the left cheek discolored and swollen. The nose had been broken by the force of a powerful blow." The detective thought he recognized Mary Anne Wysocki, one of the missing Providence women.

In a sandy area up a slight rise around two hundred feet away, the men dug through two feet of frost before uncovering a tangle of female body parts: the lower portion of a young woman severed just above the hips, the upper half of the body. The skin of the chest had been cut open and pulled back like the front of a cardigan. The face was swollen and badly mauled, but the detective had pored over the photos of the two missing women enough to know the body in the grave was Wysocki's companion, Patricia Walsh.

The base of the tree was where Tony Costa hid his drug stash. That and other evidence linked the victims to Costa, who was convicted of the murders. At the time, no one imagined the intelligent, serious-looking young man with gold-framed glasses capable of such horrific crimes. Meads had known Tony Costa since the youth started spending summers in Provincetown with his aunt, a local resident, and Meads thought it was too bad the kid had married at nineteen and gotten mixed up in Provincetown's drug scene.

In fact, Meads had recruited Costa as a police informer for a drug bust. In return, Meads wrote a letter recommending early parole for Costa, who was serving six months in the Barnstable County Jail and House of Correction for nonpayment of child support and was due to get out in March 1969. Meads's letter helped free Costa in November 1968.

Two months later, Pat Walsh and Mary Anne Wysocki were dead.

In May 1970, Costa was convicted and sentenced to life in prison at the former Massachusetts Correctional Institution-Walpole. Four years after his incarceration and two months before the Lady of the Dunes was found, Costa hung himself in his cell.

One of the things Jim Hankins recalled about the dunes was how, despite wide-open vistas of sand and sea, the dense vegetation — taller than a man in places — created a maze of secret nooks. No one, he imagined, had ever explored all of them.

He had now arrived at such a spot, a protected cove where the victim was laid out on a blanket. She lay on her stomach, and both of her hands had been hacked off at the wrists, which had been jammed into the sand so it looked, according to several media reports, as if she were doing push-ups. Rangers and specially trained dogs who searched for her hands for four days found nothing. One side of her head was caved in. Her head had been dealt a terrific blow with a blunt instrument, and more than likely the blow had occurred while she was asleep or someone was lying next to her, Hankins said.

I thought nature-loving Jim Hankins was deeply affronted that the killer, in addition to senselessly ending a life, had defiled a beautiful spot that he was charged with keeping pristine. I had taken him back almost four decades, but Hankins's memories seemed clear. I sat at my desk, phone propped at my ear, typing as quietly as I could while Hankins's words unfurled like a ribbon.

"The only instrument that could have been used to hack off her hands was an instrument carried by almost all dune buggies. It was common in all surplus stores; it was a handy tool for the camper. It was a folding shovel called an entrenching tool. It was a standard-issue item for anyone in the infantry; soldiers in World War II and Korea carried them.

"It was very sturdy, made out of heavy metal, semi-pointed, spade-like. The blade could be folded down on the handle, or it could be raised to a perpendicular like a hoe, or you could make it into a shovel with a straight handle around eighteen inches long. In hand-to-hand combat, you could use it to fight your enemy.

"I still have a couple, as a matter of fact,

and I use them quite often for gardening. We insisted that anyone who got a permit to drive on the beach carry certain equipment, such as a board to put their jack on — you can't use a jack in the sand — and a shovel to dig out if you get stuck.

"We never knew how she got there. Throughout the dunes at that time there were well-defined sand trails where beach buggies and sand taxis — vehicles with four-wheel-drive capability — would haul as many as eight people. They would take visitors and people would go fishing out there.

"She could have been let out by dune buggy. It was very uncommon for people to be out in the dunes alone like that. It wasn't unheard-of, but it wasn't a common occurrence. It was quite possible she could have parked out in the visitor center or someone brought her. Or she could actually have walked from town, or she could have come from the beach. They discovered from the contents of her stomach that she had had a hamburger and french fries. That means she had recently been in town.

"It wasn't evident how she had selected this place to sunbathe. She secreted herself back in there. She was away from where any member of the public could see her. But someone knew she was there, or . . . some-

72

body from one of the shacks stumbled on her . . . Even if there was someone who lived in one of those dune shacks who was offended by that kind of activity and either watched her go in there or stumbled upon her, for them to beat her like that and cut off her hands, why would they do that?

"If it was a person who was offended by her nude sunbathing or was some kind of sex maniac and they killed her, why would they cut off her hands? It doesn't make sense." Hankins's monologue slowed, as if he'd suddenly become aware that he'd been rambling. He had one last thought. "Whoever killed her knew who she was," he said, "and killed her for a purpose."

Several years into the investigation of the Lady of the Dunes murder, all the usual avenues of police and detective work had yielded almost no results, so in a desperate measure, Provincetown selectmen found town money to send Chief Jimmy Meads to New York City to visit a psychic.

Meads drove six hours, battled Manhattan's weaving, honking taxis, and made his way to a rather elegant address. A doorman ushered him in and Meads took the elevator to an apartment where he placed on a table a stack of bulging envelopes. Yolana

Bard, known as the "queen of psychics," had for years offered her services to politicians, celebrities, and law enforcement officials. Now she bent over the case materials Meads had placed before her.

Suddenly she shrieked, "I sense blood!"

"I had a cup of tea on a saucer in my hand and I damn near spilled it," Meads recalled.

Yolana had come across a sealed package containing a bloody object from the site where the Lady of the Dunes had been murdered. She then reported a vision of water dripping, indicating a location on the beach where she said the victim's hands had been buried. Meads was elated. The hands would provide a key piece of evidence — especially if they could lift a set of prints. He thanked the genial redhead and sped back to Provincetown.

Yolana's unfamiliarity with Provincetown — she had never been to Cape Cod — didn't seem to impede her ability to weigh in on the case. But she could give Meads only vague directions to a place that he took to be the west end of Commercial Street. This street overflowed in the summer with tourists strolling in and out of waterfront galleries and funky shops, ice cream cones in hand. There was the occasional sighting of Norman Mailer, Kurt Vonnegut, Tennessee Williams, celebrated artists, and flamboyantly dressed drag queens working the nightclubs. At home, piecing together the tidbits that Yolana had divulged, Meads went to the phone book. He decided, finally, that the place the psychic had alluded to must be the old Ace of Spades.

The Ace of Spades was one of P-town's first lesbian bars, remembered by a patron as small, dark, and cozy, with wooden barrels as bar stools, redolent of stale liquor. During the 1970s, the place had morphed into another gay bar, the Pied Piper, that attracted visitors from as far as Montreal and Kansas City. It was a weathered, gray building on the water's edge. In those days, drainage from the bar sinks trickled directly through rough wooden floorboards onto the beach below. Dripping water, sand, a location in town — all seemed perfectly aligned with Yolana's vision. But when Meads got there, it turned out that a basement had been added to the structure two months earlier. What was once accessible space was now a solid block of cement.

On the phone, Jim Hankins and I fell silent for a time. The next time he spoke, his tone had changed.

"What I did discover that day, the police

didn't pursue," Hankins went on, more animated, as though recalling something he hadn't thought about in years.

While the chief and others waited for an ambulance to collect the body from the lonely, windswept spot, Hankins walked up the beach alone, away from where she had been found. Perhaps he watched the waves crashing in that magical evening light that makes everything look so pure and cleanly defined, trying to clear his head of the shocking sight of the woman's mutilated body. Within a short distance, he spotted something odd.

He saw what looked like large words and pictures drawn in the sand. Beaches by day's end are tableaux of children's abandoned sand construction projects, but this didn't look to him like the kind of thing kids would do.

He wishes now he had paid more attention, trusted his instincts, gone home and fetched his camera. But he didn't, because despite his many responsibilities, he knew investigating a murder was not one of them. He deferred to the pros.

But today, Hankins is convinced someone had been very close to where the body was found shortly before the girl and dog had stumbled upon it, because the wind would have erased the strange markings in a matter of hours if not minutes. Had he spotted a message from the killer, scouting out the scene as killers sometimes did? He wonders about that odd, fleeting sight all these years later.

Something in Hankins's voice was familiar to me. He sounded like others who, in the midst of relating the details of a cold case, suddenly went distant, perplexed, helpless, almost angry. To those with a personal connection to a case — or those who developed a connection by becoming immersed in its details online — the intractability of the facts could be infuriating.

As I listened to Hankins speculate about murder weapons, motives, and mysterious sand writings, I found myself getting sucked into the alluring notion that I could play a role in solving the case by mining disparate clues from participants' long-dormant memories. It was as if the facts were a jigsaw puzzle that many before me had put together in different ways. If the right person had all the pieces everyone else had struggled with for years, perhaps he or she could assemble them in a new way so that the end result was clearer, if still incomplete. Hankins had stumbled upon a clue — the sand writings — no one had ever considered before. If the puzzle had included this piece from the beginning, would it have come together differently?

Clearly Hankins and others had been replaying the facts in their minds for years. Todd Matthews told me he wished he could abort the Tent Girl loop the way you'd change the radio station when an overplayed song came on. Despite confronting dead end after dead end, Meads, Hankins, Matthews, and dozens of others couldn't stop thinking about "their" victims. By the late 1990s, the Internet was beginning to serve as a centralized place where the cold-case-obsessed could input all known clues so that others might catch something the original players missed or couldn't have known.

In 1999, a Canadian man used emerging web resources to do exactly that for a victim he knew only as Cali.

# 3
# IT'S THE ETHERNET, MY DEAR WATSON

Amateur detectives are a mainstay of popular culture. Literary ones have been around since Edgar Allan Poe's impoverished medical student Le Chevalier Auguste Dupin deduced that an orangutan was the culprit in *The Murders in the Rue Morgue*. Eccentric, brilliant, cleverer than the police, motivated by the intellectual challenge, Dupin became the model for every literary and pop culture sleuth that followed: Poirot, Jane Marple, Perry Mason, Nancy Drew, the Hardy Boys, Encyclopedia Brown, Sherlock Holmes.

In "A Scandal in Bohemia," Holmes observes that Watson has "a most clumsy and careless servant girl." An amazed Watson asks Holmes how he knows this. "It is simplicity itself . . . My eyes tell me that on the inside of your left shoe, just where the firelight strikes it, the leather is scored by six almost parallel cuts. Obviously they have been caused by someone who has very carelessly scraped round the edges of the sole in order to remove crusted mud from it. Hence, you see, my double deduction that you had been out in vile weather, and that you had a particularly malignant boot-slitting specimen of the London slavey."

Holmes never let Watson forget that he considered himself strictly an amateur. "I claim no credit," he says in *The Sign of Four.* "My name figures in no newspaper. The work itself, the pleasure of finding a field for my peculiar powers, is my highest reward."

With the help of newsgroups, online databases, and message boards, a new breed of amateur detective evolved, modeled on the famed detectives of fiction but with one big difference: the real-life amateurs were dealing with real-life crimes, real-life bodies, and real-life tragedies. And not all sought only personal satisfaction as their reward.

Every amateur sleuth toiling in the realm of Jane and John Does has a pet case. For Canadian photographer Troy More, it was Cali, also known as Caledonia Jane Doe, a teenaged girl shot execution-style in an upstate New York cornfield in 1979.

When I set out to write this book, I tried

to identify the origins of the first site to list details of unidentified remains, but found it was like trying to name the inventor of the intermittent windshield wiper or first explorer to reach the North Pole. The answer depended on whom you asked.

When I asked Todd Matthews about the early days of the Doe Network, he pointed me to an archived corner of the Web where I found a treasure trove — every post since the inception of a cold cases newsgroup, accessible only through a little-used back door. Google doesn't get you there.

That's how I learned that in 1999, More used Yahoo! — then a relatively new domain offering free hosting and other services — to create a newsgroup dedicated to the missing, the murdered, and the unidentified. He called it ColdCases, fashioned a fingerprint-and-handcuffs graphic, and flung an invitation into cyberspace: "Want to discuss unsolved cases? Subscribe to our list."

A handful of web denizens made their way to the newsgroup. Reading the moderator's messages, I got a sense of the man who first summoned the web sleuths to Yahoo! Yet, as elsewhere on the Web, the newsgroup was a veil and More's identity was indistinct: I saw only what he chose to reveal, sketchy details that emerged piecemeal in random posts meant for an audience that, as far as he knew at the time, did not yet exist.

More described himself as a jaded news photographer who had seen "a few too many bodies." He likened photographers to snipers, locking their lenses on the faces of victims' family members, hoping to capture a moment of agony. In his view, the police, the media, and nonprofits were all useless when it came to missing persons: law enforcement bungled cases, the media ignored "forgotten" victims, and nonprofit organizations fought over donation dollars with the same cutthroat mentality as corporate moguls.

On ColdCases, he was adamant about including only cases that had fallen off the mainstream radar. He dismissed a prospective member who made the mistake of expressing interest in the murder of fashion mogul Gianni Versace: "We don't normally deal with celebrity cases here as I'd like to think that people who aren't rich and don't wind up on *Entertainment Tonight* also deserve justice," he wrote; he preferred to champion victims who weren't well-known but who had died "just as violently as any celebrity." Two years before launching Cold-Cases, More had created a site he called

E-clipse Network's Unsolved Case Files —
"in search of the lost, the hidden, and the
forgotten."

Around the same time, in 1998, Todd,
inspired by Tent Girl, compiled details on
unidentified remains and missing people on
a site he called The Lost and the Found.
Independent of both More and Matthews, a
Michigan woman, Jennifer Marra — describing herself as a former journalist and
using the screen names "Jenni" and
"Stormy" — launched yet another site,
Stormcritters.com, to document American
and Canadian disappearances and unidentified victims prior to 1989.

For Troy More, Caledonia Jane Doe —
whose reconstruction shows an attractive,
perhaps sassy and tomboyish girl with a pert
nose and cleft chin — became a personal
challenge. An extremely frustrating one,
judging from his posts.

The official report stated:

Victim was found in a field near Route 20
by a passing motorist, on November 9th,
1979. Murder weapon a .38 caliber hand-
gun which was recovered at the scene.
No information available suggests a sexual
assault took place. Clothing worn was

corduroy pants, plaid shirt, blue knee socks, and red windbraker [sic] jacket. Victim was 5'3" tall and weighed 120 pounds. She had brown, wavy hair that had been frosted several months prior, a rather deep tan, and tanlines indicating that she had worn a bikini frequently.

One of the most mournful clues in Cali's case was a key chain dangling from a belt loop on the girl's tan corduroy pants. One half was a tiny key; the other a silver heart with a key-shaped cutout inscribed, "He who holds the key can open my heart." Web sleuths typically pored over details like this. Hercule Poirot would approve. Agatha Christie's famed character did not scour crime scenes with a magnifying glass (although some web sleuths would if they could). Instead, the brain's "little gray cells," Poirot claimed, are all one needs to solve any crime. Sit in an armchair and think, he advised the admiring Hastings. The puzzle pieces will fall into place.

Unfortunately, that wasn't happening in Cali's case. As I read back over months of posts, I saw that More surmised that Cali had known her attacker. It was unlikely, to his mind, that she could have been brought to this remote place near the Canadian border unless she was traveling with her assailant, especially given that there was no evidence she was sexually assaulted or restrained.

The murder was not premeditated, or if it was, it wasn't intended to happen where it did, he reasoned. The Finger Lakes region of New York contained many remote haunts that would seem more logical for a planned homicide than out in an open field along a moderately busy road. Shot in the back before the fatal gunshot pierced her right temple, Cali may have been fleeing from her attacker. The weapon, a .38 revolver, was left next to her in the cornfield, where a passing motorist found her shortly after daylight.

The victim was most likely not a runaway, More believed. She was simply too well-groomed. Her clothing, hygiene, jewelry, and physical condition all suggested that she had been well cared for. Her tan meant she might have lived in the Southeast, the Gulf Coast, or California. A summer tan would have faded by November.

More checked 1979 business directories for tanning salons, then a relatively new phenomenon. Even if one had been operating in upstate New York and the girl had happened to visit it, he suspected she would have opted for a full-body exposure rather than to create bikini tan lines.

A thorough search for the manufacturer of Cali's clothing turned up no such company in the United States at that time, and although More's research into missing-person files in Canada, Europe, and Australia also led nowhere, he considered the possibility that she was Canadian. November ninth was part of the annual Remembrance Day holiday weekend in Canada, and she was found only an hour from the Canada border, in an area frequented by tourists.

An event ten thousand miles from where she died may have sealed her fate as an unknown, More suggested. While Cali lay dead in the field, Iranian militants stormed the U.S. embassy in Iran, holding fifty-two hostages in a standoff that lasted 444 days. By the time media coverage of the hostage crisis had died down, the news of Caledonia Jane Doe's death had been buried. More was determined to find a way to resurrect it.

In early 2001, Jennifer "Stormy" Marra's site Stormcritters.com evolved into the Doe Network, and around that time she simultaneously developed a new, similar site, the Missing Persons Cold Case Network, or

MPCCN.

MPCCN collected an impressive four thousand listings for missing and unidentified individuals from North America. During its relatively brief existence, a user named Carol Ann Cielecki would help solve one of its most perplexing cases. Meanwhile, the knowledge that Carol had been seeking in the first place would elude her for another four years.

In early 2003, Marra's Missing Persons Cold Case Network was still a few months away from being hacked into oblivion. In a small Pennsylvania town, Carol scrolled through the network's database, looking for a mention of an unidentified body that might be that of her hunky, daredevil ex-husband.

I visited Carol in her compact two-story house in Allentown, the post–steel-industry blue-collar town that Billy Joel had made famous. Carol was ready for me, kneeling on her living room rug surrounded by photo albums and loose-leaf notebooks packed with articles and flyers documenting a decade of web sleuthing — and, in Carol's case, more than twenty-five years of loss and pain. In jeans and a sweater, straight dark hair flipped over one shoulder, silver-gray shadow highlighting baby-blue eyes, she looked like she couldn't possibly have married Todd Martin Smith more than a quarter century ago. When she pulled out the wedding photos, it made more sense. I saw that she and Todd were very young back then, just kids who, fittingly, went to Disney World on their honeymoon.

When Carol first started searching for Todd online, she hadn't seen him since the day in May 1989 that he stopped by the car dealership where she worked to pick up their two-year-old daughter. Later that day — without dropping so much as a hint about leaving to Carol; to his girlfriend, who was taking care of the toddler for him; or to his parents — the twenty-five-year-old motocross racer, sports car enthusiast, and skilled golfer sold one of his beloved motorcycles, abandoned his car on a city street with the motorcycle trailer still attached, and vanished.

Even after fourteen years, Carol didn't believe Todd was dead — if he was, she was certain someone would have found his body and notified her and his family — but she lived with a constant, gnawing doubt. She peeked out her windows at night as though he might be lurking in the bushes and wondered if he was keeping tabs on her and their daughter. Once, briefly, she was sure she had spotted him in a crowd photo, a pea-sized face in *Parade* magazine.

She and Todd had met in their early twenties, selling Hondas at a New Jersey dealership not far from where they grew up. Mont Blanc pens tucked into the pockets of their suits, Carol and Todd competed with the rest of the sales team to see who could move more Civics and Preludes. This wasn't overly difficult — the practical, fun-to-drive cars were popular in upscale Somerset County — but Carol recalled that, for Todd, it was practically effortless.

Tall, with tight blond curls and a chiseled jaw, exuding confidence and athleticism, he'd stroll over to a potential customer. He spoke softly — no hard sell here — blinked his cornflower-blue eyes, and flashed his boyish grin, and before you knew it, the customer was signing with the Mont Blanc pen.

Todd expected to succeed — in the showroom, on the racetrack, on the golf course. The first time Todd picked up a tennis racket he beat Carol, who for years had played the tournament circuit. She was infuriated. But life with Todd was never boring. Once, even though Carol thought he was low on money, a Corvette showed up in the driveway. Carol pictured herself in the passenger seat, the top down, wind whipping her long hair. "Is that a lawn ornament?" she chided.

You didn't need to goad Todd Martin Smith into an adventure. He folded his six-foot-three frame behind the wheel and they sped off down the New Jersey Turnpike. They stopped only when the car broke down somewhere in Death Valley and Todd suggested they get married in Vegas. "Not here," Carol laughed. They made it to California, where Todd ogled the Aston Martins and Porsches on Rodeo Drive and Carol flew home to go to work.

When Todd returned to New Jersey, they had a church wedding. In the photos he's leaning down in his tux — Carol is more than a foot shorter — to kiss her, his light curls against her smooth dark hair.

Marriage didn't change him. He'd still take off alone to race motorcycles or sky-dive or escape the chilly Jersey winters. He brought home new sports cars when Carol couldn't afford maternity clothes. He left for one of his spontaneous trips when she was almost eight months pregnant, and Carol realized then that Todd was probably never going to embrace the responsibilities of fatherhood.

They split amicably soon after Ashley was

born. On May 17, 1989, the day Todd saw Carol at work, he was picking up the two-year-old for a visit. They wrestled her car seat into his car, then stood around shooting the breeze, as Carol recalled years later. He peered over her shoulder. "What do you have there?"

"I've got doughnuts. Would you like one?" Carol, then service manager at the Honda dealership, often bought doughnuts for the mechanics. Todd held a coconut-sprinkled one in his teeth while he strapped Ashley in, buckled his own seat belt, waved to Carol, and drove off. Later, Todd's girlfriend, who kept Ashley for the day with her own kids, dropped off the little girl with Carol. The next day, worried because Todd hadn't come back that night, she phoned Carol, who advised her not to be surprised by the disappearing act. Todd did this. He'd probably turn up in a few days.

None of them ever saw him again.

Carol and her daughter moved from New Jersey to Pennsylvania. She remarried and got a job as a paralegal. She had a son with her new husband and stayed in touch with her former in-laws.

By 2003, Carol had been poking around the Internet for a few years. She had learned how to probe its little-known corners to uncover the useful esoterica buried there. Finding bits of information on the Web reminded her of scavenger hunts, Nancy Drew mysteries, and trivia contests. As a child, she'd loved math word problems. The Internet was similarly challenging: you had to sift through the irrelevant dross for clues that led to the solution. Years later, she'd remember the pulp detective magazines stacked on her grandmother's bedside table and wonder if she had inherited a hankering to be a private eye.

Besides, Carol, divorced for a second time, with Ashley approaching college age, thought their daughter deserved to know her father's story. Or at least collect Social Security death benefits. Carol found her way to Missing Persons Cold Case Network, where she saw nothing related to Todd. But she became riveted by photos of another young man, missing for seven years, who'd lived not far from where she and Todd grew up in New Jersey. There was something about his pronounced jaw that reminded Carol of her beloved, developmentally disabled little sister.

In 1975, Sean Lewis Cutler, seven years old, was living with his divorced mother in an apartment complex in Kentucky. A carbon monoxide leak killed Sean's mother and plunged Sean into a months-long coma. When he awoke, doctors told his father, Lewis, that Sean's brain had been severely damaged. He would be blind and wheelchair-bound for life.

The owner of the apartment building and the contractor who caused the accident settled with Lewis Cutler for $1.6 million. After lawyer's fees, around $800,000 was set aside for Sean's care. Lewis Cutler remarried a few years later. His new wife legally adopted Sean.

In 1992, shortly after Lew gained control of his handicapped son's trust fund, his life started unraveling. He told his wife that he saw no reason to go on living because planetary forces would destroy the world in May 2000. Calling him deranged and emotionally abusive, she filed for divorce and moved to Florida.

In 1994, Lewis rented a house in Wayne, New Jersey, for himself and Sean, but the next year he told family members that he had signed custody of his disabled son over to a nursing home in Canada.

In July 1996, Lewis Cutler was arrested for drunk driving, drug possession, and providing false information in the form of a driver's license in his son's name. An investment firm wired him the fraction of the trust money that he hadn't frittered away. A week later, Lewis Cutler's rented house burned to the ground.

Arson investigators picking through the rubble found the bodies of Cutler and a man named William Spitzer, a friend of Lewis's. They determined that someone had intentionally ignited a natural gas line in the basement. The windows had been tightly sealed and a battery to a smoke alarm was tucked in Spitzer's pocket.

At first, investigators who found the driver's license in Sean's name believed Sean, too, must have died in the fire. But they found no trace of him.

When Carol spotted Sean's photo in MPCCN, she read that Sean's family believed he was in a nursing home in Canada. If that was the case, Carol knew that there would be a paper trail. *Somebody will find that boy,* she thought, and moved on to the next web page.

That same day, Carol happened upon an online notice posted by the Vermont State Police that included an artist's rendering of a young man who had a strong jaw and a shock of dark hair. She scanned the details: the remains had been discovered in 1997 in a remote area of southern Vermont when a Labrador retriever had trotted home one day with its teeth clamped around a human skull. A day or so later, the dog brought back a lower jaw, then a femur. The police outfitted the dog with a radio collar, but no more bones turned up. Based on certain characteristics of the thighbone, the medical examiner thought the deceased might have been disabled.

Carol went back to the missing-person listing for Sean Cutler. The skull and bones were discovered less than a year after the suspicious fire. The clay model based on the remains showed a dark-haired young man with a prominent brow, an unnaturally jutting chin, slightly parted lips. "There were so many things in common: the geographical similarities, the look, the disability," Carol recalled later. "I looked at it, and I knew."

A man named Patrick Harkness, Sean's cousin, had posted an Internet plea for help finding Sean. Carol e-mailed Harkness.

Carol learned from Harkness that Lewis and Sean Cutler had lived for a time in upstate New York in the early 1990s, not far from rural, woodsy Readsboro, Vermont. Harkness told her about the carbon monoxide poisoning that disabled Sean, the settlement, and Lewis Cutler's cutting off all ties with the family in 1995.

Exactly how and when Sean Cutler died is still a mystery. To Harkness and others who reconstructed the last few years of Lewis Cutler's life, a picture emerged of a troubled man who, while taking good care of his son, was also gambling away his trust fund in the stock market. Lewis lost more than a hundred thousand dollars in 1995 alone. Police speculated that Lewis, desperate and running out of money, killed his son, buried his body in the Vermont woods, and then set fire to the New Jersey house in an attempt to cover his tracks before he fled the country. Spitzer's brother told police a pilot was scheduled to pick up Lewis Cutler a day after the fire and fly him to the Caribbean. But something clearly went terribly wrong for the two men inside the burning house.

Six months after Carol's tip to the Vermont State Police led to Sean's identification, Carol attended Sean's memorial ceremony in upstate New York. A woman who identified herself as one of Sean's aunts approached her. "What you did made it possible for all of us to be here today," she told Carol.

Harkness, who during his search for his cousin had become a follower of the Doe Network, persuaded Carol to join the group. She perused it daily, over time joining its administrative board and helping vet other members' matches.

Carol still hadn't accomplished what she had set out to do: find her ex-husband.

In 2008, four years after Sean Cutler's memorial service, Todd Smith's sister phoned Carol. "Are you sitting down?" she asked her former sister-in-law.

"He drowned," she told Carol. "They found him in the ocean at Daytona Beach, and he had flippers and a flashlight."

Carol felt her heart in her throat. "Oh, my God. Oh, my God."

On the Doe Network, she had come across a listing for a young man wearing flippers whom she had once considered a match for Todd. But too much didn't line up. For one thing, his age was cited as somewhere between eleven and twenty; Todd Smith was twenty-five. The dead man's eye color was gray; Todd's was bright blue. But the real deal-breaker, as far as Carol was concerned, was that the dead man had been found in the water. Todd wasn't keen on the beach and never swam in the ocean, even on summer family trips to Martha's Vineyard. "If this Doe was found on a golf course with a nine iron, I would have jumped on it, but the flippers and the flashlight? It made no sense," Carol said later.

On May 18, 1989, on the 300 block of South Ocean Beach in Daytona Beach the day after Todd left New Jersey, witnesses reported a man struggling in the water. Rescuers were unable to locate him, even with the use of a helicopter. His body washed ashore early the next morning.

Nineteen years later, scrolling through the Doe Network's listings for missing men, a forensic technician in Volusia County, Florida, working her way through the county's cold cases spotted a report for a tall man, over six feet, with curly hair. She scanned a poster showing Todd Smith in a tux at his wedding; a second photo of him with a trim little mustache; a third in which he was clean-shaven in a plaid shirt and oversized pink-tinted sunglasses. She looked at all four photos — the postmortem photo of a drowning victim who had never been identified, the ones online, the dates, and the description: white male, eleven to twenty years old, over six feet, 175 pounds. Greenish/gray eyes, curly brown/blond hair.

White-and-black patterned swim trunks; on his left wrist was a diver's flashlight on a strap; swimming flippers were on his feet. Mustache; circumcised; a two-inch surgical scar on the left lateral chest.

Todd's missing-person report listed him as six-three, 160 pounds, dark blond curly hair, blue eyes, with a small scar on his neck. The age, eye color, and scars didn't jibe, but still she said to herself, *That's my John Doe.*

She sent New Jersey police a fingerprint from the body. The prints pulled off Smith's car were confusing; the cops were never certain which were his. But the drowning victim's dental records matched Todd Smith's.

For days, Carol and Todd's family walked around asking one another: "Flippers and a flashlight? What was he doing?"

Looking for a document among Todd's things soon afterward, Carol found snapshots of her ex perched on a motorcycle in a parking lot surrounded by palm trees. Then she remembered that after they separated, Todd had gone to Aruba on one of his jaunts. In the next photo, date-marked July 1988, less than a year before he went missing, he was pictured underwater in full snorkeling gear.

When Todd left his car behind, Carol guessed he was embarking on one of his solo trips, this time to Daytona Beach, where he'd decided to snorkel, apparently alone and — given the fact that he had a flashlight — at night. The Atlantic was not the serene Caribbean, and Todd, an inexperienced ocean swimmer, was likely no match for the unforgiving waves and riptides.

After Todd's remains were positively identified, his sister and daughter flew to Florida to retrieve them. In New Jersey, they collected the suitcase containing his cremated remains from the baggage carousel. His sister put the suitcase down, fell to her knees, and said, "Todd, you're home."

When, as a little girl, Ashley had asked about her father, Carol told her that her father loved her and wished he could be with her. She was relieved when Ashley, who grew up tall, athletic, and blond like Todd, seemed to accept her vague reassurances. When she learned Todd's fate, Carol was relieved that he hadn't abandoned his child or his family after all, and that nobody had hurt him. But as Carol and I sat in her living room among papers and photos that pieced together strange truths about lives that would never have intersected if it weren't for MPCCN and the Doe Network,

Carol told me a story that indicated that she hadn't really been aware of what was going through Ashley's head.

Ashley once heard Carol remark about a friend, "It's like she fell off the face of the earth." Eight-year-old Ashley pictured the ground opening up in a yawning abyss. That, she thought with satisfaction, finally explained what had happened to her dad: Todd was walking along, minding his own business, when he took one false step and *whoosh,* he was gone.

In the decade after the first newsgroups appeared, Yahoo! groups such as Troy More's ColdCases logged tens of thousands of posts and signed on thousands of members seeking to play armchair detective with the burgeoning amount of information becoming available online. The web forum became their sitting room; its members played Watson to incarnations of Holmes. The new breed of sleuths spent hours a week, sometimes hours a day, surfing sites, typing "unidentified remains" and "missing persons" into search engines. Some forums were logging thousands of hits while Google and Wikipedia were in their infancy and YouTube didn't even exist.

In the 1940s, psychologist Harry F. Harlow discovered that monkeys would solve simple mechanical puzzles even if offered no rewards at all. They seemed to do it for the sheer fun of it, and Harlow speculated that human motivation also operated by what he called intrinsic drive. The clues people found on the fledgling Internet provided them with opportunities to use their powers of deduction in a public forum. Like Holmes, armchair detectives appreciate an admiring audience. Real-life mysteries are rarely clear-cut or resolved as neatly as fictional ones. But, like the monkeys' puzzles, they fascinate, maybe because of their ambiguity and complexity. Some amateur sleuths say working on a challenging case is like exercising a strong muscle. A twenty-three-year-old musician, posting on a blog, noted that he once thought he did puzzles because of the euphoria he experienced when he solved them, but then realized the process was just as satisfying as the solution.

Through a site that included official photographs, maps, forensic evidence, and copies of original missing-person reports, ColdCases users in the early part of the millennium second-guessed the police investigation into the Green River serial killer and other famous cases. Not only did the site provide an insider's perspective into how cases should be investigated, visitors could see where police completely dropped the ball.

The late James Q. Wilson, author and public policy expert, believed that cold cases are especially appealing precisely because early efforts to solve them have failed, intensifying the challenge. It's exactly the kind of game — trying to outsmart a clever murderer — Agatha Christie set up so irresistibly in tale after tale.

For generations weaned on Christie, John Grisham, Sue Grafton, and dozens of others, this was heady stuff. If Betty Brown or Troy More or Todd Matthews — or any of the other accomplished web sleuths I'd meet, such as determined Ellen Leach, eagle-eyed Daphne Owings, and sharp-thinking Bobby Lingoes — managed to match a missing person with unidentified remains, there was glory in accomplishing what no one else had managed to do. There was the exhilaration of outsmarting the police, who may have been uncooperative and dismissive, if not downright rude, when the web sleuth called with a question about that very case. There was fifteen minutes of fame if the local paper or *48 Hours* came knocking.

Sometimes, if a financial reward accompanied a solution, there was even money in it. No need to live vicariously through some fictitious detective; you could dabble in real deaths, complete with the occasional dismembered or torched corpse or serial killer victim.

Creating ColdCases was like throwing a fishing line into a pitch-black pond on a moonless night. But More built it, and many, including Todd Matthews, came.

It quickly became apparent to More who the regulars were. He enlisted Todd — who was researching missing women for chatty church ladies from Indiana who'd met and befriended him at Tent Girl's grave — to keep a lookout for inappropriate comments on ColdCases; frequent contributor Jennifer "Stormy" Marra to keep up E-clipse's website and answer e-mail; and an avid member named Helene Wahlstrom, who lived in Sweden, to populate the site with cases from around the world. Wahlstrom came across ColdCases and Marra's Doe Network at a time in her life when she was unable to leave her house alone. A rape and stalking survivor, she suffered from post-traumatic stress disorder and had been forced to terminate her studies at a Swedish university. At the time, using an e-mail address in which the word "turtle" stood in for her name, Helene was clearly hiding in her shell, living a quiet life at home with her father while scouring the Internet for cold cases.

When I tracked down Wahlstrom in Sweden, she told me that at first she was mystified by the power the missing and unidentified exerted over her. Later, she could see that she had identified with all those victims. By volunteering to help others who had suffered a loss, she said she hoped something good would emerge from her pain and self-imposed seclusion.

Meanwhile, Todd, recognizing that Jennifer Marra's site was more polished and technologically advanced than his own, joined the Doe Network in 2001 and closed down The Lost and the Found. That year, Marra decided to spend more time with her family and turned the day-to-day maintenance of the Doe Network over to Wahlstrom, who not only posted daily on Cold-Cases but who had also become Marra's second in command.

With no need to divulge one's identity, background, or motivation, it was hard to know exactly who these web sleuths were and why they flocked to sites like Cold-Cases, Websleuths, and Official Cold Case

Investigations. Voyeuristic? Creepy? Sociopathic? Were these Sherlock Holmes wannabes doing a good thing or a bad thing?

The doubt stemmed in part from the cloak of anonymity the Internet conferred on its users; there was no way of knowing who wickedprincess222 really was. You needed a Sherlock Holmes just to distinguish the good guys from the bad guys. "It's like the KKK," Todd once commented. "You can post anything you want wearing that hood."

One exchange I unearthed went a long way toward illustrating the disturbing anonymity of those who read and contributed to cold case forums.

In July 2007, a member of Websleuths sat at her computer in Phoenixville, Pennsylvania. The users of the forum typically gave themselves screen names — Magnum P.E., momtective, Twindad, latenightRN, MidwestMama — or some version of a real name, such as Darlene735. The one near Philly called herself Gina M. She threw a question out into cyberspace about a mystery almost four decades old: Whatever happened to Elizabeth Ernstein?

In 1968, officials in Scott County, Kentucky, focused for a time on a missing teenager who seemed to fit Tent Girl's description — around five foot five; 105 pounds; short, dark bobbed hair — who had disappeared almost exactly two months before Tent Girl was found. Nearly fifteen-year-old Elizabeth Lurene Ernstein lived in Mentone, a town near Redlands, California. On the morning of March 18, 1968, she set out for school wearing a blue dress with a white flower print, a small gold chain necklace, and tennis shoes, carrying a red algebra book and a blue notebook, with a quarter in her pocket. Friends would say later that Elizabeth, called Liz by her friends and Betty Lu by her family, had seemed depressed for the past few days.

She had said something about joining a "hippie colony" near San Francisco, but her mother knew her daughter to be so meticulous about personal hygiene that even if Liz had decided to run away, which was un-imaginable, she would have taken along a change of clothing. Liz left school at 3:40 p.m. to walk home two miles through blossoming orange groves. Someone had spotted her that afternoon on a palm tree-lined street amid the groves, the blue notebook and algebra textbook under her arm. She never arrived home.

Her parents, a Lockheed chemical engineer and a psychiatric social worker, offered five thousand dollars for any information that would help them find their daughter. They sent word of her disappearance to a reported ten thousand newspapers. An Associated Press photo datelined San Bernardino shows the couple — both dark-haired and slender, their faces tense and drawn — gazing up at a towering pile of boxes containing the circulars about to be mailed nationwide. Dozens of papers, in Texas, Massachusetts, Missouri, Pennsylvania, Minnesota, and other states, including Kentucky, ran the story. The Georgetown, Kentucky, papers ran breathless headlines anticipating a solution to the Tent Girl mystery, but no proof materialized that Liz Ernstein was Tent Girl.

After an initial flurry of coverage, no further details emerged. That silence would not be broken for almost forty years, and when it was, it would be through a medium no one living in the era of black-and-white television in 1968 had envisioned.

It wasn't unusual for a post such as Gina M.'s to be followed almost immediately by speculative comments from fellow users. If someone dug up a scrap of information — a newspaper story or some other tidbit — they'd often post it. As the more experienced web sleuths knew, missing children who returned home unharmed didn't generate press coverage, so it was conceivable that Liz had come home with little public fanfare, or with fanfare that had been obliterated by time. On the other hand, Liz had never been reported dead. That would have made the papers.

A few months after Gina M. posted her query and rehashed the details of Liz's disappearance, she received an answer that seemed to ring with authority. "We never found her body or any evidence of her running away," wrote someone who signed himself Jeff E. "We"? The writer identified himself as Elizabeth Ernstein's younger brother, Jeff Ernstein. He recalled that, in 1968, California was the pinnacle of the hippie movement, when some teenagers ran away for a weekend — or forever. Abductions, rapes, murders, he wrote, "just hardly ever happened back then."

He related how his parents had paid a private detective to work for the family full-time. Norman and Ruth Ernstein, despite their science-based careers, were so desperate, they contacted psychics and even checked in with NASA and the U.S. Air Force in case there had been any reports in the area of UFO alien abductions. The Ernsteins ran out of funds. Volunteers helped raise money for ads, for the detective, and for a reward that eventually totaled twenty thousand dollars — the equivalent of more than a hundred grand today.

Search-and-rescue teams and hundreds of volunteers combed the orange groves and surrounding countryside, to find no trace of Liz except a bra in her size, washed in the same detergent the household used. The family held a memorial for Liz in the early 1990s.

The next few posts by Websleuths members thanked Jeff for his post and encouraged him to send details about Elizabeth to the National Center for Missing & Exploited Children. Jeff E. did not respond.

Scanning later posts in the thread, I saw one from another Websleuths user named James G. It was dated December 2009, a full two years after Gina M. and Jeff E.'s exchange. James G. gave his location as Southern California.

"I just stumbled by accident on this site after Googling your sister Elizabeth's name," James G. wrote to Jeff E. What came next sent a chill down my spine.

"I was her boy friend at the time of her disappearance. You may remember me. I went with her and your mother and a friend of your mom's up to the mountains not very long before Elizabeth disappeared. One of her brothers went along but I am not sure of his name. It seems to me I remember the name of the boy being Jeff but I'm not positive of that. I know that he was about 10 or so. We had a picnic and a good visit. I remember what she said to me as we walked around. I even remember the conversation in the car going up and coming back. Do you have any memory of this?

"Also, only a short time (maybe a week) before she disappeared, Elizabeth called my family and told them that she needed to meet me and tell me something very important. She wanted to meet me in front of Redlands Community Hospital, but I went there and waited for Elizabeth for over an hour, and she never showed up."

Was it possible that new information about the days before Liz's disappearance would surface this way, on an obscure page of public web posts? It would be like a document concerning a crime in New Mexico turning up stapled to a supermarket bulletin board in Hoboken, New Jersey. It might be significant, but the chances of someone with any connection to the original investigation seeing it were practically nil.

James G. went on to request specific details about the family, the circumstances of Elizabeth's disappearance, and the investigation.

"I'd especially like to know if Elizabeth's older sister is still alive. Also is your mother still alive? I'd like to know where the orange groves were located where she was last seen. Are there still orange groves there or have they been replaced by houses and streets? Where was the bra found?

"It would be great to be able to talk with you. I live not very far from Redlands. I always think of her when I drive on the freeway near where she and your family lived at that time. I hope to hear from you soon. James G." The post included links to Facebook and to a Myspace page. To my disappointment, they were defunct.

The nature of relatively anonymous web postings forced me to wonder: Are both Jeff E. and James G. who they claim to be, a grieving brother and a curious ex-boyfriend?

I came across a 2009 obituary for a Stephen Ernstein, a 1970 graduate of Redlands, who could have been Liz's older brother; the Jeff E. who posted on Websleuths could have been her younger brother. (At the time that Liz disappeared, newspaper accounts said she came from a family of five, in which the oldest son had died of polio in 1962.)

At first it struck me as almost unbeliev-
able that Jeff Ernstein would happen upon
Gina M.'s posts about his sister, who had
been missing for thirty-nine years; but Jeff
commented in his post that he had been
watching a program about the impact on
families of a murder of a child, and that got
him thinking about his sister and prompted
him to search for her on the Internet. The
thread surprised him, because news of her
disappearance, as far as he knew, had
dropped off the radar by late 1969.

Having your sibling disappear and growing up with parents obsessed with and
emotionally drained by efforts to find her
could not have been easy. Jeff himself may
not ever have given up hope of finding his
sister alive. Like others who had had a loved
one go missing, he may have been drawn to
the cold case message boards' tantalizing
bits of information that dangled in cyberspace, available to anyone who happened
along.

But as for his claim that abductions, rapes,
and murders "hardly ever happened" in the
1960s, well, that was wishful thinking.

Serial murderer Charles Hatcher, for one,
confessed to fifteen child murders dating
back to 1969 in four states, including
California. The Zodiac serial murderer, who

claimed to have killed thirty-seven people, started his reign of terror in California the year Liz went missing. In 1970, Mack Ray Edwards told police that he had killed six kids over a twenty-year period in and around Los Angeles.

Before Edwards died in prison in 1972, his claim had increased to eighteen children. It seems not only possible but likely that Liz was abducted, perhaps by a stranger or by someone she knew, murdered far from the orange groves, and hidden so well — perhaps in the nearby San Bernardino National Forest or the San Jacinto Mountains, or in the Pacific Ocean, only around an hour's drive away — that no one ever found her body.

There was no indication that Jeff E. ever saw James G.'s post, and if he had, he might have dismissed James G. as a wacko, as I was inclined to. There's never any way of knowing who you are dealing with on the Internet, whether what people post is real or delusional, or why they are posting in the first place. I mulled the possible implications of Elizabeth knowing James G. when she was fourteen and seeking him out to tell him "something very important." It sounded like something out of a bad suspense novel. Was it possible that the private investigators working for the Ernsteins had never interviewed this man? Was this a clue to a murder investigation, or nothing at all?

Why did James G. want to know if the orange groves were still there, and where the bra was found? If he still lived close to Redlands, as he claimed, wouldn't he know whether the groves were there, or couldn't he drive by himself to look?

James G.'s questions struck me as creepy if not downright alarming. He referred to "Elizabeth." If they'd been as friendly as he claimed, wouldn't he have called her Liz, as her other friends did?

I never found the answers to my questions about James G., but incredibly, in 2011, half a lifetime after Liz Ernstein disappeared, remains that had been discovered in 1969 in a shallow grave near Wrightwood — a sparsely populated town nestled in a pine-covered valley in the San Gabriel Mountains around fifty miles from the orange groves — were reexamined. At the time, the coroner had characterized the remains as those of a young male.

Acting on a suggestion from a web sleuth who questioned the original forensic analysis, the San Bernardino County coroner exhumed the remains, which had been buried in a mass grave in a county cemetery.

In 2012, DNA confirmed that the remains were Ernstein's.

Once again, Jeff Ernstein surfaced briefly, this time to comment on a 2012 news story about his sister's remains posted by *Mail Online,* a wildly popular offshoot of the British tabloid *The Daily Mail.* Liz was very slender, he wrote, and he could see how she was mistaken for a teenaged boy. Besides, many young men then had long hair. Liz had had no dental work done besides cleanings, hence no records. "My mother, father, and older brother all passed away without knowing for sure . . . Thank you all and pray we catch an old killer, if still alive," signed "her brother. - J Ernstein, Jackson, United States."

The posts by Jeff E., James G., and Gina M. spanning more than five years were like a dialogue between actors performing an existential play before an enormous audience that came and went at will. An actor might speak a few lines one night, fall silent for years, and then pipe up again in front of a group of people who had completely missed the first act.

In 2013, ColdCases lived on — having logged a total of more than seventy thousand posts since 1999, with two thousand per month at its peak between 2005 and 2007 — although its creator, Troy More, was long gone. In one of More's final posts on ColdCases, in 2001, he reported to his loyal following that he had moved to New Zealand and was hot on the trail of one of the oldest unsolved cases in New Zealand history, that of an unidentified woman discovered floating in Wellington Harbor in 1902.

ColdCases accomplished what More originally set out to do: spread the word about Caledonia Jane Doe. As a result of More's efforts, sixteen hundred people from newsgroups around the world, some as far afield as Israel, Australia, Kazakhstan, and New Zealand, offered an assortment of theories and tips about her murder. Unfortunately, none of them helped identify her.

Both More and Doe founder Jennifer Marra seem to have vanished from the Web. Perhaps if you know how to maneuver within little-known corners of the Internet, you're equally skilled at making yourself invisible.

There was no question that web forums exposed cold cases to fresh eyes, resurrecting them from obscurity; but ironically the people behind these efforts receded behind the Internet's potentially insidious veil.

Faces, identities, and motives became as opaque as the facts of the cases themselves. The forums reminded me of Alice in Wonderland. It was perpetually teatime in the virtual world, and conversations were as out of sync as Alice's and the Mad Hatter's. And Alice, the White Rabbit, and the Mad Hatter could be anyone at all.

# 4
## GHOST GIRLS

Livingston, Tennessee, is plopped like the yolk of a sunny-side-up egg in a valley roughly midway between Nashville, home of country music, and Knoxville, birthplace of Mountain Dew and the Dempster-Dumpster. The Highland Rim, an escarpment of stratified bedrock, encircles the region like an ancient fortification that defined Todd Matthews's world for the first half of his life.

Livingston's downtown looks like someone stopped the clock in 1955. Even in 2012, a citizen who votes to allow liquor to be sold within county lines runs the risk of being accused of openly and willingly courting the devil and is ostracized accordingly. *The Jeffersons, The Dukes of Hazzard, Knight Rider,* and *I Dream of Jeannie* provided the only proof to young Todd that there was civilization beyond the mountains. He didn't encounter blacks until he was eight years old and his family sought medical care for his congenital heart condition in Nashville, a hundred miles away. The city, talking cars, a genie in a bottle, a middle-class black family — all seemed equally fantastical to a boy growing up in small-town Tennessee in the early 1970s.

Athletic fields and parking lots dwarf Livingston Academy's low brick academic building, much as they did during Todd's time there as a student in the late 1980s. In those days, the football queen wore a strapless white gown with a hoop petticoat overlaid with lace. The dresses of her royal attendants were tiered pastel affairs as big as pup tents. In the yearbook's head-and-shoulder portraits, the girls' big hair fell in bangs curling like spiders' legs over their foreheads. The boys' hair, with the exception of Todd's, was conservatively short. Todd's wavy 'do reached a height that rivaled some of the girls'. And he was the only student with a chinstrap beard.

In the South, men pride themselves on their toughness and self-reliance. Boys grow up with a football in one hand and a hunting rifle in the other, but Todd, born with a bum heart, wasn't allowed to play sports or hunt. The closest he got to running with the rah-rah football crowd was announcing the members of the marching band, team, and cheerleaders at games.

When it was time for animal dissections in biology lab, some girls groaned while the boys, accustomed to shooting and skinning deer, squirrels, rabbits, and raccoons, were unfazed by the cardboard box full of dead cats, each in a plastic bag secured with a rubber band. The animals were sliced lengthwise through the belly, the arteries and veins injected with red or blue dye. At the beginning of the year, Todd had struck a deal with his lab partner, Wayne Sells: Todd, the more talented artist, would sketch the splayed animal's innards, while Wayne did the actual cutting. Nothing would have induced Todd to lift a scalpel.

Todd — imaginative, artistic, stubborn — stymied his father, the Fort Benning recruit who had shipped out to Vietnam soon after Wilbur Riddle stumbled on Tent Girl.

Just before Todd was born, Billy Matthews brought home a Purple Heart from his stint in the Special Forces. He was driving alone on a Tennessee highway when an oncoming vehicle veered into his path, demolishing both cars and breaking both of Billy's legs. Years later, on his forty-sixth birthday, Billy was driving a tanker full of diesel on a short-haul circuit between Nashville and Knoxville when the fuel caught fire on Highway 111 in Cookeville. He escaped by kicking out the truck cab's rear window with the heel of his cowboy boot. His neck, arms, and chest were badly burned but he was not killed, as the news reported that day. He became known as the man with nine lives.

When I met Billy Matthews, he was still wiry and fit, a Clint Eastwood look-alike in jeans, athletic shoes, and a dark oxford shirt with a ballpoint pen in the pocket. Practically vibrating with nervous energy, he patted his receding hairline, fiddled with his watch, and cheerfully reminisced about how he used to give Todd whippings for being "hardheaded." Daddy, as Todd and his brother Mark still call him, hadn't demanded that his sons take on many household chores but when he said be home by nine o'clock, you'd better be home. Todd didn't dare drink or smoke pot in high school; Billy Matthews would have killed him.

In October 1987, Todd had just started his senior year. He was having lunch with a friend in the cafeteria when he spotted a girl he had never seen before. She was petite, with soulful brown eyes. Her dark hair fell in perfect waves just past the shoulders of her burgundy rain jacket emblazoned with the name of some other school.

Even if the sixteen-year-old girl noticed Todd gazing at her across the room, she was unaware that she had unwittingly become his personal quest, and that this would change her life. Meanwhile, there was no question in Todd's mind that this girl, whoever she was and wherever she had come from, was his future wife.

Word got around that the new girl had moved to Livingston from northern Kentucky; her name was Lori Ann Riddle, and she was a junior. Todd spent the hours after lunch wondering how to insert himself into Lori's path. The last period of the day, he walked into study hall and saw her seated there. He gave a slight nod of acknowledgment to some higher being before walking over and sitting down next to her.

Lori and Todd started dating. If Todd had a premonition about his future father-in-law as he had had about his future wife, he never mentioned it. But his first meeting with Wilbur Riddle would prove as life-changing as his first glimpse of Riddle's daughter.

Swapping spooky tales on their first Halloween together, Lori told Todd her best real-life ghost story: the one about her daddy finding a dead body in Kentucky.

The day Wilbur Riddle and I made our pilgrimage to the Tent Girl site, Riddle decided we must drop in on his old friend Bobby G. Vance, the former sheriff of Scott County, the man Wilbur had raced to phone when he saw what was encased in the tarp. Sheriff Vance's office back then was in the imposing nineteenth-century brick courthouse adorned with a non-blindfolded Lady Justice that still stands in the heart of historic downtown Georgetown, a straight shot down Route 25 from Sadieville. Tall, solid, with dark hair, Vance, although still a young man in 1968, had served two four-year terms as deputy sheriff in the three-person department before being elected to a four-year term as sheriff. Most locals knew Vance by sight. Georgetown was — and is — small-town South, where the sheriff shook his forefinger at rowdy boys and threatened to tell their daddies on them. Vance knew Wilbur Riddle may not have been the straightest arrow, but he wouldn't joke about a corpse.

It was around ten in the morning on that day in May when Vance pulled his cruiser in beside Riddle's truck. The two men hustled down the embankment to the spot by the creek where the bundle lay. They peered at it as if it had fallen to earth from outer space. Vance was wearing a suit, white shirt, and tie. The odor had gotten worse, and as Riddle remembers it, Vance was promptly sick in the bushes.

"Will you open it?" Vance said to Riddle.

"Yeah, I'll open it."

Among his many avocations, Riddle traded knives. He typically had one or two new bone-handled Case Canoe penknives in his pocket, but he chose an old, rusty blade; he didn't want that smell on his knife. He didn't think it would ever come off. Done, he placed the knife on the ground. Riddle had sliced the fabric at a place that happened to expose the back of a neck.

The flesh looked petrified, like shoe leather. In a corpse, the intestinal bacteria that help break down food start to produce a foul-smelling gas that flows into the blood vessels and tissues. The gas bloats the body and blackens the skin. Even seasoned coroners can find it harrowing to encounter a neglected body at close range.

"What is it?" Vance said, still queasy.

"It's a girl."

"White or black?' "

"White," Riddle said.

At around eleven, Vance phoned Kentucky State Police Post 12 in Frankfort. Detective Edward L. Cornett picked up the phone. The report he typed up a few days later said that Bob Vance, sheriff of Scott County, stated that a body tied up in a tarpaulin had been found in a rural area beside US 25 thirteen miles north of Georgetown by one "Wilburn" Riddle, and Vance had requested that the state police help with the investigation.

Meanwhile, deputy coroner Kenneth Grant, Deputy Sheriff Jimmy Williams, and a newspaper reporter arrived. A photographer captured the incongruous scenes I later saw of men in black suits and narrow ties kneeling on the brush-covered ground and conferring in groups like accountants lost in the woods.

The bundle was loaded onto an ambulance and taken to Johnson's Funeral Home near downtown Georgetown, then to Saint Joseph Hospital in nearby Lexington, where the autopsy commenced in a basement room at five o'clock in the afternoon.

Murder was not a common occurrence in Scott County in the sixties. During Vance's entire twelve-year tenure, there had been only one besides Tent Girl: an irate wife shot her drunk husband to death in bed. The

Tent Girl case was, Todd would tell me later, like "murder in Mayberry." By the time I met him, Vance even looked like Andy Griffith.

Vance lived in a big, stately brick house at the end of a long driveway in a subdivision of stately houses on spacious lots not far from his former office in the courthouse. He was long retired from the sheriff's department as well as from his second career, as county tax assessor. He answered the door with his wife, Maxine, at his side. His hair was gray and he walked with a hesitant step, but he was as tall and striking as in the news photos taken at the edge of Route 25 forty-three years earlier. With all the flourish of a Southern gentleman, he escorted me to a seat in the dining room, where a vinyl-covered photo album sat on the table. "It's been so long, I don't know what I can remember," Vance apologized. "My head don't work like it used to."

Maxine, round and affable, was as quick and lively as her husband was deliberate and slow. As soon as we sat down she urged him, "Why don't you tell her what you did?" Vance fanned open the pages of the album, which turned out to contain a collection of newspaper clippings, police reports, autopsy results, and a copy of the 1969 *Master Detective*.

Vance gripped each yellowing page in its plastic sheath like a lifeline, perusing them through smudged bifocals. After a lengthy pause, he intoned as though quoting scripture, "We went down there, the coroner and I, and Wilbur, it seemed like, had found this body over a rock wall and he sort of kicked it and maybe it rolled down the hill. Maybe an arm rolled out."

Vance remembered joining Riddle at the scene. He recalled that the body, severely decayed, smelled terrible. Paramedics took it to Johnson's Funeral Home and then to a hospital to conduct the autopsy.

"You went to that, didn't you?" Maxine prompted.

"I very well did," Vance said.

"Johnson was there with you. He wanted to go eat and you were sick." Maxine didn't try to hide her amusement at her husband's weak stomach. Vance probably wished he had skipped breakfast that day.

"It smelled up the whole bottom of that hospital, to tell you the truth, it was that bad. I remember it was a hot, muggy spring and it was just terrible, seeing the maggots around her," Vance said, peering at me with the glasses slipping down his nose. "I hate to tell you that, but it's true."

A grandfather clock ticked.

Maxine leaned forward and put her hand on her husband's arm. "She wants you to tell her the rest of the story, Bobby," she said.

With Vance, state police detective Ed Cornett, a deputy sheriff, the deputy coroner, and two hospital employees gathered around the autopsy table, Dr. James T. McClellan made the first incision, in the neck, near the spot Riddle had exposed by ripping open the bag. The color and texture of the skin struck him as skinned and raw. Peeling the rest of the fabric away exposed flesh churning with fly larvae.

"When the body is placed on the autopsy table, it is seen to be that of a young white female whose age is estimated to be near eighteen years," McClellan wrote. "She is five foot one inch in length. The hair is reddish-brown and fairly short. The eyes are decomposed and their color cannot be determined. The scalp is partially decomposed but is dried. The right side of the face is partially decomposed and sloughed away. The mouth hangs open." No fillings, but a line of decay was visible along the edge of an upper front tooth, a fact that became

129

important much later.

In his official report, McClellan noted that the tarpaulin was made of a thin green waterproof canvas, both ends tied with heavy cotton rope of a type that might be used for tents, awnings, or clotheslines threaded through the eyelets. She was naked except for a slightly ragged hand towel draped across her right shoulder, back, and lower right neck, McClellan noted. It was a mystery why it was resting on her shoulder, Riddle said later. The police report called it a small white towel similar to ones used by motels, with spots of blood on it, but at various points the cloth would be identified as the kind of towel found in roll-up dispensers common in service station lavatories and later, most significantly, as a baby's diaper.

There were no flesh wounds to indicate choking, hanging, or trauma. X-rays revealed no evidence of bullets or broken bones. McClellan removed the fourth finger of the left hand for fingerprints, and stored organ specimens in a refrigerator. Eight days later, the organ tissue was delivered to Cincinnati for toxicological tests.

A state police sergeant took photos during the autopsy. In one photo, a figure — presumably McClellan in a white lab coat — is visible at the edge of the frame. With his hand encased in a light-colored latex glove, he grips the corpse slightly below the right shoulder, supporting it upright for the photographer. The ravaged face — nose gone, teeth bared in a gruesome grin, left eyeball melted away, right glowing white in its socket, a swath of hair matted to the cratered, blackened forehead — is turned toward the camera over what remains of the left shoulder. The effect, despite the horrific state of the corpse, is oddly coquettish, the toothy smile almost cheerful.

McClellan tried to determine how much time had elapsed since the young woman's death, but he conceded that the presence of fly larvae was not very helpful. Flies descend on a corpse and deposit eggs that hatch into larvae in eight to fourteen hours. Larvae burrow into the decaying flesh and produce large crateriform cavities, he wrote, and leave a dirty gray slough on the surface of the skin. After nine to twelve days, the larvae morph into pupae, but no pupae were found on the young woman, leading McClellan to surmise that the larvae were present for no more than twelve days.

Yet, the fact that the organs were intact but that the blood in the vessels and heart had completely disappeared suggested a time interval of a month, with the greatest interval possibly no more than two months, he wrote. This didn't jibe with the insect evidence. On the other hand, the bag covering the body may have protected it from flies for quite some time, McClellan noted. There had been both warm and cool periods in the preceding weeks; these would have affected the rate of decomposition, the cold slowing it down, the heat speeding it along. In the end, McClellan seemed uncertain. He settled on "six weeks to two months" preceding May 17, the day the body was discovered, as the likely time of death.

Trooper Cornett's report reiterated facts from the autopsy: The young woman weighed between 110 and 115 pounds. Her reddish-brown hair was cut short in a "bubble" style. She had been crammed into the bag with her legs folded and her torso bent double, almost in a sitting position.

Peering over McClellan's shoulder during the autopsy, Cornett, who had a cleft chin and a sharp part in his Brylcreemed hair, jotted details that he undoubtedly hoped would help determine her identity and aid in a criminal investigation. "It should be noted that the victim's hair was cut short and her fingernails was [sic] long but neatly kept," Cornett wrote. It was impossible to say if her intact face had been pretty or plain, the deputy coroner told *The Kentucky Post,* but for his part, he thought the girl would have been "very presentable" because of her elegantly kept nails.

Newspapers would later report that her right hand was clenched, the fingernails shattered as if she'd try to claw her way out.

On his official report, under "Accused," and "Suspects," Cornett wrote, "None." Under "Motive," he wrote, "Unknown."

After Wilbur Riddle drove home that day and announced to his wife, Julie, that he'd found a body near a creek, he recalled that not more than a week or two earlier he'd dreamed about finding a dead girl. "And I told her there's going to be detectives, the state police, the sheriff all coming around" because that's the way it happened in his dream, he told me. But no one came around. Riddle made phone calls, demanding to know what they did about that dead body he found.

He reached Ed Cornett, who told him that more than a hundred missing young women matched the description of the body in the tarp. In the following days, weeks, and months, he returned to Sadieville, driving "real slow down through there to see if anything lying on the road looked strange," he said.

Alone one day, he spotted tracks that looked like they had been formed by a little car, perhaps one of those Volkswagen Beetles, backing up to the rock from the road. He called the state police to report leaves mashed down in the mud in the shape of tire tracks. But the police didn't seem interested and the reporters and photographers, who had snapped away as he posed peering at the weedy spot now devoid of a lumpy bundle, had stopped calling. And still he could learn nothing about the progress of the investigation.

He was irked by the silence. If there was any news, he figured he should be the first to know.

Sheriff Bobby Vance and Ed Cornett dodged tiresome Wilbur Riddle, and equally insistent reporters, by retiring to Vance's house in town to work on the case. Despite Cornett's apparent brush-off of Wilbur's tale of muddy tire tracks, he did think that the young woman's body had been transported by car. Apparently the body had been placed inside the bag, hauled or brought to the scene, lifted across the fence, and placed at the foot of an elm tree approximately one foot from the wire fence, Cornett had written in his report.

To reporters from *The Kentucky Post &*

*Times-Star,* he theorized that it must have taken more than one person to tie up and lug the awkward, misshapen bundle forty feet from the gravel turnoff to the edge of the embankment. He and Vance suspected that the body had been dumped at night, because — despite the existence of the new highway — US 25 was a well-traveled road and passing drivers might have easily spotted one or more men engaged in the grisly task. Based solely on the fact that the girl was discovered close to the interstate, Cornett declared to reporters that she was definitely from outside Scott County and probably from out of state. Vance concurred that it was possible that she was killed somewhere else and brought to Scott County. Investigators from Philadelphia, where another girl had turned up murdered and dumped in a bag a few weeks earlier, pointed out that it was possible to drive from Philadelphia to Cincinnati, and then south to Scott County, Kentucky, without exiting a highway.

At the time, towns newly connected to the interstate system worried about the highway bringing a new, threatening, unknown presence into small-town America: their turf was being invaded by strangers with no connections to the region.

This fear would be borne out years after construction of I-75 was completed. Twelve unidentified women would be found nude and stabbed in rural wooded areas adjacent to the highway starting in the late 1990s. One theory was that these crimes were committed by the same person, the I-70 Killer, or a copycat. The I-70 Killer was a serial killer who had committed a string of murders within a few miles of the interstate in several Midwestern states in the 1980s. A serial killer, perhaps working as a truck driver, was picking up women from truck stops or bars along I-75 and then dumping their bodies just off the main thoroughfare in Tennessee and Kentucky. But although investigators in 1968 envisioned Tent Girl as this type of victim, it would turn out that her presumed attacker was someone she knew well — or thought she did.

The city editor of *The Kentucky Post* asked a patrolman in Covington, where the newspaper was based, to sketch Tent Girl. The patrolman, Harold Musser, an amateur artist, had previously been called upon to create likenesses of suspected criminals and drowning victims. Musser spent almost a week poring over photos and slides of her melted, decayed face, quizzing Cornett about what he had seen at the autopsy, speaking with bone specialists, and studying the dead girl's facial structure.

The paper ran Musser's black-and-white pencil sketch of a young woman with bobbed hair, high cheekbones, arched eyebrows, and a gap between her front teeth; the image also circulated as a nation-wide bulletin under the heading "Do you know this girl?"

The mother of fifteen-year-old Doris Dittmar of Maryland saw the sketch and tear-fully told investigators she was sure the girl was Doris, who had been seen leaving town with a group of "swingers, hippies and un-desirables."

The FBI said hair samples from Doris and Tent Girl were a nearly certain match. Doris's family summoned her older brother home from Vietnam to attend the funeral. They made arrangements to have Tent Girl's body transported to their home in Pasadena, Maryland, for services and burial at the Methodist church where Doris had attended Sunday School for the past three years.

The problem was, Doris was far from dead. Her family soon discovered she'd run off with her boyfriend to Pennsylvania, where the couple lived in a shack and pretended to be married. Doris arrived home wearing fake wedding and engagement rings, her nails bitten to the quick and her reputation ruined. Her mother was so humiliated that she said she would rather Doris was dead.

Cornett was swamped by inquiries from others who thought they knew Tent Girl. A maintenance man from Newport, Kentucky, drove more than seventy miles to Georgetown to see if the body was that of his wife, who had left their apartment earlier that month and hadn't been heard from since. A man came to Vance and Cornett with a rambling story about picking up three hitchhikers. He seemed to be confessing to something, but Vance wasn't sure what. Cornett ruled out other leads based on glaring discrepancies in height, weight, age, and dental structure.

Meanwhile, the green canvas bag, the rope it was tied with, and the small piece of white cloth found over one of Tent Girl's shoulders were sent to the FBI's Washington, D.C., laboratory for examination.

On March 9, 1968, sixteen-year-old Candace Clothier, a high school junior and daughter of a Philadelphia firefighter, went to visit friends in nearby Mayfair. On April 13, a few weeks before Tent Girl was discovered, two fishermen found a black cloth bag containing the decomposed body of an unidentified female floating in a creek around a hundred yards south of a bridge in what was then rural Northampton Township. The victim's skull showed a slight discoloration of the skin in the same spot on the right side as on Tent Girl's skull; both corpses were wrapped in canvas bags tied with rope from top to bottom and the feet tucked under the torsos.

Both bodies had been dumped off main roads near creeks and had remained undiscovered for four to six weeks. Scott County attorney Virgil Pryor, Cornett, and others believed Clothier's murderer might lead them to Tent Girl, but no leads panned out in the Clothier case.

(Candace Clothier's murder would remain unsolved for forty-two years. In 2010, a woman identified the bag in which Clothier was found as a black laundry bag she had owned in 1968 and had given to her then husband. She saw him hand the bag along to two men in a car. All three men, who police believe had taken Clothier to a house where she died of a drug overdose before they disposed of her body, died between 1975 and 2000. Barring the strikingly similar methods of disposal of the bodies, there was no apparent connection to Tent Girl.)

Liz Ernstein, the missing California teen who popped up on Websleuths decades later, was considered and ruled out.

Meanwhile, the FBI lab tests on the canvas bag, the rope, and the cloth all drew a blank. The material was a sturdy, water-resistant fabric made by a number of manufacturers and distributed throughout the country. The rope was unremarkable.

And the white toweling was actually part of a baby's diaper, a point that Todd, for one, would latch onto years later to argue that Tent Girl may not have been a teenage girl at all but a young mother. At the time, all three items were too widely manufactured and distributed for their sources to be narrowed down.

State police were able to get one good fingerprint from one of Tent Girl's badly decomposed hands, a print they hoped to compare to those of missing girls or a missing girl's personal effects. Later, the finger amputated for this purpose would mysteriously disappear.

After a time, frustrated investigators called in the coroner of Hamilton County, Ohio, to perform another autopsy. He found no trace of poison or toxic material, only a slight discoloration of her skull. "We now think," Cornett said, "the girl was rendered unconscious by a blow to the head, then tied up in the tarpaulin to die a slow death by asphyxiation."

Although there is a possibility that she had never regained consciousness, Cornett suspected that Tent Girl died a horrible and lingering death, clawing at the tough canvas with her elegantly manicured nails.

As Bobby Vance relived those days in his dining room, he was still frustrated decades later by how hard he and Cornett, who died in 1977, had worked just to come up dry. "I wished it could have been resolved," he said. "You want to close the case."

Cornett's boss, state police lieutenant Algin Roberts, held out hope that one obvious physical feature — the space between Tent Girl's two upper front teeth, and what might have been decay — would lead to her identification. Roberts told reporters that someone who knew her might recall a dark spot there that would become visible whenever she smiled.

Roberts had no way of knowing that he was right: that distinctive gap and dark spot would lead a forensic anthropologist to agree that maybe there was a match between Tent Girl and a young woman, depicted in a grainy Kodak snapshot, with a similar mark between her front teeth. But that conversation wouldn't take place for another three decades.

The first time Todd met Wilbur Riddle, it didn't take much urging to get Riddle to launch into his ghost story. Riddle was known for telling waitresses and checkout clerks about Tent Girl while friends and family rolled their eyes. Todd didn't roll his eyes. Who was she? Todd asked during his next visit. Nobody knows, Riddle told him. He pulled out of his pocket a dog-eared magazine with a red cover depicting a screaming young woman in a dress and high heels, covering her face with her handcuffed hands.

Riddle smoothed out the pages of an article headlined "Urgent appeal to *Master Detective* readers. Kentucky police ask for your assistance in the most baffling case in the state's criminal history." In the piece, Riddle, as the fictitious "Bart Cranston," finds the corpse and alerts the authorities.

Todd read: "Who is the 'Tent Girl' . . . and who killed her? She was murdered in the Blue Grass State, but she could have come from anywhere. YOU might even have known her — as the girl next door." As he

142

had with Lori, Todd felt an almost instantaneous connection.

Like Todd, the clan of eight Riddle children born to Wilbur's third wife, Julie, had lost a brother and sister, twins who died years earlier. Lori's mom didn't talk about them. She seemed to Todd to have stored away the knowledge of her dead children in a quiet, secret place. As far as Todd knew, she never visited their graves, which a teenage Todd found harsh and unfathomable. At home, his parents talked about his dead siblings, Sue Ann and Greg, as though they'd stepped out and would be back any moment.

To Lori and her siblings, Tent Girl was a scary thing that their dad had found. Todd didn't believe they ever absorbed the tale the way he did: they saw her more as a mystery and he saw her more as a person. Todd knew that even though he was a kid, he was closer than most to the netherworld of the dead. As a child, he had overheard doctors, in hushed tones, warn his parents he might not survive childhood. Todd didn't find the notion of death particularly alarming. "The way I saw it, I could live here" — he gestured around him — "or there" — in the cemetery with his siblings. He sensed this outlook made him a bit of a freak.

But he couldn't hide his excitement at a magazine article that suggested he might know a dead girl. He did know dead people. He was related to them.

One April day, Todd Matthews and I set out from Livingston in my rented car. In the rural South, it's not uncommon to drive past privately owned cemeteries without ever realizing they're there. Over time, as families move away or die out, vegetation swallows grave markers and blurs the edges of plots. As Todd put it, nature consumes us in more ways than one.

Although Todd isn't crazy about power tools, he swears that as long as he's alive he'll maintain his Tennessee ancestors' plots, where his siblings lie under spare rectangular stones and his beloved grandfather Thomas Clark "Papa" Vaughn, who lived to nearly eighty, shares a stone carved with entwined wedding bands with his first bride, Della Mae.

The cemetery is located squarely in the Bible Belt but the plaque of Della Mae's daddy, Todd's great-grandfather Willie Joe Pryor, is enigmatically engraved with a Star of David. The Conner-Pryor cemetery of Todd's mother's ancestors is tucked into the foothills of the Cumberland Mountains in an area called, depending on whom you ask, Taylors Crossroads or Barnes Ridge, that straddles the border between Overton and Pickett counties.

In the genealogy room of the Overton County Public Library, a compact, graying man introduced himself as Elmo C. Garrett. Five decades ago, Garrett's grandparents and Todd's great-grandparents lived less than a mile apart. Everyone was acquainted with — and very likely related to — everyone else. Garrett recalled men with names like Willis "Scissors" Clark, Herman "Terrapin" Holt, "Ticky Joe," and "Bigun" Johnson who'd gather at the general store, spit tobacco juice into a can, play checkers, whittle, trade knives, and wager on whose glass Coca-Cola bottle was stamped by the most distant manufacturing plant. Women came in to buy dry goods, sacks of dried beans, and cured hams; they supplied Livingston markets with locally picked strawberries and wild blackberries. Almost everybody grew and sold tobacco.

Some New Yorkers, like me, head outside city limits and immediately envision ax murderers lurking behind trees and secreting themselves in bushes. Todd reinforced my urban anxieties by describing middle Tennesee's car-swallowing sinkholes that unexpectedly open up in the pavement, tornadoes with deadly winds and flying debris, and venomous copperheads and cottonmouths that slither underfoot and lurk in caves. Poisonous hemlocks grow taller than a man. Todd called it the land of the lost.

We pulled over next to a farm gate of tubular metal struts latched to wood posts. An adjacent field had been recently mowed, the brown hay neatly rolled like enormous rugs. Strands of barbed wire encircled a half acre where the descendants of John William Pryor, Armitage Conner, and others are buried beneath small granite and limestone slabs. Native American graves scattered helter-skelter were marked only with flat rocks, mossy and lichen-covered, that looked like a garden stepping-stone path. I glanced over at Todd, picking out traces of Cherokee in his mocha-brown eyes, his prominent cheekbones.

There were limestone, shale, and sandstone markers buffed blank by decades of rain and wind and positioned like a drunken game of dominoes — an attempt, Todd suspected, to point them east, the direction from which Jesus is predicted to return. The cemetery was located on an old piece of hallowed ground where Todd's mother's family had always been buried, and where he expected to be buried.

During Todd's childhood, on Sundays after church the whole family headed to the cemetery. While his father maneuvered an old-fashioned push lawn mower around the stones, Todd and his cousins played tic-tac-toe with broken shards of yellow sandstone. If they were lucky, they found shiny hunks of quartz that could pass as precious diamonds, or tiny woodpecker eggs in a nest in a hollowed-out fence post.

Now, among the manicured grass plots, Todd stopped before two small stones of polished granite set flat in the earth next to a few stems of iris in a Mason jar. An angel, hands clasped and bordered by flowers, is carved on one of the rectangles along with "Baby Sue Ann Matthews B&D April 17, 1972" and beneath that: "Pray the Lord my soul to keep." The stone next to it says only GREGORY KENNETH MATTHEWS NOV. 21, 1979, NOV. 22, 1979 in bold capital letters outlined with a thin black rule. If someone asked Todd how many brothers and sisters he has, in his head he says two brothers and a sister. Out loud, he says one brother.

In contrast to Todd's lovingly maintained family plot are the nation's enormous, anonymous potter's fields where the unidentified are often interred. The New Testament named the first potter's field. Judas, to make amends, surrendered to the chief priests the thirty pieces of silver he had collected for betraying Jesus. They bought a plot of land in the valley of Hinnom near Jerusalem where potters once scraped up clay. The land was useless for farming. Strangers and foreigners got buried in the red soil also known as Aceldama, Aramaic for "field of blood."

It was only from the early modern period onward that we began to shield ourselves from death. Bodies started to be masked, shrouded, hidden in coffins, and buried deep in the earth. It wasn't until the nineteenth century that coming into contact with decomposition was recognized as a public health risk. A physical and symbolic separation ensued between the living and the dead.

Potter's fields of the eighteenth and early nineteenth centuries were slivers of existing church graveyards or community burial grounds designated for paupers, foreigners, slaves, prisoners, and the unidentified. By the 1800s, every major city — San Francisco, Philadelphia, Memphis, Cincinnati, Omaha, New York — had its own separate cemeteries devoted to the unidentified dead. Two men are listed in Tombstone, Arizona's Boot Hill cemetery as "Hung Mexicans," with no date or details.

Section H of the Minneapolis Pioneers and Soldiers Memorial Cemetery contains seventy-eight people identified as "unknown" or "Unknown German Man." The paupers' section includes three mass graves with the remains of 355 people whose bodies were used for research by the University of Minnesota Medical School in the early 1900s. More than 10 percent of the total number of burials are in that single section adorned with only a couple dozen markers. Some potter's fields, such as Chicago City Cemetery, were once the targets of grave-robbing medical students seeking cadavers to dissect or to sell to body traders.

Around the turn of the twentieth century a number of the unidentified dead were known as "boxcar Willies." Today they're called the homeless and indigent. In 1911 in Prescott, Arkansas, a man known only as Old Mike hawked pens, paper, and thread out of a leather satchel to homes and businesses near the railroad tracks in the center of town. He arrived on the southbound three o'clock and pushed on the next day.

One day he was found dead under a tree in a city park. Local morticians with a questionable sense of humor and a deficient sense of respect embalmed Old Mike and propped him upright in a wide-open pine box.

For more than sixty years he was displayed behind a curtain in a funeral home, dressed up in a suit, white shirt, and a tie weighted down by a silver dollar. One of his skeletal hands was positioned near a pull string for a lightbulb. Skin blackened with age and rot, glass eyes staring, mouth frozen in an O, Old Mike became a popular tourist attraction. Kids dared each other to touch the "petrified man." Wise-guy fathers urged their little girls to dance with him. Because Old Mike lacked an identity, embalmers turned him into an object of curiosity akin to a freak in a carnival sideshow. He wasn't buried until 1975.

I never imagined mass graves underneath American city streets, but they exist in Philly and New York. A Philadelphia public square near Independence Hall was once known as the strangers' burial ground and "Negroes' ground" where dead inmates from the nearby Walnut Street prison, yellow fever victims, Revolutionary War soldiers, and free and enslaved African Americans were stowed until the first quarter of the nineteenth century.

I'll bet not many of the college kids, dope dealers, and tourists who wander through Greenwich Village know that thousands of New York's indigent — some sources say 20,000, some say 100,000 — are buried underneath Washington Square Park. The iconic arch framed a gallows for public executions from 1797 to the 1820s.

Remains were then shuttled uptown to Fifth Avenue and Fortieth Street, later to another site on Fiftieth Street, and still later shipped across the East River and deposited on seventy-five acres in Wards Island, which now contains parks and recreation areas but once was the dumping ground for all sorts of New York City detritus.

In New York City today, few know of the existence of Hart Island, a ghost town of abandoned missile silos, asylums, an old church, and shuttered dormitories among meadows, woodlands, and dunes. You can get to the island only by ferry. Inmates from nearby Rikers Island, one of New York's most notorious prisons, volunteer for the grim duty of burying more than a hundred dead every week in communal plots three deep and ten across. Around one-tenth of the million-plus buried there are unidentified; most are unclaimed.

Once, Todd Matthews accompanied a woman to a neglected public cemetery in Texas where, she had learned, her son had been buried as a UID. Scandalized by the sight of grave markers sinking under tire ruts and overgrown grass, Todd had a brainstorm: he would open the world's first private potter's field in his backyard. "What if I bought an acre of ground in Tennessee? I could bury them in lots with numbers. All you need is a two-foot plot with a headstone and a little concrete vault to place an urn in. Whoever wants to can send them here," he said.

I couldn't help picturing Lori's reaction as caskets and pots of ashes started showing up on the doorstep. But I knew Todd was serious. "I might get two or I might get two thousand," he continued earnestly. "All you need is a shovel and determination."

In 1988, in his future father-in-law's living room, eighteen-year-old Todd couldn't take his eyes off the lurid cover of *Master Detective*. When he asked to borrow it, Riddle was loath to let it out of his sight. He finally agreed to let Todd take it to the library to make a photocopy.

While still in high school, Todd drove

three hundred miles to Georgetown, Kentucky, with a friend named Donny and a pile of awkwardly folded maps in his father's green and tan Chevy pickup. The visit was the first of dozens for Todd. They found the cemetery where Tent Girl was buried, just down Route 25 from where Riddle found her. They parked on a narrow asphalt road that snakes among the plots and spotted her gravestone off by itself in a grassy section in front of a fence.

Todd got out of the truck alone. It felt surreal to finally gaze at her headstone. In Georgetown, Todd learned, Tent Girl was a local legend. Like Lori, children told ghost stories about her on Halloween. College students were dared to visit her grave at midnight. Young women traveled from all over Kentucky and Ohio to leave flowers at her grave.

In the days after Tent Girl's body was found, she was too decomposed to be embalmed. Following the autopsy, the body was interred in the county-owned section of the cemetery marked only "No. 90," near the grave of a young man found dead outside Georgetown thirty years earlier. Townspeople had bought him a grave marker that read: "Someone's boy. About 19." By the time Todd went in search of

Tent Girl, the owner of a local funeral home — who would later serve as county coroner and lobby to have Tent Girl exhumed — had paid to replace the "No. 90" rock with a much grander headstone.

Unlike Sue Ann Matthews's stone, it had no angels or flowers. Instead, Musser's pencil sketch of a young woman's smiling face — round, with a short bobbed haircut and a gap between two front teeth — was carved into the red granite intended to match her reddish-brown hair. The words underneath were cold, clipped, official — a police report, not an epitaph.

The gravestone read:

TENT GIRL
FOUND MAY 17 1968
ON U.S. HIGHWAY 25, N.
DIED ABOUT APRIL 26 – MAY 3 1968
AGE ABOUT 16 – 19 YEARS
HEIGHT 5 FEET 1 INCH WEIGHT 110 TO
   115 LBS.
REDDISH BROWN HAIR
UNIDENTIFIED

It's all too easy to put the dead out of your mind and declare them gone, Todd told me later. A year after he underwent open-heart surgery at age eight, his brother Greg was born. He recalls the call about his brother's death: "The sound of the phone, my dad's voice talking to the hospital, the smell of breakfast my granny had made for supper . . . I can sit quietly, shut my eyes, and relive that moment in vivid details." Greg lived two days. As painful as the memory is, Todd fears that one day it might vanish. Todd remembers his mother flinging herself on the new grave and clawing at the red clay earth. Later, Todd accompanied his mother to the family plot. She clutched his hand. Together they arranged a few stems of roses or irises in a jar and pushed back the grass that crept around the edges of the stones. The graves somehow made his brother and sister real to Todd; Tent Girl's grave now accomplished the same thing for the nameless girl. She had been a human being, not a monster crammed into a bag. She was about his and Lori's age, and he felt that he was beginning to know her. He had a strong urge to put her back where she belonged.

In 1988, not long after swirling around the dance floor to "(I've Had) The Time of My Life" at Livingston Academy's junior-senior prom, Todd, in the same white tux, minus the pink tie and pink cummerbund he wore to the prom, and Lori, resplendent in white, were married at Livingston's Standing Stone State Park, atop the eastern section of the plateau-like upland that surrounds the Nashville Basin.

Months after Wilbur Riddle had moved his eight kids to a house on a country road outside Livingston, the Riddles' house burned down, struck by lightning.

Lori alone among her siblings lost everything in the fire. The Riddles planned to move to Indiana, but Lori didn't want to leave.

Nine months after Todd met his ghost-story girlfriend, Lori's long train trailed behind her as she glided over a swinging bridge and past a waterfall on a beautiful July day. Someone played the guitar. The reception — attended by Wilbur and Julie Riddle, Lori's crew of siblings, Billy and Brenda Matthews, and Todd's brother, aunt, and maternal grandparents — was held at a covered picnic shelter just past the bridge.

Billy Matthews bought a single-wide trailer for his son and seventeen-year-old bride, had it installed in the side yard of his own small, immaculately kept house, and told the young couple they were responsible for the monthly payments.

There they were, a family in middle-class

America: Todd's parents, his wife, his living brother, his dead siblings, and Tent Girl. At that point, Todd couldn't have predicted which one would have the biggest impact on his life for much of the coming decade.

# 5
# BRING OUT YOUR DEAD

It was a dreary November day, but inside the historic Union League of Philadelphia, I milled among a gathering crowd in a warm ballroom done in rich shades of burgundy and mahogany. Chandeliers twinkled far above our heads and massive floor-to-ceiling velour drapes dripped with tassels the size of dismembered hands.

At a round table set for a formal luncheon, three men introduced themselves as FBI agents. At the next table sat a woman with unruly black curls and very red lips who said she helped law enforcement interpret gang-related symbols, tattoos, and the scenes of ritualistic slayings. Serial murderer profilers mingled with experts in blood spatter and the use of hypnosis for crime scene recall.

Seated at my left was a short, round woman in a shapeless navy-blue pants suit, sensible black shoes, and metal-framed eyeglasses: the famed Dr. Marcella Fierro. To my right, Todd Matthews perched in a shirt, tie, and pea jacket, looking uncomfortable and a little deflated. His usual chest-forward strut was gone; his hands — typically open-palmed in mock surrender, index fingers like drawn pistols, slapping his thighs for emphasis — drooped at his sides. Todd was out of his element north of the Mason-Dixon Line; he confessed later he was worried everyone would consider him a redneck.

In the Union League ballroom, the lights dimmed as an Alaska cold case investigator described to the attentive audience the case of the day: the murder of a twenty-year-old woman found dead in a communal dormitory bathroom at the University of Fairbanks in 1993. He displayed a photo of the victim sprawled in a white bathtub, pants yanked down, sweater hiked up, the back of her head shattered by a .22-caliber bullet, stab wounds to her right eye and cheek. Blood covered half her face. I fell into a reverie as the investigator droned on, unable to tear my eyes from the young woman's smooth skin and small bare breasts. Her legs were bent at the knees, her arms raised as if in surrender.

"Would you like the cream?" Startled, I

looked down and saw Fierro offering me a small glass pitcher. Waiters in black suits poured coffee from long-spouted silver pots and served chocolate mousse garnished with sprigs of something slender and green.

I was at a meeting of the Vidocq Society, the exclusive group of crime solvers profiled in Michael Capuzzo's best-selling book *The Murder Room*. The society was named for the brilliant eighteenth-century French detective Eugène François Vidocq. The group — originally limited to eighty-two, one for each year of Vidocq's life — today claims more than a hundred volunteers who apply their collective forensic brainpower to unsolved homicides. I was there because a handful of Vidocq Society members, such as my host, forensic dentist Dr. Warren Tewes — who, in the wake of 9/11, had searched for teeth to identify victims in the charred wreckage of United Airlines Flight 93 in Shanksville, Pennsylvania — were driven by the subset of cold cases involving nameless victims. (The Vidocq Society typically takes on cases involving known victims.)

As Virginia's chief medical examiner, Marcella Fierro worked on some of the nation's most notorious crimes, including the Virginia Tech massacre and Richmond's

Southside Strangler killings. Now retired, once a month she takes the train from Richmond to Philly to share her expertise at the Vidocq Society meetings because, she told me, you never know what little piece of information might lead to an inference, a correlation, or a solution to a cold case.

Fierro had been speaking for the unidentified dead since the 1970s, but until her message got an unexpected boost from a little-known government agency and a former TV producer, it reached only ears as unhearing as those on her autopsy table.

Matthew J. Hickman's first cubicle at the Bureau of Justice Statistics was a GS-9, a step up from the entry-level GS-5 that had made him feel like he was working in a fishbowl. At least the GS-9 had tall partitions. By the time he had almost completed his PhD, Hickman was a GS-14 with his own office. He found it demoralizing that the size of his cubicle walls corresponded with his pay grade. Right out of *Dilbert,* thought Hickman, who has blue eyes, the trusting nature of a Seattle native, and a shock of dark hair across his forehead.

One day in 2004, the boss walked into Hickman's second-floor office with its glass-front bookcases and window overlooking

161

D.C.'s Chinatown and plunked himself on an unyielding government-issue chair. "We have to find out how many unidentified dead people there are in the United States," he said to the young statistician. "How can we do that?" It was the royal "we."

Hickman had done plenty of surveys. He had counted people locked up in prisons across the country and people victimized by crimes. He had never been asked to tally dead people. It turned out that no one else had, either, perhaps because for decades the medicolegal establishment had, by intention or accident, shrouded the unidentified and unclaimed dead in neglect and secrecy. The task Hickman's boss described was literally counting skeletons in closets.

Hickman decided the first order of business was to get his hands on a master list of the more than two thousand medical examiners and coroners in the country. "You'd think that would be easy," he said ruefully. After calling around D.C., he ended up on the line with the Centers for Disease Control and Prevention in Atlanta. They had a list but warned him it wasn't up to date or accurate. Hickman took it anyway.

To his surprise, some coroners flatly refused to cooperate. They accused him of being part of a conspiracy to eliminate the much-maligned office of the coroner. Often culled from the ranks of former cops, police chiefs, and death investigators, coroners often ally themselves with local law enforcement and can be distrustful of the feds. Hickman's alma mater, Temple University, conducted a study that showed that coroners, who are elected, reported 15 percent fewer suicides than medical examiners, who are appointed. "Coroners would . . . be worried about antagonizing local community stakeholders who might bad-mouth them," says the study's author, sociologist Joshua Klugman. The fact that Hickman was no J. Edgar Hoover and took no stand in the coroner-versus-medical-examiner debate didn't seem to matter.

Hickman and colleagues developed an eight-page questionnaire, which was faxed, e-mailed, posted to the Bureau of Justice Statistics website, and snail-mailed around the country. Slowly, in response to hundreds of follow-up e-mails, letters, and phone calls, results started trickling in to RTI International, a North Carolina–based research institute that had helped oversee the survey's creation and was responsible for processing the raw data. Send us what you've got, Hickman begged RTI almost weekly. ("We do get excited by this stuff," he admitted. "It's kind of nerdy.")

Around this time, he spoke at a meeting of the American Academy of Forensic Sciences where attendees were in a highly uncharacteristic state of excitement — actually in an uproar, as Hickman put it — to learn the results of the survey. He was afraid they were going to rush the podium when he and the RTI reps insisted they couldn't tell them anything concrete about the numbers of unidentified remains in the United States — not yet, anyway — because the Bureau of Justice Statistics didn't release preliminary findings.

It was one of the roughest presentations he'd ever attended, Hickman said later, but he understood the forensic professionals' impatience.

His survey was akin to what doctors refer to as a gold standard test — the best available under challenging conditions. Overnight, Hickman had switched from feeling like a character in Dilbert to one in Dick Tracy. He'd become one of the enforcers. Hickman experienced that sublime realization that surfaces all too rarely in a data collector's career: his results were going to make a difference in the real world. Maybe even change people's lives.

■ ■ ■ ■

Hickman had been launched on this challenge partly because of a woman named Cheri Nolan. Nolan, blond, blue-eyed, and supremely effective, had toiled behind the scenes for three presidents and probably knew her way through labyrinthine federal government politics better than many elected officials. Early in her career she worked with John Walsh, the driving force behind the creation of the National Center for Missing & Exploited Children, which as of 2013 had a volunteer and paid workforce of five hundred in several states and had aided in the recovery of more than 175,000 children. During her eight years at *America's Most Wanted,* Cheri Nolan handled everything from requests for Walsh's autographed headshot to his contract negotiations. She'd see viewer mail begging Walsh for help finding a brother, a sister, or another family member. Nolan was stunned by the volume of such requests — and of missing-person cases in general.

Nolan felt for the families, but the show focused on fugitives, not the missing. Then, in 2001, she returned to government as a deputy assistant attorney general for the

U.S. Department of Justice. She was sitting in her spacious, well-appointed office one day, thinking there she was, with great resources and responsibility, while a parallel universe of people were looking for loved ones who were very likely dead and investigators were frustrated by the lack of resources for these cold cases. She decided to find out if she had stumbled across a national problem, something the federal government might play a role in correcting. In 2002, she invited homicide investigators, sheriffs, police chiefs, Atlanta forensic pathologist Dr. Randy L. Hanzlick, members of the Department of Justice, and family members of missing people to a conference room at NCMEC's Alexandria, Virginia, offices. Was the proliferation of the missing and unidentified a problem? The unanimous answer was yes, Nolan recalled. "Is it a national problem? Yes. Is there a role for the federal government? Hallelujah, yes."

Coroners such as Mike Murphy from Las Vegas, who detailed his bureaucratic struggle for me as we toured his county morgue, were starting to go toe-to-toe with the FBI over the fact that coroners and medical examiners, who were responsible for documenting thousands of unidentified deaths each year were denied direct access to the National Crime Information Center (NCIC), the official law enforcement database of the missing and the unidentified. "We had some issues," Murphy said bluntly. The FBI told him every coroner's and medical examiner's office in the country had access to NCIC. Murphy said, "Really? Because I don't." Marcella Fierro, who was at the meeting, joked that if Cheri Nolan could fix such issues, she, Fierro, could retire.

Nolan knew that before the government allocated money to a problem, it needed numbers. Gathering numbers required money. The attacks on the World Trade Center would be the unexpected impetus for federal money to make its way to Nolan and Fierro's cause.

DNA has the potential to identify criminals with incredible accuracy, as well as to clear suspects and exonerate those accused or convicted of crimes they didn't commit. As of 2013, DNA testing had exonerated more than three hundred people in thirty-six states; eighteen of those proven innocent had served time on death row, including Kirk Bloodsworth, who served eight years in a Maryland prison for a rape and murder he didn't commit.

In the late 1980s, the federal government had laid the groundwork for national, state, and local DNA databases for the storage and exchange of DNA profiles. The Combined DNA Index System (CODIS) compares crime scene evidence to a database of DNA profiles obtained from convicted offenders and links DNA evidence from different crime scenes, thereby identifying serial criminals. States began passing laws requiring those convicted of certain offenses to provide DNA samples. Eventually, all fifty states would require DNA samples from some categories of offenders.

Public crime labs were becoming overwhelmed by backlogs of unanalyzed DNA samples. A month before 9/11, Nolan's boss, the U.S. attorney general, directed the National Institute of Justice to come up with a way to deal with the backlog in the criminal justice system's analysis of DNA evidence.

As the rubble of the collapsed Twin Towers smoked, the need for fast DNA analysis took on an even greater urgency. Representatives of the nation's forensic community struggled to identify bodies that were in some cases little more than fragments. If Cheri Nolan's initiative wasn't already vast in scope, on September 11, 2001, the biggest mass fatality identification effort in U.S. history would begin.

That morning, I was at my desk in a cubicle at the Massachusetts Institute of Technology, where I worked as a science writer. It was a spectacular, clear-blue-sky late-summer day in Cambridge — an ordinary Tuesday, it seemed — and I and a dozen colleagues were engrossed in e-mail, typing, phone calls, and heading to or from the café housed under one of MIT's majestic domes. Someone heard the initial newsflash: an airplane had flown into New York's World Trade Center. It soon became clear it wasn't a small private plane or an accident, as the media first reported, but a deliberate move by a hijacked jet that had taken off from Boston's Logan International Airport. Had we known, we might have spotted from our office windows the ascent of American Airlines Flight 11 with one of MIT's own on board.

We would learn later that among the dramas playing out in the sky that morning was a thirty-one-year-old MIT mathematician's heroic attempt to foil one of the hijackings. Software entrepreneur Daniel M. Lewin had not only started a company that helped revolutionize the way content is

169

delivered over the Internet, he was also a former member of the Israel Defense Forces' Sayeret Matkal, a top-secret counterterrorist unit. Lewin was seated in 9B and reportedly stabbed from behind by one of the hijackers when he tried to stop ringleader Mohamed Atta from taking control of the plane.

For the next two hours, we crowded around a small TV in our boss's office and watched the gut-wrenching events taking place two hundred miles away. We wept, we covered our mouths with our hands, or — when it became too difficult to watch people leaping to their deaths and see the south and then the north tower collapse amid smoke, debris, flames, and white ash — we paced the deserted cubicles.

In the days and weeks following 9/11, the search was on to identify the victims. Fewer than three hundred intact bodies would be recovered from Ground Zero. The rest were body parts, flecks and fragments of tissue and bone. At first, Robert Shaler, director of forensic biology at New York City's Office of the Chief Medical Examiner, decided his team would test only samples from body fragments the size of a thumb or larger. But when he saw how small many of the fragments were, he changed his mind. They would analyze everything that came along. Some of what came along was barely recognizable as human. On more than one occasion technicians realized they were trying to extract DNA from bits of plastic.

A few years earlier, maverick biotech entrepreneur J. Craig Venter of Maryland-based Celera Genomics had launched a highly publicized race to see whether his privately held company could sequence the entire human genome faster than a public consortium made up of talented scientists from around the world, including DNA pioneers James Watson and Francis Crick. Cloned sheep, human organs grown in petri dishes, genetically modified foods — biotech in 2001 had reached a pinnacle of promise and controversy. Mapping the blueprint of human life was expected to revolutionize medicine, opening the floodgates to a host of new drugs for everything from cancer to diabetes, and Venter wanted to lay claim to that cash cow.

I was rooting for Venter's rival, MIT scientist Eric Lander, who headed up the publicly funded international Human Genome Project. Lander — a Brooklyn-born former Rhodes scholar and recipient of a MacArthur "genius" grant — led a consortium that, unlike Celera, was committed to making its results freely available online and in scientific journals.

Venter declared victory in the sequencing race in April 2000. Lander's "hard-core" group of bioinformatics specialists published the draft genome in the prestigious science journal *Nature* in 2001. (The two factions subsequently joined forces.)

Venter, who flew to New York the day following the attacks, had met forensic expert Shaler just months earlier, at a museum reception. They had been a short cab ride away from lower Manhattan, at the American Museum of Natural History. Now the elegant affair seemed like it had occurred on another planet. Venter offered Shaler his expertise and the use of Celera's gene-sequencing facility to help identify the New York City victims. At the time, DNA profiling — determining the likelihood that genetic material came from a particular individual — was not as advanced as the science of sequencing. Documenting the 30,000 genes of the human genome had taken even speedy Celera almost three years. The challenge in New York City was fundamentally different but comparable in scope, a Herculean task outside the realm of anything previously attempted with existing technology and tools.

September 11 became the world's largest forensics case, illuminating the need for fast, accurate DNA fingerprinting. Three years later, in 2004, President Bush signed into law the Justice for All Act — known as the DNA Initiative — which established rights for crime victims; provided for post-conviction DNA testing that might set the innocent free; and helped state and local law enforcement get access to DNA analysis labs.

The DNA Initiative had one more provision.

Almost a footnote to the National Institute of Justice's list of requests in that year's $232.6 million proposed budget was $2 million — less than one-hundredth of the total — that Cheri Nolan had slipped in for "missing persons identification."

It went through, she told me, still sounding surprised almost eight years later.

"From there," she said, "we rocked."

Matthew Hickman, toiling away at tallying the nation's unidentified dead to help Nolan and others make a case for government aid, had no statutory authority to require anyone to turn over anything, so he was gratified to find that — aside from a handful of recalcitrant coroners — agencies and individuals seemed to see the situation as a matter of public policy and offered up what they had. The problem was, what they had was often incomplete and inaccurate.

Some agencies had lists dating to the early twentieth century; others had sketchy files going back only a few years. It wasn't unusual for records to go out with the coroner leaving office and start up again with the new one coming in. Only around half of the offices even had policies on whether to keep records, X-rays, fingerprints, DNA — or the bodies themselves.

Medical examiners or coroners serving larger jurisdictions were more likely to have such policies, but Dr. Randy Hanzlick, the outspoken chief medical examiner from Atlanta, said bluntly that most agencies disliked even admitting unidentified cases still existed and would far rather forget about them than think or talk about them. Only 30 percent of offices serving jurisdictions of less than 2,500 people (read: small-town coroners) had policies governing the unidentified.

Some agencies buried the remains; others cremated them. In more than one office, staff discovered dusty bones in cardboard Bankers Boxes. Hurricane Katrina forced a complete halt to Hickman's data collection efforts in Louisiana as the state was forced to ship bodies to whichever facility would take them. Three years after Hickman's boss first approached him, Hickman and his colleagues were finally ready to announce their findings.

RTI had delivered Hickman's questionnaire to 2,000 coroners and medical examiners across the country. Around 1,600 actually responded, a rate of return that allowed statisticians to extrapolate that the nation's medical examiners and coroners had investigated almost one million human deaths during 2004. Of the estimated 4,400 dead who came in unidentified across the country every year, 1,000 or so tended to remain unidentified after one year. Hickman had eked out records of almost 13,500 unidentified human remains, some decades old. But he and others knew this didn't tell the full story.

Shortly before the final results were in, National Institute of Justice staffer Nancy Ritter wrote, "If you ask most Americans about a mass disaster, they're likely to think of the 9/11 attacks on the World Trade Center, Hurricane Katrina, or the Southeast Asian tsunami. Very few people — including law enforcement officials — would think of the number of missing persons and unidentified human remains in our nation as a crisis. It is, however, what experts call 'a mass disaster over time.'

"More than forty thousand sets of human remains that cannot be identified through conventional means are held in the evidence rooms of medical examiners throughout the country," Ritter wrote in a National Institute of Justice journal in January 2007. The actual study, published a few months later, cited Hickman's total of 13,500. According to Hickman, 40,000 is a "mythical" number, an extrapolation that took on a life of its own.

The phrase "silent mass disaster" and the 40,000 figure spread virally through media outlets. No one questioned the higher figure; after all, as Cheri Nolan pointed out, numbers are crucial in the funding game. Nolan herself believes that because so many remains went unrecorded for decades, the true figure actually tops 40,000. George Adams, a former Fort Worth cop now with the Center for Human Identification, the world-renowned DNA forensics lab at the University of North Texas, agrees, suggesting the real number may be in excess of 60,000, because each time he calls an agency and asks how many unidentified remains it has, the number goes up.

After Hickman digested the initial shoc of there being so many unidentified bodies lying around all over the country, he acknowledged that a coldhearted rationalist might argue that Americans take for granted homicides and car crash fatalities that account for similar numbers of lost lives each year (around 15,000 and around 34,000, respectively). But, he said, when you make the link between the unidentified and the missing, that's when it hits people: Wait, there's a connection here. People are looking for missing persons. Medical examiners may have those remains. There are lives hanging in the balance.

Web sleuths helped put two and two together. They provided answers that, however painful, ended the paralyzing doubt that many claimed was even worse than hearing about a loved one's death. There suddenly existed the possibility, Hickman said, for closure.

In the end it was the numbers, Hickman believes, that got a lot of players interested in the unidentified remains real fast. Who the players would turn out to be was the real surprise.

# 6
## INSIDE REEFER 2

It was only seven in the morning but I was wearing the desert heat like a lead suit. My throat, eyes, and sinuses had shriveled up like a slug doused in sea salt. Somewhere to the west the Vegas strip hummed, but the taxi had deposited me on a seemingly deserted street of low buildings of the type favored by personal-injury lawyers and insurance agents. I pushed a buzzer next to the mirrored door of 1704 Pinto Lane and admired a Japanese-style sand garden of swaying grasses, flowering desert plants, artfully placed boulders, and cacti. Excellent landscaping is not something you expect at the morgue.

When Mike Murphy opened the door, nothing about him dashed the illusion that I'd come to inquire about life insurance or a timeshare. Marcella Fierro complained to me once about "Joe Coroner from East Wherever" — the elected official who's also the local feed store operator or a farmer who milked cows before signing the day's death warrants — but she wasn't talking about Clark County coroner P. Michael Murphy, known to pals as Murf. He's an FBI National Academy graduate and holds a doctorate in business administration. Vegas's death chief likes to say he's in the people business. The day I met him, he was revved and brisk, clearly prepared to interact with someone with a pulse.

Clark County, Nevada, encompassing the world-renowned Las Vegas strip, serves two million residents and forty-two million visitors a year in an area the size of New Jersey. What happens in Vegas may or may not stay in Vegas but it always takes on a sordid tinge. Murphy's predecessor had fielded a storm of media calls in 1996 when a mysterious assailant gunned down rapper Tupac Shakur in a drive-by shooting, and again in 2002 when, in bed with a stripper at the Hard Rock Hotel and Casino, The Who guitarist John Entwistle died of a cocaine-induced heart attack. The Clark County coroner's office is the model for the original *CSI,* at one time the most-watched program on American television.

Dealing with more than ten thousand deaths a year doesn't seem like a dream job, but during the sixty-plus years the county coroner's office has been in existence, only three people have held the top post. Murphy's two predecessors each served for nineteen years. In late 2003, Murphy was elected only months before he launched what turned out to be a very controversial website that would serve as a turning point for the web sleuth movement. He was simply too naïve, he said later, to realize that posting actual photographs of dead people on the Internet might not have been a good idea. For a time, he was sure he was about to become the shortest-tenured coroner in county history.

The day I met him, his dark suit, crisp white shirt with a monogrammed cuff, and sharp tie were set off by mother-of-pearl cuff links in rich blues and greens — almost as reflective as his bald head — that glinted as he offered me his hand. He wore a heavy gold-link bracelet and two rings: a thick, stone-embossed band from the FBI Academy and the other with a claddagh design engraved "Mike," a gift from his wife. These rings, he noted in the same confiding tone he might use to give me a promising stock tip, were exactly the kind of distinctive details that came in handy when identifying a body.

Murphy became the public face of Clark County's radical Internet experiment, an effort to enlist the public's help in identifying the disturbingly large backlog of unidentified bodies he inherited in 2003. But he told me that if I really wanted to understand the story behind the website, I needed to know about Jane Arroyo Grande Doe and Rick Jones.

At nine o'clock at night on October 5, 1980, a driver was speeding along a lonely dirt road just south of State Route 146 and west of Arroyo Grande Boulevard in Henderson, Nevada. Henderson back then consisted of a whole lot of nothing; vacant, arid land dotted with scrub and an enormous sky punctuated with telephone poles and electrical lines. Through the deepening dusk the driver spotted what looked like a nude female form lying facedown in the desert.

An autopsy found the young woman to be between fourteen and twenty years old and dead for around a day. She was petite, five foot two and a hundred pounds. In the coroner's photo, she looked peaceful. Her long-lashed hazel eyes were closed under finely shaped brows. Her wavy shoulder-length auburn hair, pulled back from her high forehead, framed her perfectly oval

181

face. Her classic, delicate beauty struck me; she looked like she might have been a silent movie star of the 1920s.

Being dead may have accounted for her alabaster complexion, but her ginger hair and brows suggested the fairness typical of a redhead. Her ears were small and her mouth wide, the lower lip protruding slightly as though her last expression was a puzzled frown or a look of disgust. Her strong round chin would have been particularly noticeable when she smiled or laughed. The letter *S* was tattooed on her right forearm.

Her assailant or assailants struck her on the head and stabbed her repeatedly in the back. With not even one piece of clothing as a clue to her identity, she became Clark County Coroner Office case 80-1221. She was buried in Henderson under a flat rectangular marker surrounded by palm trees and inscribed "Jane Doe, Oct. 5, 1980. From your family at the Henderson Police Department." In the coroner's office, she became known as Jane Arroyo Grande Doe — the case, Murphy says, "that started it all for us."

Offices lined the walls and enclosed a corral of cubicles on the administrative side of the

Clark County coroner's building. A posted sign read: "Remember . . . Families entrust us with one of their most precious possessions . . . The body is dear to them . . . treat it reverently." I trailed Murphy to a cubicle occupied by a man with close-cropped light hair, a goatee, wire-rimmed squarish glasses, and blue eyes. A coroner investigator, Rick Jones had donned maverick black Western boots under the gray polyester slacks of a civil servant. His solid build befit the former cop and onetime casino security guard but his voice was gentle, almost a whisper.

Rick Jones and other coroner investigators were among the first to arrive at the scenes of suicides, accidents, murders, and deaths due to natural causes; an alarmingly large number of Vegas's forty million tourists a year go there to check out of life. A Harvard sociologist found that residents of Las Vegas had a 50 percent higher risk of suicide than folks living elsewhere in the country. You increased your suicide risk just by moving into the city, and lowered it by moving out.

If someone hangs himself during Jones's shift, he drives an official white SUV to the scene. After snapping pictures to document how the body was found, he talks to the cops and slices the rope off the suicide's neck.

I'd become aware that some people seem more at ease around corpses than others. A coroner once told me the ability to handle bodies — physically and emotionally — is a matter of exposure. The more you do it, he said, the better you tolerate it. But I think it comes down to something innate. You either have the squeamishness gene or you don't. I've found that there are those who are repulsed by an out-of-focus image of a dead person on a computer screen and others who are entirely blasé about hoisting a severed limb into the back of their pickup truck or peeling bits of human beings off pavement. Jones turned out to be in the latter camp.

He and around thirty other full-time and part-time death investigators were available around the clock to accompany police on emergency calls, often enduring years of sporadic, limited shifts before being hired as full-time coroner investigators. It's a great job, Jones insisted the day I met him at the Clark County office. "I love the work that I do. We're blessed to be thrust into a family to help them go through the ordeal they have to go through. It's not that we like to see people hurting. But it's a necessary part of the job. We do things and we see things that most people don't ever have to see or think about."

"How do you know — when do you know — if you're capable of this job?" I asked him.

"You actually have to do a few ride-alongs to see if it's something you can handle," he said. "There are calls that test us and see if we can truly stay in this field or not." Like all who passed the test, Jones had a few scenes permanently etched in his brain, scenes he didn't often talk about but couldn't erase. He remembered the first SIDS death he attended. He remembered how a woman, backing out of the driveway, didn't see her two-year-old trying to get into the passenger door and crushed the toddler's head under the wheels.

Jones will never forget talking to a father at the scene of an accident in which two teenage girls were thrown from a motor home on the freeway. "I had to meet with the father and ask him to help me ID the girls. The father told me one girl's name and then dropped to his knees and started crying and said, 'I couldn't find Alexis's head.' She had been decapitated at the scene.

"These are deaths we keep to ourselves

and keep in the back of our heads. We do appreciate life. We take every effort in our home life to make every hour, every day, count because you never know when you may not have a chance to see your family again. We encourage people, 'Before you leave your circle of loved ones, make sure they know how you feel about them, because life can be short and death can happen quite suddenly,' " Jones said soberly.

After gathering information at the scene of each death, Jones arranges to have the corpses brought to the coroner's building. Each body wheeled through the side bay doors is fingerprinted, photographed, X-rayed, and examined. A driver's license doesn't cut it for positive identification. If the person is not identified at the scene, someone must come in and identify him or her, or the fingerprints are run against those in the FBI system. Fingerprints are a powerful identification tool — if you can get them. Crackheads sometimes literally sear off their prints by handling red-hot glass pipes. Skin on the hands of a badly decomposed or bloated corpse can slide off like a glove, requiring the person conducting the autopsy to slip their own hand inside to try to recover prints.

(To rehydrate dessicated fingertips, pros

suggest soaking the hands or individual fingers for ninety days in embalming fluid or Downy fabric softener. Then press on an inked wad of Silly Putty — just as good as the expensive stuff in the medical supply catalog — and transfer to paper.)

There are a number of separate fingerprint repositories, and investigators may not check them all consistently. The military uses the same fingerprint system based on arches, loops, and whorls developed by Sir Edward Henry in the late nineteenth century. To check a body against military records, you need all ten digits intact. The FBI stockpiles and compares fingerprints — seventy million criminal prints and thirty-four million civilian prints — through the Integrated Automated Fingerprint Identification System databank, known as IAFIS. Homeland Security has its own fingerprint database.

Bleached bones discovered outside make up most of Clark County's unidentified. "Bodies found in homes, hotel rooms or apartments give investigators more to go on; they can identify a person by his papers and possessions. People found outdoors are often homeless, and have no identification at all," Abigail Goldman wrote in the *Las Vegas Sun* in 2008. "Or they've been dumped, victims of foul play."

Of the hundred-plus Jane and John Does that turn up in Clark County every year, investigators identify the vast majority within twenty-four hours by talking to locals, checking with cops, looking at lists of missing persons. If the family lives locally, Jones goes to their home, knocks on their door, and informs them in his soft voice that their loved one is awaiting them in the adobe building on Pinto Lane.

Soon after Jones became a coroner investigator for Clark County in 1998, he was leafing through the cold cases — the unidentifieds — and came across Jane Arroyo Grande Doe. He sat for a time gazing at her photo. His daughter was around her age. "I kind of took it personally," he said of the cold case. "If it had been my daughter who was missing, there'd be no end to my searching for her."

Was Jane Arroyo Grande Doe a runaway? Was she in the foster care system? Why was no one looking for her? Every week he checked descriptions of missing teens from the 1970s in the hope that someone, somewhere, was looking for a girl with auburn hair and an S tattoo on her arm. No one seemed to know her. But Jones did know, as he said later, that "she's a young gal and a pretty gal and she doesn't deserve to be found on the road dead."

Local newspapers had run stories, but they could only do so much. And how about the other hundred and eighty unknowns in the file? *"America's Most Wanted* or *Unsolved Mysteries —* they're not going to profile a hundred and eighty persons for us,"* Jones said. But Jane Arroyo Grande Doe's picture had given him an idea.

One morning in 2003, soon after Murphy took over as coroner, Jones stepped into Murphy's office. "I've got something to talk to you about," Jones said. "You know our John and Jane Doe cases, our cold cases? They're just sitting. There's not much that can be done with them. We're at a standstill. We need help." He described his idea to his new boss: Why not post pictures on the Internet of "facially recognizable" unidentified corpses such as Jane Arroyo Grande Doe?

Murphy blinked. "Why would we want to do that?"

Jones admitted it was risky. At the time, the only public displays of death were sordid, underground affairs, like the controversial 1978 film *Faces of Death,* which purported to show real people and animals in various stages of dying or death, narrated by a "pathologist." Whether the film or its sequels used real or fake footage, it elicited a firestorm of criticism, and enough notoriety to turn it into a cult favorite with a sizable worldwide audience.

Paradoxically, despite the high level of violence Americans tolerate in entertainment films, U.S. audiences have low tolerance for graphic real-life images. Images of death both fascinate and repel us. While village folk used to lay out the corpses of neighbors and relatives, most people now only experience fantasized versions of death through movies and art, be they zombies or nineteenth-century American photographs of well-dressed, romanticized bodies that appear to be peacefully sleeping. It was acceptable for people to view such images privately, but public display of the kind Jones was proposing was controversial.

Then again, there was a precedent in American history for images of the dead serving a higher purpose. After one of the bloodiest Civil War battles, at Antietam in September 1862, photographers Alexander Gardner and James Gibson reached the battlefield not long after the fighting ended and created seventy photographs, nearly a third depicting corpses. It was the first time the American public viewed its war dead, and the ensuing shock and horror may have helped speed the end of the war. Some of the Antietam photographs were exhibited in New York City within a month after the battle. An anonymous writer for *The New York Times* provides the following description:

> Of all objects of horror one would think the battle-field should stand preeminent, that it should bear the palm of repulsiveness. But on the contrary, there is a terrible fascination about it that draws one near these pictures, and makes him loth [sic] to leave them. You will see hushed, reverend [sic] groups standing around these weird copies of carnage, bending down to look in the pale faces of the dead, chained by the strange spell that dwells in dead men's eyes.

These days, we're bombarded by media images of death in catastrophes and wars. We manage to convince ourselves that those extreme situations will never happen to us. The individual dead are harder to contemplate, perhaps because we imagine ourselves in their place. Like Woody Allen, we might not be afraid of death; we just don't want to be there when it happens.

191

In Murphy's office, Jones kept pushing for a website. He sensed that his new boss could be convinced. It wasn't Jones's intention to shock anyone with gory images. As far as murder victims go, Jones thought Jane Arroyo Grande Doe was pristine. What the coroner's office needed, he insisted, was the public's help in identifying her and the other 180 remains. They needed more sets of eyes. Vegas was already associated with grisly images through the TV series *CSI*, Jones argued. (The Clark County coroner's office was part of the backdrop for the original series.) Why not use the exposure from *CSI* to accomplish something good?

The sense that I was in an office building evaporated as soon as Murphy escorted me through a heavy airlock door. The subdued pastel rooms where family members identified their loved ones from digital images, the gift shop display case filled with black T-shirts with a slot machine and "Cashed Out in Las Vegas" on the back, the toy skeletons, the desk calendars, fax machines, and wall-to-wall carpeting were gone and we were in what looked like a hospital with an antiseptic smell, tiled walls, and a linoleum floor.

Murphy gestured to rooms where police

look over suspicious cases and forensic experts "prep" each body, taking photographs, measuring trajectories of bullets through flesh, analyzing knife tears through clothing and organs. Farther down, what looked like pickles sat in cloudy fluid in gallon-size Tupperware vats; these were hearts, lungs, livers, and intestines awaiting shipment to a lab for testing.

There was movement in one of the rooms, people in scrubs and face masks, a form on a silver table. "Can you please pull this door closed," Murphy admonished two women in scrubs chatting to one another in low tones. They closed the door, but not fast enough. On the table lay a slight figure wearing knee-length cutoff jeans and a T-shirt with a colorful logo. Her bare feet were mottled and pale, her toenails painted pink. The face was turned away but I could see a shock of straight black shoulder-length hair. A young woman. Later, I sat in on the morning staff meeting and learned she was fourteen, a suicide. She had come home from school, posted a message on Facebook, and hanged herself on a trampoline.

In the autopsy room, one of the women started to snip the neckline of the girl's T-shirt with a pair of scissors. I hurried after Murphy.

In 2003, before Jones had approached his boss with an idea for a website, veteran coroner Ron Flud accompanied the newly elected Murphy down this same corridor. They walked through the thick metal door, past wrapped bodies with protruding, discolored, waxy hands and feet to a small room where boxes and body bags and brown paper evidence bags were stored on racks.

They were in what the coroners knew as a secondary refrigerated unit — reefer 2 for short. Some of the inhabitants were no more than a single bone; some were just skulls; some were what was known as PHRs — partial human remains; some were complete bodies, skeletonized or in full decomp. The oldest had been found three decades earlier.

Clark County had more than 180 unidentifieds back then, more than some coroners and medical examiners see in an entire career. There was Jane Cordova Doe, the little girl found in a Dumpster at the Villa Cordova apartments. John El Cortez Doe had died of a heart attack in the El Cortez Casino. Jane Oakley/Fremont Doe was found at an intersection, and Jane Canyon Cliff Doe was only bones. Jane Sahara Sue Doe turned up in 1979 in the parking lot of what was then the El Rancho Casino. A murder victim, she wore a complete set of dentures even though she was only around seventeen to twenty-one years old.

Reefer 2 was crowded in 2003, partly because Las Vegas's population had almost doubled between 1985 and 1995. So many people were moving into the city, if you brought in a U-Haul, you'd have to pay extra to have it taken out. Murphy was all too aware that people came to Vegas to make a fresh start, to reinvent themselves, often under assumed names. He also knew escape was one of those things that works better as a dream than a reality.

Murphy says of his time as a cop, "I can't tell you the number of times I went to handle a domestic disturbance, or pull someone causing trouble out of a bar, only to hear the guy say, 'Gosh darn it, I came here to make a new start.' The problem was, they brought themselves with them." Flud and others in the coroner's office were left holding the body bag when those who came to hide from a troubled past died inside county lines.

Newly armed with a business administration degree, Murphy considered himself a hands-on manager, a take-action kind of guy.

"What do you do about this?" he asked Flud, gesturing toward the bags of bones. Flud had been coroner for nineteen years. He knew what happened to cold cases when every day brought new deaths and urgent demands. "They were here when I got here, and there'll be more here when you leave," Flud told his younger colleague. "There is no one, and no way, to deal with this."

Relieved that I hadn't had to see the face of the girl being autopsied, I followed Murphy down the hall. We stopped to don baby-blue booties, sliding in the toes of our shoes and pulling them over and up in back. He handed me a face mask like those worn by surgeons and showed me how to place it over my nose and mouth and edge it down so there was a space to breathe. We went into a receiving bay with garage doors and around a dozen gurneys neatly lined up. We walked past whiteboards listing the previous night's incoming. I scanned for female names, knowing the girl's was probably up there.

We reached another heavy metal door and he said, "Are you okay with this?" I wasn't sure what he meant. I had asked Murphy to show me where the unidentified remains were kept. Why wouldn't I be okay with seeing a closet? I was clutching my digital camera; he instructed me not to take any pictures of what was on the other side of the door.

I realized then we were walking into the morgue itself. In movies, morgues are walls of stainless steel drawers containing bodies hidden within or zipped up neatly in what look like black fabric garment bags.

A few steps through the door, which slammed behind us with a metallic clunk, and I was uncomfortably close to a row of gurneys. There were at least six, maybe more, but I couldn't bring myself to study them closely enough to count. I thought: *All these people, just from last night?* Each body was on its own gurney, wrapped in something white — plastic, maybe — and they were not smooth and uniform but cinched at the middle, lumpy, vaguely human-shaped packages.

Faces were covered but feet protruded from at least two of the packages. One set was narrow and pale, clearly a woman's, with painted toenails. The other was bigger and mottled greenish brown. I learned later that the coroner does not embalm the bodies or preserve them in any way other than by stowing them in the refrigerated unit; embalming is the undertaker's job, when the body makes its next stop at the mortuary. Refrigeration only slows decomposition that began hours or in some cases days ago.

I was startled to be so close to them. And I was startled by my reaction. The emotion hit me first. I felt so very, very sorry, an overwhelming pity for these people in the bags, which didn't make a lot of sense. Whatever they might have suffered was over.

I became aware that Murphy was talking to me, his voice indistinct through the mask covering his mouth. He pointed to brown paper bags, labeled in black marker with numbers and letters, on a table opposite the row of corpses. "You can take a picture of this," I heard him say. He held up one of the labeled bags, which looked like something you'd bring a six-pack home in but apparently held human remains.

I aimed the camera. It took a superhuman effort for my spinning brain to instruct my finger to press the shutter.

Murphy returned the bag to the table and walked away. I saw where he was heading; the doorway to reefer 2 was on the right-hand wall, just past the last of the gurneys. I followed a few steps. I tried to edge away from the row of bodies, but they took up a lot of space in the narrow room and were less than an arm's length away. *Breathe,* I told myself. *You need to breathe.* It was then that I became aware of the smell. Sour and acrid, it was there when we'd entered, of course, if somewhat dulled by the face mask, but it hadn't affected me — I thought — as much as the waves of sadness and horror that settled in my chest and throat.

I didn't think I was in danger of passing out, but I didn't want to take another step into the room; I was especially loath to walk past the bodies whose feet were visible. I had an irrational fear that they might move, or get up, or try to touch me if I got too close, like zombies with ravaged, reaching hands. I was ashamed of this reaction, but I knew that if asked to touch one of them, I would have been powerless to so much as raise my arm. In fact, I couldn't take another step.

I looked over at Murphy, around ten paces away, a gap that seemed at that moment about as easy to navigate as the Grand Canyon. He turned and peered at me over his face mask and I thought he was going to say something sympathetic about my sorry demeanor but he barked, "You're not taking a photo, are you?" I realized then I was frozen in place, in as advanced a state of rigor mortis as our compatriots on the gurneys, still holding the camera up in the air. "No, no," I said, lowering my arm.

I knew then I was not going to make it all the way inside. My brain was cajoling: *Follow the nice man. Don't be such a sissy. What kind of reporter are you, anyway?* But my feet were heeding some ancient impetus that demanded, pretty clearly: *Get. Out. Now.* My feet were not open to discussion. "Um, I don't think I can go any farther," I said weakly through the face mask.

Back outside the metal door, I slumped against a wall, gulping down untainted air and peeling off the face mask and booties. "Do you remember your first time . . . in there?" I asked Murphy, who was tossing his own booties and mask into a trash can. He had been in and out of the coroner's building many times when he worked as a local cop and police chief, he explained. He recalled his first time was a hot summer day, the hundred-plus-degree kind that's more the norm than the exception in Vegas. Other cities have climates that support human life, but Vegas's atmosphere seems best suited to those single-celled organisms able to withstand heat emanating directly from the earth's core.

Murphy followed the then coroner inside the well-chilled thirty-eight-degree room.

"The place was packed," he said, meaning more than the six gurneys I had just seen. "The coroner's looking at a toe tag or something and I started to lose my peripheral vision."

The smell doesn't help, he said. "Not to be inappropriate, it kind of reminds me of when I was a kid and went to the butcher shop in back of the grocery store. It is meat. The smell is a combination of things — sweet, acidic, putrid. In some instances it has a landfill kind of smell." It sticks to hair and clothing. Murphy offered to have his secretary sniff us before we headed back into the outside world, but I wondered what would happen if we didn't pass the test. Would she douse us with Lysol or Chanel No. 5?

Urban legend has it that you can mask the smell by dabbing Vicks VapoRub in your nose or smoking a cigar, but the truth is, the only thing that works is olfactory shutdown. You just stop noticing it, Murphy said. He's a fast talker, but he paused. "Once you smell it, you never forget it."

Later, I pressed Rick Jones about the morgue's emotional jolt. He was giving me a lift downtown in one of the coroner office's white SUVs. Why do we have such a visceral reaction in the presence of death? I asked.

He signaled, turned at an intersection. His eyes didn't leave the road. After a bit he said, "Someday we're all going to pass through the coroner's office. And we understand that and that's not a problem; when you pass through it when it's your time to go. Nobody's going to live forever. But when you have people your age or younger, a fourteen-year-old girl, whatever the case is, those people shouldn't be dead.

"When you see bodies lying on a gurney with toe tags hanging out, it's kind of a reality check," he said. "All of a sudden you realize: *This could be me.*"

Murphy okayed the website. Jones and other colleagues sifted through case files for any identifiable features of the bodies in the cooler, or any of their known histories, or any clothing or jewelry found with their bodies. Like Jane Arroyo Grande Doe, some had photos, good likenesses of what they must have looked like in life. Some had striking tattoos. Jones was careful not to release sensitive information about ongoing investigations that law enforcement wouldn't want shared.

There were other hurdles. For one thing,

the coroner's office had no website and no budget to build one. County officials told Murphy if he wanted a website, get in line — for up to two years. Instead, a part-time employee on Murphy's staff used *Building a Web Site for Dummies* to develop one on his own time. Then there were the images themselves. Jones tried to be careful. Knowing he and his colleagues were jaded, they showed the photos to the administrative staff and brought them home to their spouses. If the guinea pigs yelped or cringed, Jones said okay, maybe not that photo.

For the unacceptable images, or for decomposed bodies, they substituted sketches or clay models. They included disclaimers: "No decomposed remains will be shown. Some of the photos and information in this section may be disturbing to some viewers." Users had to click through several pages to make sure they didn't inadvertently see something gruesome.

In November 2003, the website was ready to go live. Murphy sent out a press release, feeling hopeful. Finally, after years of stagnation, it was time for progress.

Murphy, like Rick Jones, speaks of "honor" and "privilege" when he talks about being entrusted with a family's dead loved one. Murphy always reminds visitors to the morgue that no matter whether a person has just succumbed or consists of a single bone found in the desert, they're somebody's child. Murphy believes that it's especially important to bring closure to families of the missing. "We know where he is" are the words he's had to say to mothers and fathers. "Your son has died. He's here with us in Clark County. What would you like us to do?"

"My stepson went missing a couple of years ago," Murphy told me that day in his office. "I spent a period of time not knowing where he was. Every day I went to work, scanned daily reports on boards. My greatest fear was that I was going to find him on that board and have to go tell his mother. It gave me just a glimpse of what some of these families go through. It gave me a new insight." Until the young man resurfaced, he said, "that was not a pleasant place to be."

Within hours of going live, Las Vegas Unidentified got its first hit.

Sure enough, as Murphy had anticipated, the phone started ringing. E-mails poured in. Reporters worked on stories. They asked coroners and medical examiners in other parts of the country what they thought of the Clark County coroner's experiment.

Sacrilegious, said one. Inappropriate. Offensive. Indecent. What if children saw it? Messages from reporters seeking interviews piled up on Murphy's desk. Twelve hours after the site went live, Murphy's elation had turned to horror. *Ruh-roh,* he recalled thinking. What the hell had he done?

"Don't you think this is rather macabre?" The reporter from the BBC sounded as if he had gotten a whiff of something nasty through five thousand miles of phone line. London calling was the just the latest in a series of incredulous, outraged inquiries since the website — the damned website, as Murphy was beginning to think of it — had gone live. Murphy posted photos online because, he claimed, he needed access to more eyeballs. Whether he knew it or not, he was onto something.

Imagine standing at the finish line of the Boston Marathon, taking a photo of the mass of runners pounding the pavement toward you. The lead runners' faces are the most distinct, but you can also make out the faces of those farther in the distance. Zoom in on that distant runner and there's very little intrinsic face-related information, such as eyes and a nose. It's just a diffuse blob. Yet, somehow we can classify that blob as a face, says Pawan Sinha, a brain scientist at MIT. What's more, the human brain can pick out a face much more reliably than even the most technologically advanced recognition systems. Maybe, Sinha concludes, we're born with the ability to recognize faces.

Just a glance at Las Vegas Unidentified was enough to pick out someone you'd known — someone like Jane Arroyo Grande Doe who, as Rick Jones put it, was "facially recognizable." That, anyway, was the hope.

At first, Murphy was horrified at the reactions he was getting to the website. Then he recalled something a mentor had once told him: As long as you're doing the right thing for the right reason, everything will work out.

Murphy thought about the day he visited reefer 2 with former coroner Ron Flud. Flud seemed regretful but resigned to the idea that these cases were dead ends and would always be dead ends. Murphy had trouble accepting that. Helplessness was counter to every action-oriented bone in his body, but he knew some of these cases didn't get as much attention as they should. It was easy to get a lot of media play for a cute little girl, for instance. Not so much for a rebellious-looking teen with a dozen facial piercings. Nobody except a family member might miss someone whose background was riddled with arrests. In Murphy's view, that didn't make them any less dead or any less unidentified. And it certainly didn't make them any less important to him.

Later, Murphy polled religious leaders — Jews, Mormons, Baptists, Muslims, Catholics — for their reaction to the site. They assured him they knew his intentions were good. He asked lawyers: Is this legal?

Who's going to sue you? they responded. The dead?

He phoned families and asked: Is this offensive? People looking for a missing family member were pleased that the coroner's office had taken a bold step. Their only objection was that after a case was solved, the photo remained on the site with "solved" plastered over it. (The site removed those photos.)

Murphy regained some of his swagger. Maybe other coroners were okay with having unidentified remains in their closets, he told reporters. He was not. Maybe other major cities had just as many unidentified remains as Las Vegas and he was the only one publicly acknowledging the problem.

But the stress got to him. He developed Bell's palsy and stood in front of TV cameras with half his face paralyzed.

Looking like Droopy the cartoon dog on national television didn't brighten his mood. But something else did. Within twenty-four hours of the site going live, a corrections officer recognized one unidentified Las Vegas man as a former inmate. Forty-eight hours later, web sleuth Daphne Owings, a mother of two, sifted through the Doe Network's catalog of the missing, using her knack for retaining visual images to absorb dozens of faces, including that of a man missing from Torrance, California. Soon afterward she spotted him on the Clark County site.

The UID's hair color, eye color, and weight were off; dates didn't match. John David Clough was last reported seen July 1, 1988, while the Clark County John Doe was supposedly killed on June 27. "Everything I'm seeing in terms of black and white said this was not possible," Owings said later. "But I really felt like I was looking right at him." Owings was right: the John Doe turned out to be Clough.

Within a year Murphy started getting calls from public agencies, including three that had initially spoken out against Las Vegas

Unidentified, asking for help setting up their own web pages. As of 2011, there were sites devoted to the unidentified — managed by law enforcement, public safety departments, coroners, and medical examiners — in Florida, Kentucky, California, New York State, New Jersey, Wisconsin, Texas, South Carolina, Georgia, Iowa, Illinois, Louisiana, Massachusetts, and Tennessee.

Many of these sites used sketches or other artist reconstructions. The city of Milwaukee joined Las Vegas in using real photographs.

Las Vegas Unidentified helped ID nearly thirty bodies, including that of a man from Ireland who had hanged himself in Vegas and was spotted on the website by his sister in Ireland. By 2009 the site had had more than one million hits. That year Las Vegas Unidentified, along with several of the other independent sites, was rolled into NamUs (the National Missing and Unidentified Persons System, pronounced "name us"), a searchable online national database accessible to medical examiners, coroners, and the public. This was the initiative that Las Vegas Unidentified helped inspire; the one that Murphy, Fierro, and others had spent years lobbying for.

While I sat across from Murphy in the Vegas hotel where he was attending a conference for medical examiners and coroners, he finished relaying what he viewed as his greatest success story and straightened the cuff links in his perfectly starched shirtsleeves. "God shines on fools and drunks," he grinned. "I won't tell you which one I am."

A year later I heard that Murphy cut a deal with Discovery Studios for ten episodes of a new reality TV series based in the Clark County coroner's office.

Clark County never cremates its John and Jane Does, in the hope that some future technology will help ID them. Back in 1980, in the case of Jane Arroyo Grande Doe, the teenage girl who inspired Murphy and Rick Jones to launch Las Vegas Unidentified, DNA testing wasn't available. They kept no samples of her hair or nails, Jones told me.

With no budget for DNA analysis of Jane and John Does, the coroner's office applied for and received a grant that paid for Jane Arroyo Grande Doe to be exhumed in 2007. Forensic specialists collected X-rays, dental information, and DNA. She was reburied and twenty Henderson police officers attended a service at the mortuary. They stood with their heads bowed under a tent, gathered around the young woman's gray casket, and asked for God's help in finding out who she was. "We recommit her spirit to you," Henderson police chaplain Gary Morefield intoned. "We hope you help reveal the identity of this person that you care about very much."

At one point Jones thought he had a match for her DNA; it didn't pan out. Along with two hundred or so Las Vegas unidentified, the identity of Jane Arroyo Grande Doe remains a mystery. "We're crossing our fingers that one day we're going to find her," Jones said. He still spends hours every month poring through missing-person records.

Every so often, Jones gets a phone call or an e-mail from a web sleuth. These callers are used to being hung up on, but never by Rick Jones. He knows there are growing numbers of them out there, spotting clues the professionals have missed.

# 7
## THE PERKS OF BEING ORNERY

Part of me badly wanted to match a missing person with unidentified remains. I anticipated the moment I'd spot the specific details that aligned like stereoscopic images and drew an object into sharp 3-D focus. I imagined making a match might feel like scanning the crowd in Grand Central station until the familiar silhouette of a friend emerged from the crowd. But I knew that the chances of making a match were slim, especially for me, because I hadn't put in the hours, developed the eye, formulated the tactics.

Probably the bigger hurdle was that I had no skin in the game. I wasn't searching for someone I knew, like Betty Dalton Brown was. For Betty, it all started with a missing brother.

Betty Brown's father had been abandoned as an infant. A West Virginia hospital volunteer brought the sickly two-pound preemie home to make his last days comfortable. He slept in a shoe box heated with coals and suckled milk from an eyedropper.

Within six months, he had gained thirty pounds. The volunteer and her husband adopted him. As an adult, John Dalton moved to Newport News, Virginia, married Mary Jane Campbell, and fathered seven children, including Betty. John had promised his adoptive mother he wouldn't seek out his birth parents while she was alive. After her death, he approached his second-oldest daughter for help finding his biological family.

Through articles, obituaries, and county property records, Betty tracked down her grandparents, aunts, uncles, and great-grandparents, all dead. Only a few of her father's nieces and nephews remained alive. But the endeavour proved to Betty that she had a knack for detective work.

Betty studied business at a community college, got married, and took a job with a company that ran fifty hog farms in several states. She worked her way up from production worker to technician to farm manager to assistant office manager. She trained new employees and managers. After seventeen years, she figured she'd be with the company until she retired.

One day in 2004, Betty was in the office when the man who was supposed to give the baby pigs their anti-pneumonia vaccinations didn't show up. Betty decided to do it herself. Inside the pen, jostling, grunting piglets circled her ankles as she held up the airgun-like syringe.

The floor of the nursery was constructed of metal slats through which manure fell into a pit below. Days earlier, she'd noticed some of the struts were loose. She'd called maintenance but the floor still sagged.

She was about to stick a pig when a strut gave way. She pitched headlong into a tumble of squealing pink bodies and the entire length of the needle plunged into her left hand. With blood running down her wrist, she yanked the needle free, washed up, and kept working. She noticed her hand getting numb, then her wrist. She thought she'd better go home.

The next thing she knew, her teenage son was on the phone, calling for help. "Am I dying?" she asked emergency medical technicians in the helicopter that airlifted her to Richmond.

She had contracted a bacterial infection that only animals get. The infection attacked the tendons in her fingers. Doctors pumped

214

antibiotics directly into her heart for six weeks. She vomited continually. Six months of physical therapy helped her regain the use of her fingers, stuck together like a claw.

She returned to work and got neither the sympathy nor acknowledgment she expected as the thirteenth person hired in a multimillion-dollar business with which she had spent almost two decades. They treated her, she said, like yesterday's trash.

She quit, took a job at a paint factory, divorced at age forty, remarried, and moved with her new husband and in-laws to Winston-Salem. She worked as a waitress at the Golden Corral and then for the big-box chain store Lowe's. But during all those years of upheaval her real passion was finding tidbits of potentially useful information tucked in obscure corners of the Internet. She's helped police close the files on at least five cases in three states; one case had not much more to go on than a pen inscribed with words in an unfamiliar alphabet.

When are you getting paid? Betty's husband asks her. One day, she says.

As we drove together through her North Carolina neighborhood, she confided, "He doesn't understand. I do this because I want to do this, whether I get paid for it or not."

Phone on shoulder, ankle propped on knee, foot jiggling, Betty tapped away at a keyboard on the desk of a den in a white clapboard house in a Winston-Salem subdivision. A photo of the brownish skull of Christmas Jane Doe, a little girl found dead behind an I-95 rest area in 1983, shared a bulletin board with snapshots of blond, grinning, bespectacled six-year-old Jonas, Betty and Joe's son.

Betty's genius is in unearthing ephemera. Using Ancestry.com and a host of other sites, Betty can find anything, a friend and colleague said. Other web sleuths and, increasingly, law enforcement agencies, have asked Betty to troll for their missing pieces.

On a typical day, someone from Idaho calls to tell her that a suspected serial killer may have moved to the Carolinas. Todd Matthews questions something about one of the hundreds of missing people and unidentified remains cases she's input into the database NamUs that compares DNA and other identifiers in an attempt to solve unidentified and missing-person cases. It provides family and friends access, for the first time, to their missing-loved ones' official records. Web sleuths and missing-person advocates use it as a resource.

A sudden, high-pitched "Say whaaaa" leaps into Betty's low, lazy Newport News drawl when someone exceeds her tolerance for foolishness, but on the phone she's all business. She promised the University of North Texas Center for Human Identification she'd collect a cheek swab from the family and told the Idaho caller warning that a serial killer may have struck North Carolina that she'd keep an eye out for any cases that fit the MO.

Yet, one mystery she can't solve is the whereabouts of her own brother.

In the late 1990s, when her dying aunt confessed to Betty she had an older brother no one ever told her about, Mary Jane Dalton refused to talk. Combing through birth certificates county by county, Betty eventually found one with her mother's name on it in Hancock County, West Virginia. Betty had never heard of the father.

According to the document, in February 1957, Betty's mother, eighteen-year-old orphan Mary Jane Campbell, married a Yemeni citizen named Khalid Mahssen Saleh. Khalid, around twenty-four years old, from the village of Murissi in the seaport city of Aden, had emigrated to the United States to take a job with Weirton Steel in West Virginia.

The couple had a son they named Seif. Khalid took five-month-old Seif to his family in Yemen. Mary Jane never saw her husband and infant son again.

On the website OfficialColdCaseInvestigations.com, Betty posted, "Please, if you can help me . . . we just want to know if [my half brother] is safe and doing okay. He has 7 brothers and sisters in the USA that would love to know him. Until this day my mom still gets very upset about this. This was her firstborn child. She never expected this to happen."

Betty went to law enforcement for help. "Are you serious?" was the only response she got from West Virginia police when she inquired about how to file a report for someone missing since 1957.

Betty found a San Bernardino County, California, deputy coroner's investigator who had made a name for himself as an advocate for the missing. The California penal code requires police and sheriff's departments to accept a missing-person report "without delay" and to submit it to the FBI's NCIC database within four hours. It didn't matter if the person had never been in California. The report was filed.

Several years and many dead ends later, a man came forward claiming to be Betty's brother. Betty asked for a DNA sample. He said he needed money. His inability to make his way to the U.S. embassy in Yemen's capital seemed fishy. Officials warned Betty that unscrupulous foreign nationals can target Americans as easy marks, and she never sent the money. She still has no definitive answer in her brother's case, but in the process of searching she forged connections to the Doe Network, NamUs, Todd Matthews, and others in the web sleuth world. "I guess I'm trying to help families get closure because I don't seem to be able to get it for myself," she said. She meant her search for her half brother, but I wondered if there were other parts of Betty's life that resisted tidy endings.

Through NamUs, Betty met fellow volunteer Shannon Vita in Arizona, who knew a Phoenix police detective named Stuart Somershoe. On Vita's advice, Somershoe asked Betty for help with some of his seventy-plus unidentified cold cases.

In 1998, a Phoenix man committed suicide. He had no ID and his fingerprints revealed no arrest history. A trace of his gun came up with the name William Joseph LaRue. Somershoe couldn't find any kin —

couldn't find anything on the guy.

"In order to find out where he ended up at, you need to find out where he started at," Betty says like a mantra.

LaRue had apparently started out in Rochester, New York, where his birth was recorded in 1952. Along with his birth certificate, Betty found he had three siblings, and convinced the state to release the name and date of birth of one of his sisters. Betty plugged her first name, birth date, and "Rochester" into an Ancestry.com search; only one address popped up. A few phone calls later, Betty had secured a promise for a DNA sample. The test showed LaRue's DNA matched his sibling's; and Somershoe had his next-of-kin.

Another time Betty, in Sherlock-worthy fashion, spotted a tiny by critical clue.

A body of a fifty- to seventy-year-old man had been found in Phoenix in 2009. A suicide note, expressing his desire to be cremated, was signed only "M."

"All they knew was, this guy who they thought was Hispanic was found dead in the street," Betty said. "He was dressed really nice." His clothes had been sold through Sears but labeled in French.

Meanwhile, a woman in Israel had contacted police in Canada. She was unable to reach her fifty-six-year-old brother living in Calgary. Police tracked him from Calgary to Las Vegas, where he had missed his return flight and stopped withdrawing money from his bank account. For some reason Vegas law enforcement had closed the case. No one had entered the man as a missing person into NCIC.

Photos of the suicide scene in Phoenix showed a pen lying near the body. The pen itself had not been entered as evidence, but from the photo, Betty could see it was clearly imprinted with words in a foreign alphabet. Thinking it was Arabic, she sent it to an acquaintance familiar with the language. He told her it was Hebrew.

She stopped in at a Winston-Salem synagogue, where someone translated for her the name of a solar hot water company based in Jerusalem. "Okay, this guy is not Hispanic," Betty and Shannon told Somershoe. He could be Israeli. His clothes were likely purchased in French-speaking Canada. Somershoe contacted the FBI, which contacted the Canadian consulate and the Israeli embassy.

FBI agents contacted an Israeli police attaché in Los Angeles, who produced the name Maurice Marciano. Marciano was fifty-six, stocky, bald, blue-eyed, photographed once on a deck in a polo shirt and jeans, unsmiling.

Dental records from Calgary confirmed Marciano's identity. "Betty did her magic," Somershoe said. He's certain the case would not have been solved without her.

On another occasion, Betty started to enter details into NamUs about a missing Arizona man named Elmer O. Sanchez. She decided to do a quick web search to see if there was anything on him.

Within an hour, she'd found newspaper articles from the late 1960s about a man by that name who had been arrested previously for public drinking and theft. He had been found dead in a vacant, burned-out building in Yuma.

Meanwhile, in Albuquerque, Sanchez's sisters, in their seventies and eighties, never knew what had become of their troubled younger brother, who had been in and out of reform schools as a teenager. In 1969 he was thirty-four. He'd sent his older sister Rose a postcard: he was hitchhiking to California to take on migrant farmwork. He apparently never made it farther than Arizona. The Yuma paper described a body, dead for six months, on a cardboard bed surrounded by unopened cans of macaroni, spaghetti, and sardines and empty wine bottles. A wallet contained two dollars, a Social Security card, a Selective Service card, and a police mug shot.

An Albuquerque police detective speculated that an incorrect address and a one-digit mistake in the Social Security number had kept word of Sanchez's death from his family.

"I found Elmer Sanchez; he's deceased," Betty told Shannon Vita, who contacted the Yuma coroner's office, which confirmed Sanchez was long buried. Betty found the name of Sanchez's father and siblings; the sisters were relieved their brother died of natural causes and had even received a proper burial, courtesy of a charitable organization. Wondering, questioning — the family had had this hanging over their heads for a long time, said Sanchez's nephew.

In 2000, a young black man had been found dead in a canal in Florida's Dade County. He had not been identified. A tattoo on his arm read "Hakim." A visible tattoo of a name would most likely be the owner's, Brown reasoned. An address search using "Hakim" as a first or middle name close to where the body was found turned up two Hakims in the young man's age range. The first one turned out to be female. The second was an alias for a New Jersey man named Eric Todd, who had been arrested once for car theft. Fingerprints confirmed his identity.

Betty found out later that the Florida police contacted the family and reached a sister who had been with Todd when he converted to Islam, changed his name, and tattooed it on his arm. Unaware of her brother's death, she thought his long silence simply meant he wanted nothing to do with his family.

After leaning over a computer screen for what felt like hours, we stood up and ventured out of Betty's study. "Whatcha doin', bubba?" Betty cooed to her son, placid after his after-school nap. Jonas has pin-straight blond hair, a captivating smile, and the round face and wide-set, almond eyes of a child with Down syndrome. "He's ornery," Betty confided affectionately. Where in the world, I wondered, could Jonas possibly have picked up that trait? Being ornery is a necessity for many parents of atypical children. Some days, advocating for Jonas took its toll on Betty. "I worry every day about my little one and how people have treated him in this world," she once wrote. "I try to not let it bother me but . . . I wish people saw Jonas for the fun, lovely child he is . . . So disappointed in life and people at times." But with her son, she's upbeat. "He's my little man," she said, ruffling his hair. Betty's husband, Joe, smiled and shrugged when I asked him about Betty's web sleuthing. "It's her thing," he said. "You help me out once in a while," Betty interjected and then turned to me. "I'll ask him: 'Does this guy look like that guy?'" Joe didn't disagree, but it was clear from his resigned manner he wasn't a die-hard fan of Betty's hobby.

It had gotten late. I told Betty dinner was on me; I offered to take the whole family out, but Joe stayed behind, sunk into a plush beige recliner with Jonas sprawled on his lap. We drove to a bar and grill in a strip mall where beefy, tattooed men perched at high-tops, drank beer, and watched the game on TV. Betty and I settled in a booth. The waitress called us "girls." Betty laughed when the high-octane margarita I was served in a plastic tumbler made me toss my head back and forth like a horse shaking off a fly.

On the way back to her house, we cruised Betty's neighborhood in her husband's silver Dodge Ram. High-voltage power poles in the distance towered above rolling, grassy hills like monstrous Erector set men. The development was so new, houses were still emerging from bare lots. Betty pointed to an architectural detail she liked on someone else's house, but the structures all looked the same to me: white or beige clapboard with pitched roofs, porches, and black shutters. They had backyards and central air and cathedral-ceiling living rooms, the American dream for $350,000, around a third of what the same kind of house would go for in Boston or San Francisco. Betty Brown had a lovely home, a beautiful boy, and a husband she was crazy about, but her life wasn't perfect — no one's ever is.

Back on her street she waved to a man loading something into a pickup. "That's my father-in-law," she said, and sighed about how Joe's parents, who moved to Winston-Salem at the same time as Joe and herself, didn't seem inclined to socialize. "In this neighborhood, if you're not born and raised here, you're an outsider," she said.

It struck me that Betty Brown's intense spell of web sleuthing coincided with Jonas's birth and her move from Virginia to North Carolina. It must have been a stressful time: the challenges of a late-in-life baby; moving to a new state with a new husband and new in-laws; leaving behind her siblings —

whom she had described to me as her best friends — and her grown children.

The Internet may have helped Betty escape to a different world, one in which she wielded power and control. "Making an identification — that's power," Todd Matthews pointed out to me one day. "You just changed something. You changed an unknown person into a homicide investigation." The local paper calls, you do a story, a family is appreciative, and for a while you're a hero. Then the hubbub dies down and you're back where you started, dealing with your own potentially troublesome life.

As Betty said, to find out where someone ended up, you need to find out where they started. "For our family, I know how long it took me to search and research and get as far as I have," she told me.

I was beginning to see how Betty Dalton Brown had ended up where she did.

# 8
## SEEKERS OF LOST SOULS

Taking a break from the Tent Girl case, I was idly searching through archives when I came across an old newspaper article about the Lady of the Dunes with a byline I recognized: George Liles.

I had worked with Liles, an amiable fireplug of a guy with basset hound eyes, at Tufts University, where I wrote about people, events, and research before I left to accept a science writing job at MIT. Liles and I had both started our careers as newspaper reporters covering selectmen's meetings that droned on about granite versus asphalt curbs and other mind-numbing small-town minutiae. Pre-Internet, reporters typically moved from the town government beat to the crime beat, where you paid a daily visit to the police station to chat up the cops, hoping they'd drop a newsworthy tidbit. If you're on the crime beat for more than a year or two you're considered a lifer, prone to becoming a cynical connoisseur of human misery and deviance. Neither George nor I had succumbed to that fate, but I knew George knew his way around an old-fashioned police log.

The byline on the article I'd found showed that in 1995, twenty-one years after the Lady of the Dunes was murdered, Liles was doing a stint at the *Provincetown Banner*. On a slow news day, he had ambled over to the station to see what was happening with the decades-old unsolved case.

He was ushered in to see tall, stocky Provincetown sergeant Warren Tobias, who struck Liles as an old-school gumshoe right out of a Dashiell Hammett paperback. To Liles's surprise, Tobias was working on a lead and willing to share. Tobias said he believed the Lady of the Dunes was an alleged drug runner and gun smuggler named Rory Gene Kesinger, who had escaped from jail in 1973, the year before the body in the dunes was found, and vanished. Liles's story had legs, as they say in the news business. Tobias's speculation about Kesinger would appear in coverage about the case until 2002, when a DNA test showed definitively she was not the victim in the dunes.

Now a veteran newsman and science writer, Liles helps undergrads from around the country hone their writing skills as part of a summer program at the preeminent Woods Hole Marine Biological Laboratory on Cape Cod. A few weeks before he and I spoke, he kicked off the seminar as he always does, by showing the students examples of his own published pieces, including the one about the Lady of the Dunes.

Under a photo of a grave marker, the headline on Liles's 1995 story read, "Is There a Killer Among Us?"

Liles told me that the headline always jarred the college students into looking up from their laptops and cell phones. They all wanted to know if the murderer had ever been found, and were surprised to hear the victim was still nameless.

Liles held that the Lady of the Dunes manifested a new twist on high-profile cases such as the Lindbergh kidnapping and reports of the survival of Anastasia, a daughter of Czar Nicholas II. Instead of a famous victim, the victim was unknown, yet the case had the same aura of intrigue as historically notorious mysteries.

Then there was the matter of her missing hands. Going to the trouble of hacking off and disposing of hands suggested the killer didn't want her to be identified by her fingerprints. But in the 1970s, processing ten-print fingerprint submissions was a manual, labor-intensive task, and only federal employees and lawbreakers would have been certain to have fingerprints on file, Liles argued. Was she a fed or a criminal?

Liles asked me if I had been to the dunes. It's an eerie place, otherworldly, he reminded me. Just a short walk away from Provincetown, this civilized little town, the dunes can feel like a different planet. The fact that the victim was found in the dunes added to her allure.

"The 'Lady on the Sidewalk' just wouldn't have the same ring to it," he said, and I laughed. I thought Liles was right: circumstances conspired to capture the public's imagination on this case while others languished in obscurity. Still, if I was ever going to get my feet wet as a web sleuth, it might not hurt to start with a high-profile case.

During a trip to North Carolina, I quizzed Daphne Owings, the most prolific web sleuth I'd encountered, on tips for how to go about sleuthing out the Lady of the Dunes's identity. In 2002, Daphne, a mother of two, had become engrossed in Sue Grafton's *Q Is for Quarry,* a crime thriller based loosely on the Santa Barbara,

California, sheriff's investigation into Jane Doe 1969, a stabbing victim discovered near a quarry on Highway 1, south of the working-class city of Lompoc. Grafton herself helped pay for the body to be exhumed, which led to a facial reconstruction. Daphne became fascinated by the image of the bucktoothed, brown-haired young woman. When Daphne's husband was sent to serve in Iraq, she started volunteering for the Doe Network to take her mind off the war. Daphne is blond, athletic, and sharp, and I quickly saw that besides the fact that I'd never catch up with her in a road race, my visual memory was no match for hers. She had the extraordinary ability to look at morgue photos and facial reconstructions and then scrutinize missing-person files until a spark of recognition, as she put it, struck her.

Daphne pointed out that, given the extensive media coverage of the Lady of the Dunes, it was quite likely she was not in a database anywhere or she would have been matched already. Instead of going to the usual websites, she advised, plug in "missing woman," "missing girl," and "Massachusetts" in newspaper archives and genealogy databases. Ignore the hair on the reconstructions, which might not be depicted in an accurate color or style, and look at the basic facial shape, the line of the nose, the width between the eyes. Start hammering away at missing persons who fall within the age range and range of time: Look first at people who went missing in 1974, backtrack a few years, and work with those, she said. If I came up empty-handed, I could look for people who went missing earlier; who were younger or older, shorter or taller; who had blue eyes instead of brown. It was easy for errors to creep into the online data.

Daphne was not exaggerating when she called it work. This was hard. What's more, she eschews relatively high-profile cases such as the Lady of the Dunes on principle. Owings said she never opted to spend any time on her case because so many others likely had. She prefers cases that haven't garnered a lot of attention: they're the ones that need it.

In 1995, my friend George Liles was one of many reporters who had written about the Lady of the Dunes. That same year, in Kentucky, almost no one was actively following the case of Tent Girl besides Todd Matthews, by then a twenty-five-year-old night shift worker in an auto parts factory.

Over and over, Todd mentally rearranged

the meager facts about Tent Girl, like the squares on a recalcitrant Rubik's cube, in a fruitless effort to force them into place.

If Tent Girl was a teenager, as he read in the newspapers, Todd figured someone must have filed a missing-person report. When he didn't find one, he convinced himself that the only reason Tent Girl's parents weren't looking for her was because they had a hand in her disappearance. These murderous parents lurking in Kentucky horrified him until he remembered they likely existed only in his imagination.

The one thing Todd couldn't seem to do was forget about the case. One harrowing incident captured what lack of closure can do to you.

It was 1995. Todd lived with twenty-four-year-old Lori in a single-wide trailer adjacent to his parents' home.

As he did every day, he yanked black curtains over the trailer's tiny bedroom window to help himself sleep, but white-hot sunlight still crept in around the edges. He pulled the bedspread over his eyes, trying to pretend that the world outside was dark and still. It was only Wednesday — two more all-night shifts at the Hutchinson plant before the weekend.

For eight years, he'd been chasing the ice-cold trail of a girl dead almost three decades. He never imagined himself as a private detective, let alone an amateur one. As a kid, he'd spent so much time in hospitals for a congenital heart condition that he figured he might have picked up enough medicalese to become a doctor. With a bum heart, he couldn't quarry limestone like his grandfather, and he didn't have his father's knack for fixing machines and driving trucks. But, married at eighteen and a father at twenty-two, Todd had a family to support.

After bagging groceries at Brown's Galaxy Market his junior year in high school and working as a bundle boy in a garment factory, Todd now commuted less than a mile to Hutchinson Worldwide, a global conglomerate that owns manufacturing facilities in Livingston. Inside a large, windowless rectangular building he plucked pieces of stainless steel off an assembly line and inserted them in a machine called a bender. The metal was curved into a cylinder, then he and high school buddy Wayne Sells fitted O-rings onto it, capped it, labeled it, and packed it on its way to automobile factories for use in air-conditioning and engine cooling systems.

Sells invited Todd to hear his bluegrass

band, but Todd was always tracking down some lead on a dead girl. Sells had never heard of such a thing. For one, it seemed impossible. And it didn't seem like fun.

Todd's night-owl schedule meant he was often alone with time on his hands to think about Tent Girl and how she had most likely been murdered and that her murderer was still at large, maybe even in Tennessee. Loneliness spilled over into depression. He feared he was losing his grip on reality. Looking back, he wouldn't say he went crazy, exactly, but he knew he wasn't pursuing healthy patterns. He never got enough sleep. Dark seemed darker, he knew, when your mind isn't the way it should be.

One morning, he was startled to see a half-empty glass of juice on the kitchen counter that hadn't been there when he had gone to bed. He didn't recall waking, walking to the kitchen, pouring and drinking the juice. Another time he'd awoken and found himself standing completely upright, propped against a cabinet in the bathroom with a book in his hand. These incidents set him on edge for days. Was he capable of lighting an oil lamp while he slept and setting the entire trailer on fire?

If you asked him if he believed in ghosts, he might say that ghosts were crazy talk.

Other times, the God's honest truth was he wasn't sure. Todd once spent a night in a city park in Harrodsburg, Kentucky, hoping to catch a glimpse of a ghost. The story goes that a young woman arrived at the now-defunct Graham Springs Hotel in the mid-1800s and signed the register with a ficti-tious name. The woman danced madly the entire night and finally collapsed, dead, on the ballroom floor. She was buried in an anonymous grave on grounds that became a park. Todd didn't cross paths that night with the Lady Who Danced Herself to Death, but if trying to see her meant he was crazy, so be it; he wasn't ashamed. Maybe, he said a tad defensively, there's a separate, unseen world out there that we only catch glimpses of.

In the state between wakefulness and sleep, the outside world felt removed, unreal. Todd had to shut down his morbidly swirling thoughts if he was going to get to sleep. He was, as usual, exhausted. The doc-tor had given him a prescription for the sleeping pill Ambien. He thought of the vial in the medicine cabinet but later swore he did not take any that day. He had just suc-cumbed to a blissful blankness when he heard a sound. This was not unusual. Some days he was awakened by scratching, banging, rattling — sounds difficult to ignore.

Members of Todd's family had had ghostly encounters before. His mother once heard a cooking pan clatter to the floor in the middle of the night. The pan rolled on its rim before finally settling with a clank of metal on wood. She got up to pick it up only to find it safely on its hook. Even Lori once insisted that an entire second-floor landing had crashed in — but nothing turned out to be out of place. Right before Todd's grandmother died, she accused Papa Vaughn of playing tricks on her when she discerned guitar music coming from the next room. But even though Tom Vaughn was known for the occasional practical joke, that wasn't one of them.

Todd heard a thump. Like a driver in a slow-motion car wreck, he felt himself propelled through space. He threw off the sheets and stumbled from the bedroom into the adjacent combined kitchen and living room.

She was there in the kitchen. He was not at all surprised to see her. The trailer's small windows were covered in a vain attempt to simulate night, but he made out the shape of a head and shoulders. Awkwardly confined by the grayish green canvas bag, she nevertheless seemed able to move about the cramped room.

He imagined himself, like her, closed up in a tarp, struggling to breathe. It was almost as if he were inside her head. He could feel her fear.

The first thing he asked her was what he most wanted to know: *Who are you?* He sensed her reproach. He should know who she was, if he truly wanted to help her. Well, then she would have to reveal herself. The next thing he knew, the bag was lying on the couch and he was leaning over it, a butcher knife in his hand. He heard a blade sawing through fabric, the way Riddle's must have when he cut open her shroud. Todd struggled to penetrate the tough fabric, finally carving a slit, an opening that he hoped would free whatever was inside from the horror in which it was trapped.

As soon as the opening was big enough, something flew out toward him. What was left of her face, streaked black and brown with decay, burst through the hole. Her short reddish hair was mussed and plastered to her scalp. The eyes were gone; the right side of her face eaten away, exposing her white, straight teeth to the roots. Her lipless mouth looked huge, the teeth bared in a horrific grin.

A few years later, in 1998, a newspaper

reporter would come to interview Todd. They stood together in the brand-new double-wide that had replaced the single-wide trailer. The reporter shuffled through a sheaf of paper, pulled out an eight-by-ten photograph, and offered it to Todd. Todd looked down at the photo in his hand.

It was just as horrific as the dozens of times it had replayed in his mind. The rotted flesh, the skin leathered over, the hair in disarray. The only difference was that the reporter's photograph was black-and-white. The image burned into Todd's memory was in full color.

The reporter was amused by the look on Todd's face. The photo was taken at Tent Girl's autopsy hours after Wilbur Riddle found her. The gruesome image had never been published, never made available to anyone outside of police investigators working on the case. "I'll bet you've never seen that before," the reporter chortled.

Immediately after Tent Girl popped through the opening Todd had cut in her shroud, he sat bolt upright in bed, shaken and recoiling from her ruined face.

After a time, he disentangled the sweat-soaked sheets and padded into the living room. The room was quiet and empty. He turned to return to the bedroom and a glint caught his eye. He spun around and scanned the room: chairs, lamps, tables, all where they should be. Then he spotted it. On the couch was an enormous butcher knife with a razor-sharp blade.

When Todd and Lori's son Dillan was born, Todd turned his mental image of Tent Girl into a young mother and the white cloth on her shoulder into a diaper. He wrote to the Scott County sheriff, the governor, and the coroner, urging them to exhume her remains and reexamine her pelvis for signs that she had borne a child.

Maybe the young woman had been pregnant and someone killed her to hush it up? Looking at Dillan toddling about, Todd wondered if Tent Girl had had a child who had been kidnapped, or killed and dumped elsewhere. Or — (and here he guessed the truth) — if she had a young child, now motherless, who had no way of knowing her mother was buried in Kentucky.

At that point, Todd even started suspecting Wilbur Riddle. He'd heard about Riddle's romantic conquests outside of his three marriages, rumors about illegitimate children. Todd decided he wouldn't put it past Riddle to "dispose" of an inconvenient lover. He was ashamed afterward of his evil thoughts, but there was no love lost between father-in-law and son-in-law. Over the years, Todd and Riddle's shared interest in Tent Girl had evolved into more of a rivalry.

Sometimes Todd's information-gathering forays dovetailed with trips to see Lori's family in Indiana. Early on, Lori waited patiently in the car while Todd rummaged through microfiche in libraries and picked up old copies of newspapers from archives. Other times Lori railed at him. "You don't think about anybody but yourself!" she yelled. "What about our son? He needs you more than some dead girl." Their fights got more heated, more physical.

There was the matter of money. Todd's friend and former coworker Wayne Sells recalled that they made no more than eighteen thousand dollars a year. They both worked overtime, but it was hard to support a family on that salary. More often than not, Todd, Lori, and Dillan ate dinner with Billy and Brenda Matthews in their house next door, so close they could practically shout to one another — too close, in Lori's opinion. And Todd often got so wrapped up in Tent Girl, he forgot he had a family, Lori said years later.

Billy was satisfied that the young couple

was meeting payments on the trailer but he didn't know that, besides the money Todd spent pursuing Tent Girl, the couple was living beyond their means, taking cash advances against their credit cards. They told one another they'd work more overtime to pay it back.

Todd was soon bankrupt. He couldn't bring himself to tell his dad. Lori, tired of Todd spending money they didn't have on detective work, moved out of the trailer and rented her own place in town. Todd, always on the computer searching for Tent Girl clues, seemed to have no time for her or their son. "I left because the Tent Girl was his life, not us," she said simply. At the plant, Todd still couldn't get the hang of working the third shift. He was physically and mentally exhausted by whatever was compelling him to seek out the name of a stranger who had died before he was born. He had to concede his family and friends were right. It was time to give up this crazy attachment to Tent Girl.

He decided to ask one last person and abide by her word.

Todd climbed the steps of a dilapidated house in Livingston, Tennessee. There was no name or shingle out front. Everyone knew where to find the lady who saw visions.

Todd's decision to call on Miz Cole was partly a whim, like the times he dropped everything to drive to a library on the off chance that they would have a stash of two-decade-old newspapers, and partly desperation. Tent Girl appearing bloody and reproachful in his kitchen, Lori moving out, filing for bankruptcy: the events of the past few months had left him shaken.

Yet, the thought of abandoning Tent Girl made Todd feel as guilty as failing to see his grandfather the night he died. Todd's fondest childhood memories were tromping through the woods with Papa Vaughn, searching out unnervingly human-shaped ginseng roots. Papa had recently moved out of his daughter and son-in-law's house next door to the trailer. Todd didn't visit as often as he planned; he wasn't there the night his grandfather died of heart failure. Since the old man's death, the words played in Todd's mind: *You should have gone. You had the opportunity to go. Why didn't you go?*

Some extolled the potency of Miz Cole's psychic powers. Others called her a phony. Then there were those who declared Miz Cole pure evil, a practitioner of witchcraft.

Inside the shabby house, a plain, tired-looking woman answered the door. Furniture covered most of the floor, whatnots such as Avon perfume bottles shaped like the Eiffel Tower crowded every surface, putting Todd, as he recalled the scene years later, in mind of an episode of *Hoarders*. Miz Cole seated Todd at the kitchen table. Todd heard children somewhere in the house or yard. Apparently accustomed to visits from their grandmother's clients, they kept out of sight.

Miz Cole opened notebooks filled with cryptic writing, scribbled verses from the Bible referring to gifts. People in the Bible saw visions, she told him. Her powers, she claimed, were a gift she was obligated to share. She listened attentively as Todd described his indecision, his anguish, over a dead girl who had nothing to do with him, the exasperation of his family, his nightmares. She talked about sprinkling holy water over his door to ward off evil energy. He rejected that idea. She finally said, "The answer lies within yourself."

If Todd hadn't sounded so serious as he related this, I would have burst out laughing. I'd often thought Todd should have lived in Victorian times, when everyone believed in witches, ghosts, and fairies. On the other hand, I'd heard Todd scorn psychics who purported to know where the remains of the missing could be found. " 'Oh, they're buried near the water,' " he mocked. "Okay, well, how many lakes are around here? Specifically north, south, east, or west? What county? They can't tell you that; they just know that the spirit is near the water. Good tip. We'll dig up the entire coastline of the United States."

But just then Miz Cole's hackneyed phrase was exactly what Todd needed to hear. He didn't know it, but the psychic's advice would help define his adult life. It gave him permission to do what he was determined to do all along: give Tent Girl a name.

At the time, all Todd knew was that he felt better than he had in weeks. After the reading, although Miz Cole didn't ask him for money, he handed her a five on his way out.

He still didn't know what to make of his terrifyingly realistic nightmare. But he was convinced he was on a quest some force in the universe didn't want him to quit just yet.

# 9
# How to Make a John Doe

I was in Guilford County, in north-central North Carolina, on the trail of a John Doe who was frustrating the hell out of Betty Brown and a local detective. On her day off, Betty, dwarfed behind the wheel of her husband Joe's Dodge Ram — tricked out with a skull-and-bones-motif rearview mirror and ox-size chrome testicles hanging from the trailer hitch — drove me to the site where the remains were found.

Detective R. Allen Cheek hadn't divulged too many specifics to me on the phone. Some things only the murderer would know, he said. He didn't want to blow his case — should he ever have one.

Trailing Cheek's unmarked cruiser south on US 421, one of many interlacing highways and secondary roads between Raleigh and Greensboro, we passed a sign for Climax Creek, invisible through the dense foliage. "A lot of people get dumped out there dead." Betty pointed through the truck's window. "In a back area of road with no houses, you can easily pull over and drag a body out and throw it out and no one actually sees you. They found three women there in the last year and a half — one decapitated, one beaten to death, one shot — all dumped on that road, all within a five-mile distance."

We looped onto a ramp for 421 and had pulled over next to a wooded area dividing the highway's northbound and southbound lanes. Betty chain-smoked in the truck while Cheek and I picked our way into the football field–size island between the two roadways.

It was a gray, misty day. The detective elbowed his way past brambles, stepped over a Dunkin' Donuts cup, and skirted an old tire in a puddle. He drew aside a swath of vegetation as if it were a velvet curtain and he was inviting me backstage. "You're going to get your shoes dirty," he warned.

One February day in 2008, a motorist pulled over at this spot to stretch his legs. Wandering into the woods to take a leak, he spotted a rolled-up tarp. Animals had ripped and shredded it to gain access to something inside. "He started looking at it and he realized he was looking at a human rib cage," Cheek told me. "So he backed out and called us."

"Us" was the Guilford County sheriff's office in Greensboro. Many web sleuths make themselves known to local law enforcement to gain trust and information. Betty Brown is no exception. "If you give me a lead, I'll work with anyone," Cheek said, though he admitted he was initially wary of Brown and her questions. I sympathized. Betty could be a tad scary.

Sometimes when cops wouldn't return her calls, Betty told me out of Cheek's hearing, she'd be forced to "harass" the police department until they entered their missing and unidentified cases into NamUs. She wouldn't let them back down. One sheriff, resisting Betty's efforts to collect a family reference sample for a missing person, told her, "I don't know about that DNA. They're kind of backwoods hick people. I don't think they understand what DNA is."

"Well, give it a whirl," Betty told him drily. "They might watch *CSI.*"

Shannon Vita, the fellow Doe Network and NamUs volunteer from Arizona who talks to Betty almost daily, agrees that Betty can be aggressive. "That's how she gets her stuff done. If there is something concerning a family's missing person or unidentified case she feels strongly about, she will not take 'no' for an answer."

Today Betty couldn't say no to yet another attempt to ID the John Doe found near US 421.

Betty had told me on the phone from North Carolina that it seemed the John Doe's assailant or assailants thought they knew something about forensics. In an apparent attempt to mask the victim's identity, they left him clad in nothing but a T-shirt and pair of boxer shorts. And they took his false teeth.

A tall, solid man with a round face and a shaved head, Detective Cheek reminded me of a young Telly Savalas. He was wearing a tweedy sports jacket, khakis, crisp blue shirt, and yellow tie — not good attire for tramping through mud in the rain. My loafers sunk into the spongy underbrush. Wet leaves on low branches slapped our faces; thorns snagged our clothes.

We were only a few dozen yards into the thicket but the world outside had disappeared. A freight train's horn wailed in the distance. Traffic whooshed by on 421, just visible through the trees. I followed Cheek as he picked his way through the brush, watching the back of his neck redden in the chilly dampness.

"If I am correct, where he was found was right through there," he said. "There's a tree. I'm pretty sure I can find it." He paced west, then south, and stopped at a spot littered with blackened, wet branches. "This is it. He was lying right here."

Cheek remembered taking the call at around five in the afternoon on the ninth of February. He had ducked out of a Sunday afternoon family party celebrating his mother's birthday and met the deputies at the northbound ramp from Highway 62 to Highway 421, where Betty's truck now sat on the shoulder behind his unmarked cruiser.

Cheek gestured at the off-ramp, where he conjectured that the murderers pulled over to drag the body out of the car. It would have been easy enough to circle around back onto the highway. The whole process would have taken no more than a few minutes.

Even midday, the ramp was far from busy. Passing drivers must have spotted our roadside foray into the brush, but they all sped by without a second glance. "If we were dragging a body into the woods, they wouldn't have paid no attention to us, either," Cheek said as we returned to the cars.

Before I climbed in Betty's truck, I stooped and picked up a black object, shiny from the rain, lying at the edge of the pavement: a rubber bracelet stamped "live-the-backwoods-life.com." It seemed incongruous, given that we were absorbed in the details of a backwoods death.

Back in Cheek's low, nondescript cinderblock building in an industrial park, he pulled out an overstuffed loose-leaf notebook labeled "Old Joe." Seeing that I noticed the name scrawled on the cover, Cheek looked apologetic, explaining that he started calling the remains Old Joe because he hated having no other name to give them.

Cheek's first job as a police officer at age twenty-two was in a small North Carolina town called Madison. He'd known he wanted to be a cop since maybe fourth grade when he realized he didn't like to see people get picked on. He'd always wanted to "get the bad guy," he said. After twelve years as a beat cop in increasingly larger towns, he started working break-ins and larcenies. He joined the Guilford County sheriff's department as a detective in 2001, graduating from property crimes to the major-crime unit.

It's hard to make a case for any murderer "respecting" his victim, but the lack of any shred of dignity for Old Joe especially irked Cheek. "This guy, he was sixty to seventy years old. Whoever did this, they stripped him of all his clothing except his T-shirt and his shorts. They tied him up, they duct-taped him, and then they wrapped him up in a tarp and then they duct-taped the tarp. And then they drug him out in the woods. And took everything, all ID, and, unfortunately for us, he was out there for six to eight months and he totally decomposed.

"I mean, why would you duct-tape somebody and put him in a tarp and hide him in the woods down the road? You know they're going to be found eventually, and if they live on that road, somebody's going to know them. But if you drive them a hundred miles away and dump them in someone else's woods . . ." Cheek trailed off.

"And they took his dentures," he said after a moment. "When I was there that night, and they were bringing him out and they said his teeth are gone, I knew right then and there, man, this is not good," Cheek told me. "You got no fingerprints, no tattoos, no wallet, no teeth. You have no idea who this guy is."

There are a lot of ways for a body to accidentally become unidentifiable; there's something particularly insidious about killers who do their best to intentionally turn their victims into John and Jane Does. It's nothing new. Tragedies from Homer's time reference "the unwept and unburied corpse" that disturbs the social and cosmic order. I turned to a longtime anthropologist to bring me up to date.

Killers who dump bodies where they will be exposed to the elements get help from nature. In the woods, scavenging animals and insects converge on — and often disperse — human remains. Kentucky's hundreds of unpopulated acres provided state forensic anthropologist Emily Craig with plenty of challenges during her tenure in the form of skeletons picked completely clean of flesh and muscle in as little as twenty-four hours. Other images of decomposition in Craig's macabre portfolio were like a gruesome version of *Where's Waldo?* "You see the body?" Craig asked as I squinted at a photo of what I thought was a mass of greenish brown vegetation at the foot of a tree. I didn't. "There's his elbow," she said, pointing.

Forensic techniques are sloggingly low-tech. The forensic anthropologist needs the skeleton free of soft tissue, marrow, muscle, and cartilage. Forensic sculptor Frank

Bender once took revenge on a recalcitrant workman by having him peer into a bubbling cooking pot on the stove in which Bender was boiling a human head to get the skull clean. Others use Crock-Pots or hot plates for the same purpose. One lab reported a time-saving alternative: dunking the remains in Super Kleen — a foaming industrial cleaner intended for "heavily encrusted soils" in the food and beverage industry — and then baking the disarticulated skeleton in chafing dishes in a large-capacity incubator.

It's not uncommon for someone to bring the medical examiner a picture to ID skeletal remains, because that's what happens on TV. "You know, they find the skeleton and somebody does a computer face and it's perfect," Craig said. "It takes three minutes and they can bring in a photograph and superimpose them and that's who it is. But it just doesn't work that way."

Craig also stressed that DNA is not the panacea some imagine. But I was impressed by investigators' resourcefulness in using it in challenging cases of lost identity. In one documented case, DNA from a Pap smear was compared to DNA extracted from teeth as reference samples. A badly burned corpse's teeth can often still be used for identification; dandruff on any remaining section of a burned scalp can sometimes provide enough DNA for analysis. Then there are deliberate mutilations. "They'll cut off her tattoo, cut off her hands," Craig says of murderers. "They know. They watch the same TV shows that we do."

I went in search of cases in which forensic anthropologists managed to stay one step ahead of killers who thought they had beat the system. A cold case investigator told me about a Virginia case in which the killer worked hard — but not hard enough — to obliterate his victim. Mark Christopher Poe, an ex-sailor, lived on the Norfolk naval base. Poe's next-door neighbors were a husband, who was deployed at sea, and his attractive young wife. After failing to hear from his daughter, her father went to the house and found blood and signs of a struggle. When police arrived, they found hair and tissue in the bathtub and surmised the woman's killer cut the body up. Black light illuminated the site of the attack. But the body was gone.

The cops' first break came when a headless, armless, and legless torso was found floating in the river by fishermen.

Next, in the appropriately named Great Dismal Swamp, a man hunting for bait kicked a sack on the ground and a head rolled out.

Then a man's truck broke down on a road running through the swamp. Another person stopped to help and began to talk about gigging frogs. The first man had never heard of it, so the man made a gig, a kind of multi-pronged spear, and showed him. The first man took the gig and ran into the swamp.

He gigged one arm. Cadaver dogs found the other arm on the opposite side of the road. At the trial, two witnesses testified that they had seen Poe throwing an army-green duffel bag from a bridge into the water. Police recovered a green duffel bag with the name of the victim's husband stencilled on the side. Fibers from the duffel bag were consistent with fibers removed from the trunk of Poe's car, which, when tested, revealed the presence of blood. A search of Poe's home revealed, among other things, a knife that both the victim's husband and father identified as belonging to the victim, and a strand of hair in Poe's underwear consistent with that of the victim. Poe was convicted of first-degree murder in 1994 and sentenced to life without parole.

In another case, in 2009, a woman searching a Buena Park, California, Dumpster for recyclable cans found a bloody suitcase with a body inside.

The victim's teeth had been pulled and all her fingers removed. But within three days the coroner identified Jasmine Fiore, a twenty-eight-year-old former swimsuit and *Playboy* model with a size 34DD bust.

The serial number on her breast implants led investigators to the manufacturer, which kept on file the recipient's name, address, phone number, Social Security number, surgeon, and primary care doctor. (Total joint replacements implanted after 1992 have traceable serial numbers, and the FDA requires manufacturers of pacemakers and defibrillators to keep track of such data as well.)

The main suspect in Fiore's murder — her husband, Ryan Alexander Jenkins, a onetime contestant on the reality TV show *Megan Wants a Millionaire* — fled to Canada and killed himself. Emily Craig told me of a killer who dismembered his victim, tucked the body parts in neatly tied plastic bags, and tossed them in the Wisconsin River. The water kept the body as cool as a refrigerator would have. The plastic bags thwarted maggots and scavengers. "Ironically, the very steps that the killer had taken to conceal his victim's identity had helped preserve it," Craig pointed out.

Old Joe's remains, mostly skeletonized, were sent to the chief medical examiner's office at the University of North Carolina in Chapel Hill. "He works on all the bones," Detective Cheek said. "He puts them back together — or tries to, anyway. I just call and say, 'Can I speak to Gibbs?' "

I made my way to the tenth floor of a featureless beige building on the campus of the University of North Carolina at Chapel Hill School of Medicine. A man slightly paler than a hospital bedsheet emerged from a back room to greet me. I recognized Clyde Gibbs Jr. from his LinkedIn page, where he'd opted to pose in a black T-shirt emblazoned with a human-size white rib cage, the kind you'd see on a Halloween skeleton costume. "Love anything horror, death, bone, and Doctor Who," Clyde's bio reads on Google+.

After decades of anonymity, forensic anthropologists are suddenly rock stars, observed Kathy Reichs, producer of the hit TV series *Bones,* based on her work as a real-life forensic scientist and her best-selling crime thrillers. Reichs, blond and tousled, could pass for Debbie Harry. Clyde

Gibbs would have to be Marilyn Manson.

Gibbs looked like a character from one of his beloved George Romero horror films. For all the hilarity in his social media presence, in person he was low-key and solemn. He wore a small skull cast in metal around his neck. His thinning hair crept back over his prominent forehead; his straggly goatee was shot through with strands of gray; his teeth — what little I could glimpse of them — looked like blackened stubs. The fluorescent light turned his hollow cheeks sallow; he was so rail-thin, he seemed to float like a wraith in a white lab coat through the cinder-block hallways. He exuded an odor of stale cigarette smoke and something sharp and chemical. Formaldehyde? Booze?

I liked Gibbs immediately.

As we sat in a conference room and talked, I pointed a camera at him. He demurely hid his coffee mug in his lap. The mug featured a pale, ghoulish girl in a prim schoolgirl outfit. Long, stringy hair obscured half her face and one of her enormous, black-rimmed, haunted eyes. Not being a fan of the horror genre, I only later recognized the iconic Kyra Schon. She played a little girl turned zombie in Gibbs's all-time favorite film, *Night of the Living Dead,* released in 1968, the year Wilbur Riddle stumbled across Tent Girl. In the movie, Schon's character, Karen Cooper, eats her father's arm and stabs her mother to death with a trowel.

Gibbs informed me matter-of-factly that his comfort level with the dead stemmed from both his parents working at a funeral home while he was growing up. He didn't see a human being on the table; he saw a challenge, he offered as an explanation to a question I hadn't yet asked — a question he apparently heard quite often. "Dealing with the skeletons, it's a puzzle. You're going in there saying what's their age, sex, race, what trauma can I find here?"

Experienced coroners and medical examiners can tell a lot from a corpse. I was surprised by how much forensic anthropologists such as Clyde Gibbs and Emily Craig can tell from just a skeleton.

Gibbs commented that being in possession of a full, intact body would seem more revealing than having only bones to work with. You'd think fingerprints, better access to DNA, eye color, hair color, skin tones, scars, tattoos, and piercings would give you more to go on. But in the end, he said, some of those bodies actually go unidentified longer than the skeletons.

Seen one skeleton, seen 'em all? Not so. A

human female skeleton has a more rounded pelvis, more rounded shoulder blades, and thinner bones than male skeletons. Women tend to have narrower rib cages, smaller teeth, less angular jaws, less pronounced brow ridges, and a smaller protuberance at the back of the skull; the carrying angle of the forearm is more pronounced in females than in males.

Hold the skull in profile, the legendary Dr. Bill Bass instructs budding forensic anthropologists, and you can determine its race. The students place one end of a pencil on or near the midline of the skull at the base of the nasal cavity. They then lower the pencil toward the face so that the point touches the chin. If the pencil hits the jaw ridge on the roof or bottom of the mouth, the face is prognathic, or Negroid. If the pencil extends to the chin, the face is orthognathic and therefore Caucasoid.

University of Wisconsin–Madison anthropologist John Hawks notes that the nose aperture of the Caucasian skull is a narrow triangle; the bony protrusion between the eyes is long and thin. Negroid skulls have little or no nasal depression and a wider nasal opening. Mongoloid and Negroid skulls also lack a nasal sill, the angulation dividing the nasal floor from the upper jaw.

Other race-related differences include the shape of the eye orbits as viewed from the front. Africans tend to a rectangular shape; East Asians, more circular; Europeans, an "aviator glasses" shape.

One of three centers in the state that perform autopsies for law enforcement, Gibbs's Office of the Chief Medical Examiner shares space with the UNC hospitals, a complex of tall buildings.

Through hallway windows, I took in views of verdant rolling hills. I followed Gibbs down a cement staircase lined with boxes of rodent poison. As he pushed open a metal door, it struck me that even though we were on the ninth floor, our surroundings had gotten starker, more basement-like.

Why did it surprise me — again — that a medical examiner would lead me to the morgue? I knew from my failed attempt to make it into reefer 2 in Vegas that I needed more mental preparation — or at least a few stiff drinks — before we went any farther. But Gibbs was already yards ahead on his grasshopper legs.

Sure enough, on the other side of the metal door, I almost bumped into a gurney supporting a human form swaddled in black plastic and duct tape. I'd barely registered this when through an open door I glimpsed people in green scrubs hunched over a silver table.

On the table was what appeared to be a solidly built black man. His chest was wide open, gaping, and very red.

With that horror to my right and the gurney straight ahead, I was in danger of repeating my embarrassing Vegas wimp-out. But relaying this to Gibbs would require catching up with him, and that would mean I had to squeeze past the gurney. Proximity, again, was setting me off. The well-wrapped body at my elbow was far worse than the bloody one in the next room.

I kept my eyes on the floor tiles and stepped around the gurney, holding my breath the way I used to when skirting a reeking homeless man sprawled on a New York City subway seat. My gaze fell on the corpse's head, taped up in a plastic bag. "Hey, he can't breathe with that on," I felt like calling out to Gibbs; but, to my relief, we had arrived at the storeroom to visit Old Joe.

A full human skeleton, it turns out, can be neatly stored in around 180 square inches. A box that size would hold a couple of sweaters or a bathrobe. Bodies found decomposed with intact soft tissue and muscle present a problem for coroners and medical examiners in the many jurisdictions that possess limited or no refrigerated storage. Totally skeletonized remains require less elaborate conditions and storage space and are generally easier to store.

Old Joe's was one of dozens of brown cardboard boxes piled haphazardly on metal shelves that reached to the ceiling. What looked like two animal skulls, perhaps once belonging to dogs, sat next to a small, unlabeled bottle of blue liquid. White labels printed with things like "801-2199" and bar codes were affixed to some boxes; others had hand-lettered labels such as "Skulls — Cleveland County." One box was stamped, presumably from a previous use, "for home canning and freezing." A single femur, Gibbs explained, would be tagged and labeled and kept in a box with other femora. "We have a femur coming in here, an arm there," he said.

Gibbs's forensic investigation determined that the John Doe whose case Detective Cheek and Betty Brown had adopted was a white male, approximately five feet nine or ten inches, with long black and gray hair, who had apparently worn dentures for years. Cause of death was "undetermined."

A few months after the remains were

found, the sheriff's department sent the skull to the forensic anthropology center at the University of Tennessee in Knoxville — one of twelve forensic anthropology labs in the United States — for a facial reconstruction. The three-dimensional clay bust of Old Joe showed a man with high cheekbones, deep-set eyes, a prominent jaw, and a high forehead.

Until Old Joe is reconnected with his name, he'll stay in the "bones room" in the company of some of North Carolina's 107 other UIDs.

So far, it didn't look good for Old Joe. Detective Cheek had checked to see if he was a convicted felon, in which case his fingerprints would be on file. He was not.

Cheek had a profile of Old Joe's DNA. "Every time I find someone who says, 'That's my relative,' I get a DNA sample from them," he told me. Twice, such tests had come back negative. Cheek entered Old Joe's specifics into NamUs and found reports of missing men who had no teeth. "I've followed up leads in other states," Cheek said. "I've pulled up pictures in NamUs where I'm, like, 'This could be my guy!' They look so close. But I'd call and say, 'Did your missing person have any teeth?' They'd say, 'Yeah, he had a whole mouthful.' And I'll say, 'It's not my guy.'"

Cheek had spent so much time pondering Old Joe that the nameless victim started to seem like someone he had once known and been fond of. To Cheek, no one, least of all a friend, deserved to get dumped in the woods. He wanted to investigate the death, collect leads, and close the book on the case so it didn't get passed along to his successor. He told me he always gave every investigation his all, pursued every lead, no matter how far-fetched. When he went home at night, he wanted to rest easy.

But without the victim's identity, Cheek was stymied.

At the UNC Chapel Hill medical school, Gibbs escorted me back past the body on the gurney, down the elevator, and along a labyrinth of hallways to the main door of the hospital. As we walked, we talked horror films.

George Romero never really explained what caused zombies to materialize in *Night of the Living Dead* and its many sequels. Enthusiasts had their theories, which included radiation blitzing the earth and reactivating the brains of the recently dead; a sort of spillover of beings designated to inhabit hell; and a nasty kind of virus or brain toxin, transmitted via a bite. Viruses, exposure to radioactivity, and brain toxins are all real enough hazards. Maybe it wasn't that much of a leap to believe they produced zombies. Gibbs had heard of people so thoroughly convinced that zombies were a plausible threat that they stockpiled food and built shelters in preparation for a zombie invasion.

Scholars who study horror films contend that the genre depicts mutilated bodies as uncontrollable forces that don't respect borders, boundaries, or the prevailing social order. The corpse, or zombie, becomes a freeing symbol, they argue, through which viewers imagine themselves breaking away from taboos and societal constraints, at least for the duration of the movie. I imagined this might resonate with Gibbs, who confronted the reality of unidentified bodies such as Old Joe's, which defied the social order by denying the rest of us the traditional coping rituals — memorials, obituaries, funerals — that accompanied other deaths.

Or perhaps Clyde just found zombie movies entertaining.

We arrived in the lobby where I had first come in. It was close to noon. Visitors, orderlies pushing patients in wheelchairs, and medical staff in scrubs bustled by. Gibbs was still wearing his white lab coat. He might have passed for a doctor, but even if he were George Romero himself, there was nothing he could do to reanimate Old Joe and the rest of the bodies in the storeroom.

"How many ways are there to become a zombie?" I asked. A passerby judging our conversation solely by its tone would have thought we were discussing the *American Journal of Medicine*.

"I don't think there are that many," Gibbs responded soberly. "Around six."

Compared with dozens of ways, I thought, to turn a body into a Jane or John Doe.

# 10
## FINDING BOBBIE ANN

A few years after his visit to Miz Cole, Todd
was promoted to quality control at the
plant. No more assembly line, no more
night shifts. He and Lori, back together for
the time being, upgraded the single-wide
trailer to a double-wide. Todd knew trailers
had a reputation as redneck, white-trashy,
but three bedrooms and two bathrooms
crammed into eighteen hundred square feet
felt palatial. Todd used a ten-by-twelve pan-
eled room — one of the back bedrooms
furnished with a laminate corner desk from
Walmart and a yard-sale rolling desk chair
— as a study.

Neatly tucked into a two-drawer filing
cabinet, interspersed with family documents
like bills of sale and birth certificates, was
his Tent Girl stash: copies of newspaper
articles and microfiche, letters he had written to the Georgetown police department,
the coroner, the mayor, the governor, the

editor of the *Georgetown News-Graphic.* He tacked a picture of Tent Girl's headstone on the monitor of a Compaq Presario. The square white clunker, with a floppy drive and a pitiable amount of memory by today's standards, sat on the desk's fake wood top.

Todd had heard fellow Tennessean Al Gore talking on TV about an information superhighway, but Todd had spent much more time on the paved kind. He had gone to Kentucky so many times, he could do the drive in his sleep. Searching for Tent Girl clues via the Web was enticing, but in the days before Livingston attracted an Internet service provider, connecting through dial-up modem racked up a pro-hibitively expensive long-distance phone bill.

The modem whistled, hissed, stuttered, and finally warbled its ear-splitting whine as the signals completed their digital Morse code and made contact. Late at night, there were no interrupting phone calls. Todd asked his parents to walk over from their home next door if they wanted to talk to him; if they called, the connection would be broken and he'd have to start over. *Beeeeep . . . wooooh . . . tooteetee . . . deedeedee . . .*

■ ■ ■ ■

Around the same that Todd started logging on regularly in Tennessee, five hundred miles away, Rosemary Westbrook of Benton, Arkansas, bought a computer so slow she named it "Come on, dammit!"

Like Todd, Rosemary found herself scouring the Web for clues until two or three in the morning. Like Lori, Rosemary's husband begged his spouse to come to bed. More technically savvy than Todd, Rosemary used an early instant messaging service and developed her own website devoted to finding her long-missing sister, Barbara Ann Hackmann.

"Hi there, my name is Rosemary," she posted in neon blue-and-yellow type on a simple home page she fashioned with early web tools. "I am known as Slick442 because of our '72 Olds 442, and I am from Arkansas." Then she waited.

In June 1957, Louise and Harry Hackmann lived in Collinsville, Illinois, a former coal mining town that was becoming a bedroom community to nearby St. Louis, Missouri, with their four daughters — Nancy; thirteen-year-old Barbara Ann, known to friends and family as Bobbie or Bobbie Ann; Marie; and Jan — and one son, Harry Junior.

Two weeks before another daughter, Rosemary, was born, Harry Hackmann took his son to Belleville, the county seat, ten miles from their home. While they were there, a flood struck. It was later called the most devastating flood in the city's history.

Almost fourteen inches of rain turned Richland Creek into a river that swept away vehicles as if they were twigs. Water breached a wall of the Samson Furniture Company, causing a surreal vista of couches and beds floating down Main Street. A pile of waterborne wooden power poles pummeled the T. J. Gundlach Machine Company like battering rams. The water damaged or destroyed hundreds of homes and fifty businesses and killed ten people. Among the dead were Rosemary's fifty-one-year-old father and six-year-old brother.

The grieving widow asked her younger brother and sister-in-law in nearby East St. Louis to take in her newborn. Uncle Charlie and Aunt Shirley became Rosemary's legal guardians, and cousins Linda and Victor became Rosemary's siblings. Rosemary saw her biological mother and sisters occasionally, but their family life didn't always include her.

One morning, four-year-old Rosemary woke up in an empty room. She was visiting the Collinsville house, where her mother and sisters lived without her. She heard the clanking of pans and the voices of her teenage sisters and older cousin in the kitchen. She sat up. "There's a fly in this bedroom," she hollered. The fly landed on the windowsill, the walls, the dresser, taunting her. She swatted at it. "We're making pancakes," somebody — maybe Bobbie Ann — shouted back, but no one ran to her aid.

"Y'all come help me!" yelled Rosemary, alone in the bedroom of a house that wasn't hers. The others kept doing grown-up things without her. She was stuck with the pesky fly.

A photo taken later that day showed the girls of the Hackmann clan circa 1961: Jan, the youngest except for Rosemary, resting both hands on the wide straps of Rosemary's jumper; the eldest, Nancy, next to them; then cousin Linda. At the far left of the frame, almost in the boughs of a decorated Christmas tree, was Bobbie, pretty and slim, dark-eyed and dark-haired. The only sister missing was Marie, who might have been the one behind the camera.

In six years, Bobbie would be gone.

A year and a half later, the carnival came to East St. Louis, bringing with it a young man who called himself George Earl Taylor.

Taylor drove a truck in the convoy that transported the Tilt-A-Whirl; the Ferris wheel; the booths of the midway, where you could shoot a bull's-eye and win a Kewpie doll; and the stands that sold buttered popcorn, pink sugar clouds of cotton candy, and grilled hot dogs.

This carnival was a fly-by-night operation, not a local fixture like the beloved Forest Park Highlands amusement park on the Missouri side of the Mississippi River. Since the 1920s, families had flocked to the Highlands to ride the steep wooden Comet roller coaster and the beautiful carousel, its horses hand-carved by European wood-workers.

A fire leveled the Highlands in 1963. The carousel miraculously survived, but the park closed and many of its former patrons made their way to the carnival that popped up during the heat of summer and moved on to warmer locales when the weather began to cool.

One day, on the Illinois side of the river,

Taylor walked into the city's social services office. Clean-shaven, he wore his cap at a rakish angle. He clutched the hand of a little girl. "Do you know where I can find someone to babysit my daughter?" he asked the woman seated behind the front desk. "Her mother's gone. Ran off and left us," he added softly, maybe looking at the floor.

The woman gazed at the pair. The man was slight but muscular, in his early twenties; the girl no more than two. *What kind of mother would leave her baby like that?* Louise Hackmann must have wondered. She volunteered her second-oldest daughter as a babysitter.

Bobbie was warm and friendly, good with kids. Her youngest sister, Rosemary, was only a few years older than Taylor's daughter, so Bobbie Ann took the little girl, Bonnie, to play on the swings with Rosemary. They all went out for ice cream, one of Rosemary's few memories of her cousin as a young child.

At nineteen, Bobbie Ann — in love, or just looking for a way out of dull Collinsville — went with Earl Taylor to the county seat in Belleville, where her father and brother had been swept to their deaths by floodwaters six years earlier, and got married. A county clerk typed onto blank spaces amid the ornate script of a St. Clair County marriage certificate: "Mister Earl G. Taylor of East St. Louis, age twenty-four, and Miss Barbara Ann Hackmann, age nineteen, wed on the sixth day of August 1963."

With fall approaching, workers packed up the Tilt-A-Whirl's greasy metal struts and the rest of the carnival rides onto flatbed trucks. The man — whose name was not, in fact, Earl Taylor — took off with Bobbie Ann and Bonnie for the carnival's next stop.

For the next few years, as the carnival migrated up and down the East Coast, Bobbie Ann called her family in Illinois collect from pay phones. A year after she had married and moved away, she called to say she had given birth to a baby boy, Earl Junior, called Sonny. Soon after, a daughter, Dorothy Michelle, was born.

Rosemary, six when Bobbie left, remembered how her mother and sisters would always hear from Bobbie about the family's travels. A photo arrived in the mail: Bobbie sitting in a straight-backed chair, her hair in curlers, smiling happily at baby Shelly on her lap. The young family settled for a time in Florida, but Taylor's work as a trucker kept them on the move.

When Rosemary was eleven, the calls and letters stopped.

■ ■ ■ ■

Rosemary's guardian and uncle, Charlie Rule, left East St. Louis to take a job with the railroad. The family moved four hundred miles to Bauxite, Arkansas, around a half hour outside Little Rock. When teenage Rosemary pulled up to the pump at a local filling station, a tall, handsome young man with a mop of light brown hair — the son of the owner — pumped her gas. Each time, Mark Westbrook (he had earned the nickname "Putt" as a toddler for a reason no one could recall) hailed the petite, pretty girl at the wheel with a cheerful "Hi, Slick!" By the time he learned her real name, it was too late: Rosemary had simply become Slick. Putt introduced her to his parents. She answered to Miss Slick and, after they married, Mrs. Slick.

The couple moved into a ranch-style house near a small but picturesque lake in the nearby town of Benton. Putt ran his own business operating heavy equipment — "doing dirt work," he called it. The couple worked, raised a son, bought vintage cars, houseboats, motorcycles, campers, and a pontoon boat. Rosemary's older sisters married and moved around the country: Nancy to Florida, Jan to Maine, Marie to California.

The mystery of Bobbie Ann's whereabouts was always in the back of Rosemary's mind, nagging at her like the fly that had trapped her in bed that morning when she was four. At one point Rosemary called all the Barbara Ann Taylors she could find listed in the country. None of them was Bobbie. Every year, if the state fair came to Benton or a carnival stopped in Little Rock, Putt and Rosemary took their son, just as Rosemary used to go with her family as a child. She scanned the faces in the crowd, especially those of the carnival workers. She grabbed Putt's arm. "Does that lady look like me?" she'd ask, pointing out a stranger whose mouth or eyes or hair looked familiar, hoping one of those women would turn out to be Bobbie, but they never did. In the back of her mind, Rosemary knew that something bad had to have happened because Bobbie had always kept in contact — until *boom,* there was nothing.

The family had at one point filed a missing-person report in Florida, where they thought Bobbie lived for a time, but there was never any news. At least one of Rosemary's sisters, Nancy, had already resigned herself to never seeing Bobbie again.

Rosemary and the others didn't know that, six hundred miles away, their sister was the bogeywoman of Georgetown, Kentucky. Buried nameless under a donated marker, Bobbie was a Halloween legend. Youngsters dared each other to run up to her grave. Upperclassmen hazed Georgetown College freshmen by sending them to visit her stone under a midnight moon.

In 1989, more than twenty years after Bobbie's family had lost touch with her, Rosemary received a call from one of her sisters. Bobbie's daughter, Shelly, whom they had seen only in a photo as the round-faced infant on Bobbie's lap, had appeared.

Shelly and her half sister Bonnie, the eighteen-month-old toddler Earl Taylor had brought with him to Illinois, didn't start to piece together the story of their mother's life until they were in their twenties. It took Sonny's death and Taylor's terminal illness to set the wheels in motion.

Initially Bonnie; her half brother, Sonny; and her half sister, Shelly knew one another as cousins, not siblings. Earl had deposited the three children on his parents' doorstep in late 1967, telling his family that Bobbie had run off with another man. They grew up in Ohio, adopted and raised by Taylor's relatives in three separate families. They rarely saw their father. In 1984 a drunk driver struck and killed Sonny, age nineteen, while he was riding his bike. The family, thinking Taylor might show up at his son's funeral, decided to tell Shelly the only fact they knew about her history: her mother's name. To Shelly, it was painful to wonder why Bobbie Ann had abandoned her as an infant and never sought her out.

Not long after Sonny's death, Earl Taylor was diagnosed with cancer. Just before he died, Bonnie and Shelly went to pump him for answers about their biological mothers.

Taylor told Shelly her family was from Collinsville, Illinois. He told Bonnie her relatives lived in Florida. He would say nothing more.

Two years after Earl died in 1987, Shelly gathered a handful of quarters and drove to Collinsville. She called all the Hackmanns in the phone book. "Do you know of a Bobbie Taylor or a Bobbie Hackmann?" she asked. No one did. Finally, someone directed Shelly to an address. An elderly woman opened the door of the two-story house her son had built for his family. She was the only one still living in it; the family had been broken apart by his accidental death. "I'm looking for a Barbara Ann Hackmann," Shelly said for what felt like the hundredth time.

"Bobbie Ann has been gone for a very long time," the woman said.

"Well, I'm her daughter," Shelly told her.

Harry Hackmann's mother smiled sadly. It had been more than three decades since her son and six-year-old grandson died in the Belleville flood and more than two decades since her granddaughter Bobbie went missing. This dark-haired, dark-eyed young woman, if she was who she claimed to be, would be her great-granddaughter. "You look just like her," Grandma Hackmann said softly.

Armed with the names and addresses of her aunts, Shelly started making phone calls.

To Rosemary and her sisters, Shelly was the image of Bobbie Ann. Shelly, seeing pictures of her mother for the first time, was also struck. It was like looking in a mirror.

The Hackmann sisters wept and hugged their niece. But they were no closer to finding Bobbie. Shelly was only eight months old when her mother disappeared. She had no idea what had become of her.

After Shelly made contact, she put her

aunts in touch with her half sister, Bobbie's stepdaughter, Bonnie, who, being older, had many more memories of Bobbie Ann and Earl Taylor.

Bonnie was seven when her stepmother disappeared. Bonnie adored Bobbie; she was the only mother she had known. She remembered Bobbie doing her hair for her before school and lifting her up to touch the bubbling water in Hot Springs, Arkansas, where Taylor took the family one winter.

Bonnie remembered that they had moved to Lexington, Kentucky, where they lived downtown in a small apartment over a soda fountain shop. Bobbie worked as a curb service girl at the Quick Draw Drive-In. Customers might have tipped her well when she delivered their burgers, fries, and milk shakes; she was pretty and her boss remembered her as "bubbly." Taylor was still a trucker at the time.

The last time Bonnie saw Bobbie Ann was the morning of December 7, 1967. Bonnie remembered that, the night before, she'd woken up in the middle of the night to angry voices and scuffling. Earl and Bobbie were arguing. As on any other morning, Bobbie helped her get ready for school. When Bonnie arrived home from school that afternoon, Taylor had packed the family's belongings into their gray station wagon.

Bobbie's purse was on the front seat. "Where's my mom?" Bonnie asked Taylor. He said, "Oh, she ran off with another man."

Bonnie remembered that Taylor took her that night to the house of a man he called the Colonel. While the Colonel's wife bathed Bonnie, Sonny, and baby Shelly before bed, Taylor and the Colonel left. Taylor returned and loaded the sleepy children into the station wagon. When Bonnie woke up, they were in Ohio, where her grandparents lived. Taylor brought the children to his mother's house and left, saying he would return soon. Bonnie thought it was two years before she saw him again.

Taylor's parents and other relatives adopted the three children. On the rare occasions Taylor stopped by to see them, he left his truck running outside. If the house phone rang with a call for him, he'd jump in the truck and zoom off.

In 1995, when Rosemary Westbrook learned that Bonnie had last seen Bobbie in Lexington, Kentucky, she called the Lexington police department, reaching an officer in the missing-persons division. On Rosemary's first visit to Lexington a few years later, she told a TV reporter about the call, but he could find no evidence a report had ever been filed. Westbrook had happened to call on Halloween; perhaps Tent Girl's reputation led the police to assume the call was a prank.

Rosemary connected with people in chat rooms: she recalls a friendly woman in China, and a psychic who told her the clue to Bobbie's whereabouts could be found on a yellow sheet of paper. "I could search this world over and find yellow sheets of paper," Rosemary snorted.

She came across a free online bulletin board maintained by a pair of Dallas private investigators. She posted a note on Crane & Hibbs and on other sites citing her sister's name and birthday, her brown hair and brown eyes and her height, five feet two inches. Barbara Ann's family lost track of her in late 1967 and she was last seen in the Lexington, Kentucky, area, Rosemary wrote. If anyone had any information, the note read, please contact Rosemary Westbrook at the posted address.

In 1998, around a year after Todd Matthews first started searching for Tent Girl connections online, he sent a note to a pink-tinted web page polka-dotted with dozens of tiny magnifying glasses called Kentucky's Unsolved Mysteries:

"Thirty years ago my father-in-law, Wilbur Riddle, found the body of a young girl. She was wrapped in a bag similar to the type used to make tents. Her identity and the identity of her murderer remain a mystery.

"I have been working to create a website dedicated to solving this mystery. A cloth diaper was found with the body. Could this possibly mean that a child was involved? Maybe even someone looking for his or her mother? She most certainly was someone's daughter. If anyone has any information please contact me . . ."

He also sent a letter to a California man who had posted details about Tent Girl on his website devoted to the paranormal. A story in the Lexington, Kentucky, newspaper — "Internet May Solve the Tent Girl Mystery" — and a local TV piece generated dozens of e-mails. Apparently there were others who had never forgotten the case. But they said nothing Todd didn't know.

On a cold January night in 1998, Todd was at his usual spot in the study.

It was one of those late nights. Five-year-old Dillan, after endless requests for one more drink of water and one more good-night kiss, was finally asleep in his room with the family's ancient white toy poodle, Lacy. Lori called, "Come to bed," and Todd hollered back, "Be there in just a minute!" Outside the double-wide, the temperature hovered around freezing and the wind gusted. Despite the Tennessee winter's uncharacteristic cold, heavy snow, and power outages, Todd was barefoot and clad in a well-worn Superman T-shirt and gym shorts.

He heard the sheets rustle and pictured Lori clicking on the electric blanket. Soon she would be asleep, and he knew he'd be free to hunt. Nighttime, quiet in the trailer except for its occasional mysterious creaks and pops, was when Todd liked to web surf, when no one would bother him.

This Crane & Hibbs board he'd found was packed with listings. He skipped the adoptees looking for birth parents, scrolled past notices for missing cats, dogs, bikes — missing everything. He could go through those quickly, like an old salt shucking oysters. Slit one open, toss it over your shoulder, and snatch up the next one, hoping you weren't going so fast you'd miss the pearl.

It was after midnight. Todd figured he'd scanned around four hundred descriptions of missing people that night: senior citizens, children, teens. Many nights he'd fall asleep at the computer, bent in an awkward posture. He was close to nodding off that night. He made a deal with himself: ten more missing persons and he would go to bed.

That was the moment he saw it: "1967 . . . brown hair, brown eyes, 5 feet, 2 inches . . . Lexington, Kentucky." He jumped up so abruptly the desk chair spun backward and flipped over.

"I found her!" he yelled.

# 11
## QUACKIE IS DEAD

In March 1991, Bobby Lingoes sat typing at a computer terminal that would have looked obsolete a decade earlier. In the fifteen years since Bobby, a teen boxing champion, started out washing patrol cars behind the Quincy, Massachusetts, police station, he had moved up the department ranks to dispatcher and, most recently, de facto computer guy. Now he was entering a missing-person report.

The report was actually about bones.

In the woods off Quarry Street in West Quincy, in a rare bucolic section of this seaside city just south of Boston, a hiker had stumbled upon skeletal remains. There was no ID. The medical examiner's report said the bones belonged to a twelve- to fifteen-year-old boy whose skull had been smashed with blows from a blunt object. Bobby stopped typing and sat back. He narrowed his already slit-like eyes, rubbed his flattened nose, and thought about the murdered youths abandoned and decomposing for years practically under the noses of oblivious drivers and pedestrians. He thought about his sister, whose own teenager, Bobby's nephew, had died just three years earlier. He tried to picture Patty's anguish if she hadn't known where her son was and hadn't been able to lay him to rest.

"Can you imagine not ever knowing whatever happened to your son or daughter?" he asked me later, his Boston accent like a truck rumbling through a gravel pit, his words punctuated by a raspy smoker's cough.

Bobby started digging.

Within Quincy's borders is a peninsula dubbed Germantown for the immigrant glassmakers who worked there in the eighteenth century. Streets named after figureheads, binnacles, and yardarms evoke the area's nineteenth-century shipbuilding industry, but now Germantown is home to the projects: street after street of identical two-story shutter-less, cement-stooped clapboard structures painted institutional beige, ash gray, and mustard yellow. A Quincy police chief once described the eighties in Germantown as a tumultuous, difficult time, rife with family trouble, fights, and assaults.

Bobby's teenage nephew and namesake, Robert — pale, dark-haired, with a narrow jaw, and a goofy, missing-tooth smile earned in a high school football game — was universally called Quackie. His mother had given him the nickname because baby Robert sounded like a duck. Patty was twenty. No father was in the picture so she named her son after her favorite brother and filled in her own last name on the birth certificate. She raised her only child in the same Germantown projects where she, her two brothers, and her three sisters had grown up. Their mother lived a few doors away. Despite her struggle with bipolar disorder, by all accounts Patty raised Quackie right; he was a good-natured, hardworking kid.

He graduated from Quincy Vocational Technical High School and landed a job with a plumber on the west side of town. He drove a beat-up Oldsmobile Cutlass convertible. "Well, it's paid for" was his cheerful response to constant ribbing about the jalopy. He once bought a prom dress for a girl he sort of knew who couldn't afford one. He adorned his room, his clothes, and many of his belongings with a signature icon: a smiley face.

Growing up in Germantown those days provided plenty of opportunities to stray from the straight and narrow. Quackie didn't stray, maybe because of his uncle and stand-in father, onetime Golden Gloves competitor Bobby Lingoes. Bobby had taken up boxing at fourteen. Under legendary trainer and promoter Cosmo "Al" Clemente, Bobby fought all over New England in makeshift rings set up at racetracks and outside hotels. He started out at 118 pounds in the featherweight division and ended his career nineteen pounds and three years later as a lightweight.

At the pinnacle of his career in 1973, Bobby was New England Amateur Athletic Union featherweight champion, earning the opportunity to represent New England in the AAU national finals alongside eighteen-year-old, 158-pound Marvin Hagler, who lived in nearby Brockton and won the Outstanding Fighter Award that year. On three separate occasions Bobby beat "the Pride of Lowell," Dicky Eklund, one of the boxing brothers portrayed in the 2010 movie *The Fighter*. Bobby competed in the Golden Gloves in Lowell, Massachusetts, ruefully quipping that all he got was a ride on the Green Line.

Out of fifty-six fights, Bobby lost only

seven. He retired from boxing at age seventeen. He wanted to be a cop, but he choked on the civil service exam. Quincy's chief at the time had followed Bobby's boxing career and gave him a job washing patrol cars. Soon he got kicked upstairs to type up the daily police log.

In 1988, Quackie was eighteen and Bobby was a dispatcher. He typically worked nights, downing paper cups of bitter coffee and fielding calls patched through to the mission control–like enclave of computer screens and TV monitors on the second floor of the brick police station on Sea Street.

As fate would have it, Bobby wasn't on duty that night in July 1988, so he didn't hear the 911 calls come in about a kid named David Compston running around the projects like a lunatic, brandishing a bowie knife.

Bobby had spent the night at a friend's place. He returned to his boardinghouse the next morning to a fellow roomer complaining that Bobby's phone had been ringing off the hook all night long. The man said people had come by looking for him — some kind of emergency. Bobby called his mother's house and his brother Mike answered. He said, "Bobby, we have trouble.

Quackie is dead."

A surreal scene greeted him at his mother's apartment in Germantown. The small home was crammed with people. Bobby pushed through. He had to find Patty. Voices humming in the background, he searched the rooms, finally finding his older sister sprawled on their mother's bed. Bobby couldn't bring himself to approach her.

Bobby later pieced together the events that took place on a very hot July night at the cul-de-sac in the center of Germantown where teens congregated. Word spread that eighteen-year-old local thug David Compston was violating the three restraining orders against him by chasing his mother around inside her house with a knife. Two neighbors called the police.

Germantown had its own officer but he was nowhere to be found that night. Later, rumor would have it that he missed the calls because he was busy smoking crack cocaine behind the elementary school.

Hearing about Compston's rampage, Quackie went home and armed himself with a miniature Red Sox bat, the kind you'd find in a variety store or a Fenway Park souvenir stand. A crowd gathered on the sparse grass in front of Compston's mother's apartment on Taffrail Road, named for an ornately carved ship railing, the kind of fanciful, elegant detail that existed nowhere in Germantown. Quackie marched over to the featureless, clapboard-covered public housing unit identical to his own, where he saw Compston focusing his wrath on a fifteen-year-old he accused of moving in on his girlfriend. "Why don't you pick on someone your own size?" Bobby later heard his nephew had scolded. "I'll stab you if you don't get out of the way," witnesses heard Compston reply.

By the time dispatchers learned the Germantown cop was AWOL and sent another car, officers arrived to see Quackie bleeding out on the sidewalk.

An ambulance raced him four miles through deserted predawn streets to Quincy City Hospital, but Compston's knife had punctured his heart. "The best kid anyone could ever lose," as one of his friends put it, was dead.

An hour later, officers caught up with Compston at a Dunkin' Donuts and charged him with first-degree murder.

For weeks, G-town mourned Quackie Lingoes. Men, women, teenagers, and children overflowed the church at his services, snaking for blocks outside the funeral home, waiting to pay their respects at his wake. They held a vigil, burned hundreds of candles, organized and signed a petition to dedicate the neighborhood basketball court in his memory, drew signs featuring cartoon ducks, tossed ten-dollar bills into a collection jar for Patty.

His friends played his favorite Guns N' Roses song and scribbled endless smiley faces on his dented car, on school walls, on the asphalt pavement of the basketball court, and on their own skin. Some drove to Rhode Island, the closest legal parlors, for smiley-face tattoos. Germantown became rife with cheerful emoticons while most of its residents stewed in misery and fury.

What the young people didn't do, thanks to Bobby Lingoes's urging, was lash out in vengeful violence against Compston's family.

"He was a good kid. He had a heart of gold," said Bobby of his nephew. Talking about Quackie two decades after his death still made Bobby tear up, every moment of his street-toughened life visible on his face, craggy and weathered as an old catcher's mitt. He and Patty had been close. Bobby had lived with her and Quackie for a time as the boy grew up. Just before the murder, Bobby was going through a divorce and had moved into a rooming house near the center of Quincy, but still occasionally spent nights on Quarterdeck Road, bolstering Patty when she was down.

The family hadn't wanted to put Patty through the ordeal of a trial, so Compston had been allowed to plead guilty to manslaughter, despite the fact that he had stabbed Quackie in the chest and then in the back as the young man turned to run for his life. Compston might have walked in three years, but every time he came up for parole, Bobby told the board that his nephew died trying to help and that his grieving sister had never gotten over the murder of her only child. He managed to keep Compston behind bars for his entire twelve-year sentence.

Bobby wasn't sure how he and Patty survived those first devastating weeks after the stabbing. He'd drive her to Pine Hill, the city-maintained cemetery where Quackie was buried, and watch her lie sobbing on the ground behind his grave, which to this day is a totem of flowers, a tiny cross flanked by angels, a miniature American flag, and a rubber duckie. On the back of the stone an enormous smiley face is carved into the granite above the words "Love,

Mommy," Patty's final good-bye note to her son.

Three years after Quackie died, the day Bobby filed the missing-person report for the youth found in the woods was like many others: he fielded radio calls, ran stolen checks, expired and suspended licenses, outstanding arrest warrants, and stolen guns for cops out on their beats. Before things went digital, he'd do this via teletype, a clattering box that spit out printouts from state and national law enforcement databases and bulletins from other agencies. Later, Bobby entered missing persons into the National Crime Information Center (NCIC) database, a central repository accessible to "authorized representatives" of federal, state, and local law enforcement who could log in to see what their colleagues from other criminal justice agencies had input about a mind-boggling smorgasbord of crimes and criminals.

The FBI's Criminal Justice Information Services Division's massive high-tech hub is housed in a glass-and-brick structure the length of three football fields on more than nine hundred acres in the hills of Clarksburg, West Virginia. Within is the NCIC, the Big Brother of crime. When your passport is checked at the border, it's being run through the NCIC. Want to be a DEA agent? As part of your job interview, someone will run a "deep background" check through the NCIC. Chop shop dismantle your stolen car? The parts might turn up in the NCIC. Bank robbers' getaway cars; stolen boats; stolen guns; stolen, embezzled, or counterfeited securities — bank notes, stocks, bonds, traveler's checks, money orders, warehouse receipts — all of these find their way into the NCIC.

Also logged into the NCIC are the FBI's most wanted criminals, alongside records of escaped juvenile delinquents, wanted foreigners, individuals charged with serious offenses who have fingerprints on file; individuals designated by the U.S. Secret Service as posing a potential danger to the President; members of violent criminal gangs; members of terrorist organizations; and violent felons.

In 1975, certain missing persons — the physically or mentally disabled, the senile, those who may have been kidnapped, people missing in the wake of a catastrophe, and dismembered body parts — started being logged into the NCIC. (Sets of unidentified remains began being added in 1983, but as recently as 2007 the National Institute of

Justice reported that the NCIC contained just 15 percent of unidentified human remains cases, in part because it was so labor-intensive to enter the data into the system.)

The NCIC was never open to the public, and even segments of law enforcement were not privy to the entirety of its contents. According to a 2009 National Research Council committee report on forensics in the United States, 80 percent of surveyed medical examiners and coroners "rarely or never" used the NCIC unidentified and missing-person files to match their dead bodies to those reported missing by law enforcement.

"The NCIC protocol was lovely; the only problem was, only the police had access," said Marcella Fierro, who was on the NRC panel that wrote the report and has long spoken out about the inadequacies of the NCIC for missing persons and unidentified bodies. Missing persons didn't tend to get entered promptly, or entered at all; the police figured runaways were likely to turn up in a day or so. Until 1999, it wasn't mandatory for state and local law enforcement to report the missing or the unidentified to the NCIC.

Police didn't always give families the

thirty-five-page booklet of forms and check boxes to fill out regarding their missing loved ones and didn't always collect the data themselves. They'd enter age, sex, race, and a description of clothing, and that was it. Consequently, if a skeleton had been determined to be a fifteen- to twenty-year-old white female, and that broad age range was plugged into the NCIC, the police might get five hundred possible matches — too many to deal with. They couldn't do anything with such imprecise results, Fierro contends. At that time the NCIC was better for finding a stolen car or stolen boat or stolen securities than for finding a missing person or connecting found people, dead or alive.

What's more, data entered into the NCIC wasn't easy to use. At the Virginia Beach conference where I first met Todd Matthews, one of the speakers was a tall man with close-cropped graying hair, a cleft chin, and a trim mustache. Harry E. Carlile Jr., who had taught the ins and outs of the FBI to recruits for more than a decade, explained to the primarily law enforcement audience his agency's "cold hit" system. Every morning, the massive NCIC computer in Clarksburg churns through gigabytes of data seeking to match details about the missing and the unidentified, and spits out something called $.M. ("dollar M" — the *M* is for "missing") reports.

The $.M. reports look like they are generated by a monkey at a keyboard: strings of seemingly random characters followed by a number. The number represents a point total of items that matched or came close to matching, such as a missing person's date of birth falling within the range of an estimated age for an unidentified body. You have to learn how to read it, Carlile said.

The printouts are sent each day to law enforcement agencies around the country, but they are so incomprehensible, I wasn't surprised to hear that at least one police department discarded the $.M. reports unread, like junk mail. Carlile professed to be amazed by this, and distressed that many detectives never even saw the $.M. reports. Even if detectives had seen them, from what I heard, few could have spared the time to follow up on the potentially dozens of cold case leads.

And the NCIC's matching abilities were far from perfect. At one point a Seattle dentist decided to figure out if the records stored in the NCIC were doing any good at all for the missing and unidentified. Washington state had led the country in passing a law requiring investigating agencies to collect dental records for people missing more than thirty days, resulting in the highest numbers of dental records on file for missing persons anywhere in the country.

Gary L. Bell, one of the trained forensic odontologists who coded dental records for the missing throughout the Pacific Northwest, knew that in 1982 several badly decomposed bodies and skeletons had turned up in the Seattle area. Ten years later, in 1992, Bell tried an experiment with four test cases: the dismembered remains of a woman found a hundred miles east of Seattle; the partially decomposed remains of a woman found in the woods forty-five miles from Seattle; the partial skeleton of a twelve-year-old girl; and a human cranium found near a river. Like all forensic specialists, Bell expected that dental records were the best hope for identifying these nameless corpses, and in fact this turned out to be true. Washington state investigators had used a U.S. Army dental matching system to positively identify all four bodies, suspected victims of "Green River Killer" Gary Ridgway, who pleaded guilty in 2003 to murdering forty-eight women between 1982 and 1998.

Yet, when Bell submitted dental records

from the four sets of remains and corresponding victim details into the NCIC, as he later reported in the *Journal of Forensic Sciences,* the NCIC failed to match any of them. There had been rumors that at least one of the four victims had been listed as missing in the NCIC system for "some time," Bell wrote, and had never been matched to her own remains, even though a perfect dental match for her existed.

In fact, the NCIC's online searches — the searches that generated the daily $.M. reports — had never produced even one positive identification in the state of Washington.

Bell's experiment called attention to the fact that not only was the NCIC system ineffective for matching the missing and unidentified, it was poorly populated with data. Of the 73,000 missing persons entered into the NCIC at the time, less than 2 percent had dental records in the system.

Ultimately software is no match for human discernment in connecting clues. In another case, the family of a Richmond, Virginia, runaway, believing the boy was with another family member, didn't report him missing until a certain date. By the time they did, he had been dead for three days. Despite the almost perfect alignment of physical details between the missing boy and the body, NCIC computers never recognized the two as a potential match because of the disparity in dates. A web sleuth insisted the two were a match, and DNA confirmed it.

When Matthew Hickman of the Bureau of Justice Statistics set out in 2004 to figure out just how many unidentified remains existed in the United States, he heard an earful from medical examiners and coroners about the NCIC. "Entering data into that thing is a nightmare, if medical examiners could even get access to it" was the gist of the complaints.

But Bobby Lingoes had access.

Bobby committed to memory the details contained in the official NCIC report about the skeleton found in the Quincy woods. After work, he rode his mountain bike a half mile over Quincy's asphalt streets to Thomas Crane Public Library, which had something the police station didn't have: Internet access. It was there he first stumbled upon websites such as the Doe Network. Little kids reading picture books near him grew wide-eyed when they glimpsed on Bobby's screen the photographs of the very pale people with the staring eyes. Despite Bobby's law enforcement career, he was shocked himself by the quantity of unidentifieds. He scribbled down facts listed on the Doe Network about missing individuals, then took his notes to work the next day to check against the NCIC database.

From his training on the use of the NCIC, he knew about a technique called off-lining that had been used in the aftermath of the 1995 Oklahoma City bombing. Fragments of the explosive-filled van Timothy McVeigh detonated in front of the Alfred P. Murrah Federal Building flew over a ten-block radius. Among them was a shard of the vehicle's transmission, on which investigators deciphered a partial vehicle identification number, or VIN. Having that unique identifier, investigators searched for a vehicle with those digits in its VIN that had been reported missing.

Bobby realized that if he came across information about a body with certain unique characteristics — an unusual tattoo or an artificial leg — he could search through individual records for only those details, instead of looking at broad categories such as age or race, which couldn't always be determined accurately from a decomposed corpse or a skeleton anyway.

He looked, as he put it, for dead people to "speak" to him, beckoning to him from the grave with distinctive clues to their identities.

Such off-line queries couldn't be run independently from the Quincy police station. Bobby needed a warm body at the NCIC to plug in parameters that would transform the search process from a handful of buckshot to a heat-seeking missile. In 2001, Bobby's boss gave him permission to work off-line, and almost at once things began to happen.

Perusing the Doe Network, Bobby spotted a Jane Doe who had turned up near Waco, Texas. Seeking help from citizens, the Texas Department of Public Safety had posted information online about the young woman, who had suffered a severe head injury after a train hit her on tracks off Farm to Market Road 308 in the town of Elm Mott, population 190, on July 28, 1993. After days in a coma, she had died in a local hospital and been buried in a cemetery for indigents in McLennan County. She had no identification, but the word "Tonk" was tattooed on her left shoulder.

Working with an NCIC technical information specialist, Bobby queried the system:

"Show me a missing person who is five foot four, eye color brown, with a tattoo on her left arm." Within minutes a name popped up on the NCIC technician's screen in Clarksburg. He called Bobby at work, sounding a bit incredulous. "We have a possible match." Angela Marie Parks was twenty-three, had two children, and had disappeared from her home in Bowling Green, Kentucky. Parks, who tended to vanish for extended periods of time, had not been in contact with her family since 1992.

Bobby was cautiously optimistic. He and the FBI submitted the tip to Waco and Bowling Green police. Meanwhile, he went to work on another train-related death from the Texas Department of Public Safety website, this one from 1992 involving a man in the town of Victoria. This victim, another transient, was thought to have gone by the name Kelly.

With the help of a Doe Network volunteer from Los Angeles named Vicki Siedow, a private investigator who had access to resources available only to licensed investigators, Bobby found a Social Security number for a missing Michigan man by the name of Kelly Zeazical. A set of fingerprints matched those of the train victim.

Fingerprints also sealed the file on Angela

Parks. Her prints proved that the Elm Mott Jane Doe and Parks were one and the same. "Bingo!" Bobby said. "Oh, wow, it works. Let's do it some more." (At the time, the Doe Network had been in existence for around two years. Angela Parks and Kelly Zeazical were among its first "solves.")

Soon afterward, a mental health counselor named Sheree Greenwood, owner of an embroidery store in the rural central Massachusetts town of Warren, signed on with the Doe Network after sixteen-year-old Molly Bish, a classmate of her son's, disappeared from her post as a lifeguard at a local pond. (The remains of the stunning blond girl, who had been abducted, murdered, and dumped in the woods five miles from her home, wouldn't be found until 2003, following the largest, most expensive missing-person search in Massachusetts history.)

Sheree silk-screened T-shirts at her shop, which caused her to zero in on a Baltimore case: unidentified skeletal remains that had been discovered clad in a red T-shirt depicting an Indian chief.

In December 2000, a worker moving an abandoned tractor-trailer on the eight hundred block of Roslyn Avenue in the industrial southeast section of Baltimore discovered human bones, the T-shirt, a pair of jeans, and white size-seven tennis shoes. Forensic anthropologists determined the bones belonged to a white woman, around four-ten to five foot four, 120 to 140 pounds, between thirty-eight and forty-five. She might have been strangled. She had likely been dead around a year. But without a name, the police had little to go on. They had the tattered red T-shirt, which said "Wynn Family Reunion 1997" and listed names — James, Dock, Jessie, Nick, Chief, Corinia, Bessie — and the words "children of Joseph and Estelle Wynn."

Although Sheree didn't live near Quincy and hadn't met Bobby Lingoes, she had heard about Bobby's off-line successes and thought he might be intrigued. Bobby agreed that that T-shirt seemed to be shouting out clues. But its message was opaque.

Of course, there was no guarantee that if the meaning of the T-shirt could be deciphered, it would have any special significance to the woman who died wearing it. She might have picked it up in a secondhand shop or found it in someone's trash. Baltimore police had questioned local Native Americans, but no one knew of a family named Wynn or anything about a reunion at an unspecified location held three years earlier. Bobby's first NCIC off-line search produced no results. He plugged the names on the shirt into the motor vehicle database. Nothing.

He called Vicki Siedow in LA.

More than a decade later, Vicki Siedow was delighted to revisit the case when I called. Vicki, with shoulder-length blond hair and a wide smile, was smart, outspoken, and energetic, but she would never strike it rich as a private eye. In those days she took on pro bono cases such as the one with Bobby, and others for parents of missing kids. Meanwhile, her own kids ate grilled cheese and her electricity got shut off. Vicki was a sucker for a challenge, and as she saw it, real-life mysteries beat crossword puzzles any day.

Vicki had looked at the graphic of the Indian chief and the names on the T-shirt. A family reunion wasn't just for celebrating the current generation, she said to herself. People celebrated their ancestors, people of note in the family tree.

She went on Ancestry.com and within a couple of hours had found an earlier generation of Wynns that included most of the individuals listed on the shirt. Sifting through names of survivors in obituaries, she traced history forward to a Thomas

311

Wynn, a member of a Native American tribe based in Lumberton, North Carolina, and a chemical engineer for the U.S. Department of Energy who now lived and worked in Oak Ridge, Tennessee.

Thomas Wynn was surprised and impressed that someone had tracked him down based on an old T-shirt. He said his sister, Lola Wynn Haskins back in Lumberton, had designed it. Dozens had been handed out to a sizable crowd at the 1997 North Carolina family reunion. Vicki called Lola Haskins, who recalled that one attendee had given a T-shirt to a visiting girlfriend. Police tracked down the girlfriend, who, it turned out, had given the shirt to a Baltimore woman named Crystal Wright.

Crystal had roomed with a Brenda Wright, no relation, an addict and a prostitute who had not been seen in some time. Brenda Wright's brothers had been searching for her for months, showing people her photograph, posting flyers, calling hospitals and morgues.

With that information and a DNA sample from family members, Baltimore detectives identified the body as that of Brenda Sue Wright, age forty-six. The job still remained to figure out who had killed her. But identifying her body was a crucial step, a masterful bit of detective work on the parts of Bobby Lingoes, Sheree Greenwood, and Vicki Siedow.

A 2008 TV show featured the case and quoted a Baltimore detective who sounded appreciative of the web sleuths' involvement. "Naturally, by all means we did use any help we could get," he said on camera. Bobby didn't remember it that way. He recalled it was like pulling teeth to find out whether the body had been identified; he had to call the city's mayor before the cops would talk to him. "They really didn't give a shit about responding to the Doe Network or civilians helping them," he said. "Police have that attitude, 'I'm a cop, and you're not.' "

Bobby's next three cases — solved like clockwork in 2002, 2003, and 2004 — were more akin to his first two, the Texas train casualties.

The 2002 case was geographically close to home. A man was found floating in the Sudbury River west of Boston. According to the police report, the victim — a solidly built white male with a goatee — had suffered "multiple traumas" and was found wrapped in "bedding and other items." The letters

*PK* were tattooed on his right shoulder in an ornate Old English script.

Bobby posted the details on the Doe Network. Carol Cielecki, new to the Doe Network in Pennsylvania and fresh from the Sean Lewis Cutler solve, recalled reading about a missing Texas man with such a tattoo. Bobby passed along the tip to Framingham, Massachusetts, police, who determined the body was that of Peter Kokinakis, age forty, who had disappeared from Houston earlier that year.

In 2003, a ten-year-old boy rounding up cattle on horseback discovered skeletal remains in a remote area of northeast Utah. The victim's hands had been bound with electrical tape. A Job Corps ID card with the name Arthur Wuestwald lay on the ground nearby.

Bobby traced the name on the ID card, but the birth date did not jibe with the estimated age of the remains. The Arthur Wuestwald he found by name — a Nevada resident — was much older than the dead eighteen- to twenty-year-old. Bobby notified the Rich County sheriff in Utah, who contacted the elder Wuestwald in Nevada. Wuestwald turned out to be the victim's father. Someone had bound and killed Arthur Wuestwald Jr. of White River, South

Dakota, and left him on a remote path in the mountains near Randolph, Utah. His father hadn't seen his son since the seventeen-year-old left the family home in 1984 to attend cooking school with the Job Corps.

In 2004, Bobby located a man who had been missing from Minnesota since 1979. He was safe and sound, but not interested in being found and seemingly unconcerned that his family had been worried about him for decades.

In his years of active web sleuthing, Bobby was responsible for six Doe Network success stories. He downplayed his solves, crediting his access to national missing-person alerts and the NCIC database. Vicki Siedow said of Bobby, whom she counts as a dear friend but has yet to meet in person, that he always did the right thing for the right reasons. He was a down-to-earth nice guy, not all about ego, she said. I saw that Bobby had modestly told a reporter from Quincy's *Patriot Ledger* it was pretty simple to locate someone with an unusual name such as Wuestwald. He rarely mentioned that he had helped raise hundreds of dollars to help Angela Parks's children exhume her body from the potter's field where she was buried in Texas and take her home to Kentucky.

Bobby showed me around Quincy one day in June 2011. Boston Harbor is cleaner these days, and Quincy's tony new restaurants along the city's waterfront — a disconcerting mix of natural beauty and urban wasteland — have started luring diners from downtown Boston.

Town River Bay, with its khaki-colored water, splintering old piers, and moored pleasure boats, popped into view. We rolled by the peninsula's one convenience store and we were soon in the Snug Harbor section of Germantown, once a place of safety and rest for broken-down sailors.

In the years following Quackie's murder, the Quincy court system became known for its tough supervision of batterers. Offenders' probation was revoked if they so much as called or sent postcards to women they had been ordered not to contact. Weapons were seized from abusive men. Bobby Lingoes helped implement the program, recognized as the most comprehensive domestic violence intervention program in the state and one of few of its kind in the country. If the program had been in place in 1988, it might have prevented a knife-wielding David Compston from terrorizing his mother and killing Quackie.

Germantown was largely unchanged, Bobby told me, since he had moved out. Patty died in 2010 at age sixty. Always fragile, she had never quite recovered from losing her son. She was waked by the same funeral home as Quackie and buried next to him.

Bobby, happy with his new wife, Debbie, who tended a local bar, said it was time to move on from looking at dead bodies. It was getting kind of depressing.

Even though it had been a few years since he left behind the world of the missing and unidentified, he didn't seem completely free of his former addiction. Minutes after we met in the parking lot of the Quincy police station, he thrust into my hands copies of recent Doe Network case files. He waved a printout of a case, a skeleton of a John Doe discovered a month earlier in California. On the report, the estimated date of death and the date the body was found were identical. "A skeleton?" Bobby practically shouted. "On the same day he died?"

Another report that seemed to nag at Bobby was about a man who turned up dead in 1991 near Niagara Falls. This John Doe was a big guy, more than six feet tall,

215 pounds. He had a beard, a nine-inch scar that stretched from his right ankle to his shin, and a riot of tattoos on both arms, his right shoulder, his sternum, his left knee, his chest. The tattoos were graphic, disturbing: flaming swastikas, spiders on a web, bats, the Masonic all-seeing-eye pyramid, a flaming, snake-encircled cross, a circle with four triangular, inward-facing points evocative of the symbol used by the Ku Klux Klan.

Some of these tattoos are de rigueur among prison inmates, Bobby informed me. If the man had ever been incarcerated, his fingerprints would be on file in the Automated Fingerprint Identification System used by police, the FBI, the CIA, and NCIC. "Are you telling me no one has searched prints from AFIS against NCIC?" Bobby demanded.

I learned later that, in fact, no one had. Under the same high-tech roof as the FBI facility that houses the NCIC is a repository of sixty million sets of fingerprints, none of which were compared to any available prints from the unidentified tattooed man. In fact, there are several national fingerprint databases, each separate and accessible only to a specific few.

In another case Bobby found from 1991,

a young woman was found dead in Arkansas. The Jane Doe, a statuesque blonde, was a prostitute with a criminal record who used a variety of aliases. The amount of information on her whereabouts, jobs, and acquaintances over the years, coupled with many available photographs of the woman, seemed to Bobby ample material to solve a case that had languished for two decades. Bobby believed, rightfully so, that his accomplishments as a concerned citizen made gaps in the system painfully clear. Law enforcement wasn't looking at websites like the Doe Network, Bobby said. He didn't know why they didn't search off-line for unique identifiers, as he did.

As we drove down the nautically named streets, Bobby, in a tropical-print shirt, black pants, athletic shoes, and black Adidas baseball cap, his gravelly voice like that of a character out of *The Sopranos,* talked about growing up in the projects. He sounded nostalgic, even though many of his memories were awful ones. He pointed out the sidewalk where Quackie fell, mortally wounded, then another spot a few yards away where his best friend's brother stabbed his friend to death in an argument, and another street corner where yet another friend died violently.

We pulled up next to a shabby basketball court not far from where Compston had murdered Quackie on Taffrail Road. Rectangles of fractured pavement once painted green had faded to gray with weathered, once-red three-point arcs; a partially deflated basketball was abandoned just outside the peeling foul lines. Bobby kept the TrailBlazer's engine running as he pointed to discarded soda cups and cracks in the court's surface. "It's a shit hole," he said. Just beyond the edge of the court a black chain-link fence, a strip of mud-colored sand, and weeds bordered the bay. Sunlight glinted on the calm, grayish green water.

Across the channel, a factory loomed like an iron colossus, intimidating even from a distance. A small city of rusty tanks, decrepit buildings, bulging pipes, silos, and metal catwalks framed smokestacks that looked like they emitted something toxic.

"You see that plant? That used to be Procter & Gamble, where they made Tide soap. We used to swim from that jetty" — he pointed to a tumble of rocks just beyond the fence — "to that tank with the yellow stairs" — a metal fenced-in corral jutting into the water — "and jump off. We were known as the cleanest kids in Quincy because of the soap suds that come out of that plant." Bobby chuckled.

I said I thought Procter & Gamble was one of the companies once notorious for dumping toxic chemicals into Boston Harbor. He seemed unfazed. We sat in the car, gazing at the basketball court and the bay. A lone bare-chested youth in gym shorts jogged slowly around the perimeter of the basketball court, past a patch of crabgrass between the edge of the court and the sidewalk where a gray boulder squatted, inscribed with black letters:

This park is dedicated to the memory and
spirit of Robert "Quackie" Lingoes
Jan. 22, 1970–July 31, 1988
by his friends and the youth of
Snug Harbor.

Every night, the 911 calls poured in. Heroin overdoses, breaking and entering, robberies. Once in a while, a murder.

A solution to his first case — the case that earned him the nickname "Bones Man" from the Quincy cops and that led him to the Doe Network — had eluded Bobby. He'd sifted through what he guessed were thousands of missing-persons reports for months, then years, consumed with doubt and frustration while promising tidbits strung him along like a mouse following a trail of crumbs.

If it was true that the victim in the woods had been a missing kid between age twelve and fifteen, the number of potential matches in NCIC was heartbreakingly astronomical: what seemed like every runaway in the world. He had to find a way to narrow down the numbers of possible matches.

A few years ago, a Massachusetts state trooper stowed the skeleton, Quincy's one and only John Doe, in the trunk of his car and drove it to the Smithsonian Institution for forensic analysis.

This time, instead of twelve to fifteen, the victim's age was estimated to be closer to thirty. In 2002, Bobby was certain he had found him: a man who had gone missing from his home in northern Italy whose passport had turned up in a Boston homeless shelter. But dental records did not match up, and Bobby was out of leads. The woods where the body was found have since been bulldozed for condominiums.

Bobby wasn't sure he would even want to solve the case now. He doubted anyone knew where those bones were stored. He grimaced. "Can you imagine telling the mother, 'Here, ma'am, we found your son, but we can't give him to you because we don't know where he is'?"

In a bizarre Iowa case, not knowing the body's whereabouts was only part of the problem.

# 12
# THE HEAD IN THE BUCKET

One April day in 2001, retired trucker Ronald Telfer pulled into a Kearney, Missouri, truck stop at the intersection of Interstate 35 and Highway 92, northeast of Kansas City. Telfer was curious about something. Around a month earlier, he had spied a white plastic bucket apparently abandoned in the back parking lot. He bent to pick it up and saw it was filled with hardened concrete. Now he was back and saw the five-gallon bucket was still there. He tried slamming it against the pavement. A strong odor wafted toward him.

Later, Telfer would relay to a packed courtroom that the top cracked off and he saw something that looked like meat and skin — something that smelled very bad. Thinking it was animal remains, he slid the hunk of concrete out onto the pavement and took the bucket home to use for feeding his pigs.

Months later, on August twenty-seventh, construction worker Franklin Ray Dean maneuvered his truck through the same lot. Humidity hung in the air and waves of heat hovered over the ground; it was the summer's hottest day yet. Dean saw a cylinder of concrete blocking his path. He jumped down from the cab of his truck. When he went to shove the thing out of the way, he saw hair and what looked like a human skull protruding from the top.

Kearney police detective Fred Ferguson arrived. Under peeling gray chips, it looked like a human jaw was emerging like an artifact from an archaeological dig. Ferguson made a mental note that whoever the jaw belonged to had had quite a bit of bridgework.

Dean's discovery set in motion a series of events that spanned five years and four states. It involved hundreds of thousands of dollars and a race between a web sleuth and law enforcement to solve a case with a ticking clock. It was a saga of luck, greed, family ties, karma, depravity, and, some believed, divine intervention.

Eight months earlier, in Bellevue, Iowa, an unassuming Mississippi River town four hundred miles from Kearney, Jan Buman and her boyfriend, Gregory May, were talking about sunny Florida. May, fifty-five, with blue eyes and thick sandy hair gone gray, had six months earlier moved to Bellevue from Wisconsin, where he'd led a somewhat odd dual existence: he was a pioneering tattoo artist with a passion for nineteenth-century antiques.

May owned tattoo shops and enjoyed a well-deserved reputation as one of the Midwest's fastest, most talented tattoo artists at a time when tattoo artists were few and far between. He even taught the trade to his ex-wife, who became one of the first female tattoo artists in the United States and an originator of the concept of permanent makeup. Celebrities would one day flock to Sheila May's LA salon for tattooed-on eyeliner, eyebrows, and lip color.

Greg May, long divorced, was dating Jan, an attractive blonde who lived in nearby Galena, Illinois. The couple often shared meals and drinks at a riverfront bar down the street from May's rented aluminum-sided two-story house.

"Six feet tall and distinguished-looking, conservative in his politics and polite in his manner," a *Los Angeles Times* reporter later described May, who was drawn to Bellevue in part so he could emulate Mark Twain in living on the Mississippi. May lived and breathed all things Civil War.

May was tired of Midwest winters. Pick out a house, he told Jan, tossing her a Sarasota real estate brochure. On January 11, 2001, Jan was happy and excited about the future. She had spent the past three days with May, leaving only to fetch clean clothes while May went to his chiropractor and to say farewell to a friend in Dubuque.

Right before she left, Jan, May, and May's housemate, a burly ex-bouncer with a walrus mustache Jan knew as Duke, had a smoke outside. Jan knew Greg had been friends with Duke, a fellow tattoo artist, for more than thirty years. Greg had inked many of the designs on Duke's beefy forearms. Duke and his girlfriend, Julie, who rented out the finished basement of May's house, were also planning to move to Florida, although Jan wasn't happy about it.

"I don't trust that Duke," she had once told May over cocktails.

"Well, I don't trust that Julie," he countered.

That winter night, Jan kissed May goodbye. Duke shot her a mean look, which she ignored. "See you at eight," she called to

May as she drove off.

Web sleuth Ellen Leach and a man she introduced as her boyfriend, Chip, slid into a booth opposite me. We were in a Waffle House on a busy commercial strip in Gulfport, Mississippi. The booths backed up to the kitchen and diners sat on counter stools over mugs of coffee and plates of pancakes and eggs.

Ellen planned to show me around Gulfport on one of her rare days off from work, and although I kept assuring her that she was the one I came to see — she was the one who helped identify Greg May in the nick of time, saving prosecutors from a murder case without a body; she was the local hero featured on *48 Hours* — she fretted that she was somehow disappointing me after I came all the way from Boston to see her.

I had heard that Ellen Leach was one of the most effective web sleuths around, with at least five solves under her belt. She said it had all begun with her cousin, the infamous Susan Smith.

On November 2, 1994, twenty-three-year-old Smith stood tearfully outside the Union County Courthouse in Union, South Carolina, surrounded by TV cameras. She pleaded for the black man who had stolen her car with her two young sons inside to return them unharmed: "I would like to say to whoever has my children, that they please, I mean please, bring 'em home to us where they belong."

A thousand miles away, in Texas, Ellen watched in horror as this family drama unfolded. She combed websites for any kind of clues that would lead her to her cousins' missing boys, three-year-old Michael and fourteen-month-old Alexander.

Even after Smith ultimately shocked everyone by confessing there was no kidnapper, no mysterious black man — that she had let her 1990 Mazda Protegé roll into a lake with the boys still strapped into their car seats — Ellen didn't stop frequenting the sites. She found the Doe Network and signed on as a member. She intuitively started with the lists of unidentified. "You know they're dead," Ellen said. "You know somebody is missing them, so you just got to find the connections."

Ellen hadn't yet refined her technique. She would go on to appear on national media, earn a fifteen-thousand-dollar reward, be showered with gratitude by one family of the missing, and ultimately shun the group she helped put on the map.

Ellen had grown up in a small rural farming community in Michigan and thought for a time she might like to become a fashion designer. But her parents couldn't pay for college, so instead she took a job in an automobile factory in Detroit. It closed and she followed her brother to Texas, where for more than twenty years she staffed the steam table of prepared foods in a Kroger supermarket, a job she wouldn't call intellectually challenging. Ellen found herself spending more and more time logged onto the Doe Network.

Susan Smith might have led her to the Doe Network, but I thought I knew what kept Ellen there. She may have been robbed of a college education, but her considerable brainpower — like that of many of the web sleuths I'd encountered — was completely wasted on her day job. Finding the owner of a head in a bucket of cement — now, *that* was a challenge worthy of Ellen Leach.

At around eight in the evening on January 11, 2001, Jan Buman parked in the rear of 212 North Riverview Street. To her surprise, the back door was locked. Greg had told her he would leave it open for her. She rang the doorbell. No answer. Jan walked around to the front door. The shade was mostly drawn, but she saw someone who looked like May from the rear. She could only see Greg from the waist down. He was sitting, unmoving, in a kitchen chair, legs crossed and his hands on his lap. Jan recognized Duke's girlfriend Julie Johnson, a slight, pale woman with cropped dark hair and oversized tinted glasses. Julie was pacing as if she was nervous, and wiping off something Jan couldn't see.

Jan went to the Frontier Cafe without May, ordered a bowl of soup and a beer, and called the house. The answering machine picked up. "Why won't you answer the door?" Jan pleaded into the recorder. "Are you mad at me?" She stopped by again. This time she saw nothing through the partially opened shade, but she heard thumps and crashes from within. *Greg must be mad,* she thought, to stomp around slamming doors like that.

She called the property manager, who wouldn't unlock the door for her; she wasn't a tenant. Freezing, she got back in her truck, wondering what she had done to make Greg so angry.

The next Sunday, Julie Johnson informed Jan on the phone that May had gone to Chicago and he'd decided he didn't want Jan to join him in Florida after all. Jan stopped by three days later. Greg's car, his furniture, and all his Civil War memorabilia were gone. It wasn't the first time a guy had dumped Jan unceremoniously. But she hadn't figured Greg May for a coward who snuck off without saying good-bye.

Ellen Leach's boyfriend, Keith Glass, sat opposite me in the Waffle House booth. Bald and stocky with a full salt-and-pepper beard and round metal-rimmed glasses, Glass looked to me like Santa Claus, if Santa Claus were a biker dude in a muscle T-shirt. Glass had earned the nickname Chip as a boy because his reliable chip shot always got him to first base. He ordered only a cup of coffee, patting his rounded belly apologetically; Ellen, tall and lanky, dug into her plate of waffles and eggs and bacon.

More than five feet eight, Ellen, a onetime tomboy, has a strong jaw and cleft chin, a wide, mobile mouth, and gray hair to her shoulders. That day she cut a mannish figure in jeans, zip-front fleece jacket, and black leather sneakers. Chip told me that customers at the Hobby Lobby, where Ellen worked as a cashier, approached her saying, "Excuse me, sir." Then they'd take a closer look and say, "Oh, sorry, ma'am."

Sometimes, the other way around. I snuck a glance at Ellen to see if she was taking offense, but her baby-blue eyes were crinkled in amusement. With the loquacious Chip around to entertain me, she could relax.

They met — where else? — online, on a gaming website offering Monopoly, Risk, card games, puzzles of all kinds. They played Keno. You could chat in real time with other players. What did Glass say that attracted Ellen's attention? He laughed. "Oh, ma'am, we don't even want to get into that." Being called "ma'am" usually drives me crazy, but from Chip it was charming. "There was a bunch of us that were joking around and stuff," Ellen explained. "I'm always flirting and carrying on in there," Glass said. "She just took it serious."

What clinched Ellen's move from Texas to Mississippi was a photo she sent Chip of herself in waders, displaying two ten-pound redfish like slick, speckled torpedoes. Ellen had regularly fished Christmas Bay off Galveston until one day a gar — she thinks it was a gar, scaly and needle-nosed with a mouthful of sharp teeth — as big as a canoe circled her lazily. She froze, hardly daring to breathe, until it swam away. Chip also liked to fish. "I just want something I can fight with for a half hour and not marry," he quipped.

Chip was her backbone, Ellen averred. She'd show him a case and see if he thought her match was worthy. Chip looked at his hands and said Ellen was the one who put in all the hard work. Chip told me proudly that Ellen helped identify missing Pittsburgh teen Jean-Marie Stewart, whose remains had lain nameless in a Florida morgue for twenty-seven years.

The girl's abduction and murder, the length of time she remained unidentified, and the nature of her relationship with a woman who dedicated her own web database to finding her would fuel some heated exchanges within the web sleuth community for years.

"If police in Florida had Jean's dental records, if the remains of a young woman with an overbite were discovered only a few miles from where Jean disappeared a year later, why did it take more than a quarter-century for a volunteer advocate to put two and two together?" wrote a reporter in the *Pittsburgh Post-Gazette.* Chip's version was more colorful: How come a couple of boo-funkles from Mississippi solved this case before law enforcement did?

I'd never heard the term "boofunkle" but I heard it again within an hour: it's what

Chip and Ellen named their stocky mixed-breed rescue dog, who bounded to greet us at their modest ranch in a subdivision off busy Route 49.

For a time, Ellen had parked a 1968 Cadillac hearse out front. She had picked it up at a Texas auction for a dollar. Its jet-black finish gleamed in the sun; its elongated landau roof sported a metal detail like the Nike swoosh. With a few new parts its oversized engine purred. Ellen's brother stowed a fake casket in the back and she and Chip propped two plastic skeletons up front. The car had been a hit in Texas, drawing openmouthed stares, whistles, and admiring grins.

Mississippians' reactions were different. On Halloween, Chip and Ellen noticed that trick-or-treaters avoided their house. At the drive-in, they never got served with the skeletons in tow. A neighbor who ran a hair salon out of her home complained that her customers were being scared off. Mississippi mechanics were too superstitious to work on it. After nine years of owning the iconic car, Ellen was forced to sell it.

Before we walked inside the house, Chip and Ellen warned me about the cats: there was Stinky, rescued from fueling the blood-lust of thirteen fight-to-the-death pit bulls;

diabetic Francis, who needed injections twice a day; gray six-toed Grasshopper; Cali, a calico bequeathed to Chip by an elderly lady entering a nursing home; and Solo, a tailless white fluff ball prone to ambushing people's feet. In addition to the cats and Boofunkle, since Ellen had moved in, the couple had nursed three-legged lizards, one-eyed fish, and a shepherd who lost three legs to bone cancer.

In a garage converted to a spare room, Chip's and Ellen's computers sat on adjacent desks, Chip's covered with overflowing ashtrays, video feeds from a security camera aimed at the driveway, wallets, lighters, sticks of incense, vitamins in bottles, and a ragged bouquet of pens in an old flowerpot. Cali sprawled on my lap and Ellen started poking the power button of her Hewlett-Packard like a parrot pecking a tough nut. In front of her were two monitors that allowed her to compare, side by side, a missing-person report with details about unidentified remains.

A few years earlier Ellen had been at her computer, the predecessor of the one with the balky monitor, perusing the Doe Network. She spotted a photo of a bust. At the time, she didn't know that forensic artist Frank Bender was legendary for his uncanny representations of the dead based on nothing more than a skull. This one, created from a skull found at a Missouri truck stop embedded in a bucket of concrete, depicted the head and shoulders of a kindly-looking middle-aged gentleman. It was so lifelike it could have been done from a living model. Ellen had sat back in her chair, absentmindedly stroking one of the cats.

She knew the case wouldn't appeal to your everyday web sleuth, who tended to scrutinize identifiers such as height, weight, hair color, eye color, tattoos, personal effects, broken bones, and previous surgeries. Without a body, there was no quantifiable description for this victim; almost everything Bender had done was a guess. No self-respecting web sleuth would waste time on just a skull. It was crazy. It was so crazy, such a stupendous long shot, that Ellen was instantly intrigued. She liked the challenging cases. She adopted them like abandoned kittens.

By mid-January 2001, Greg May's son, Don, was worried. The last time Don saw his father had been at his grandfather's funeral in Chicago the previous April. Don lived in California, but father, son, daughter, and ex-wife were in frequent contact. Don and his sister, Shannon, both in their thirties, hadn't heard from their father in more than two weeks. They changed their phone answering machines to say, "Dad, if this is you, leave us a message." It wasn't unheard-of for Greg May to be temporarily out of touch. He led a nomadic existence, living in forty or fifty different places in his lifetime. It wasn't uncommon for his children to get a message listing yet another new number and address. He often traveled the country seeking out Civil War treasures.

In addition, he'd told friends he was considering moving to Florida. Bellevue had turned down his request to open a tattoo shop; perhaps he was unreachable because he was scouting out other potential locations, or driving south. But Don couldn't shake the feeling that something was wrong. The last straw came in mid-February. Greg May's phone was disconnected. Don and Shannon May flew from Santa Monica to Iowa to file a missing-person report with the Bellevue police.

Soon after the grisly discovery of the skull in the bucket, Kearney police enlisted cadaver-sniffing dogs to scour the Kearney truck stop. They didn't locate any other body parts. Later, dogs trained to pick up the scent of human cadavers would detect such a scent in an older-model black Volvo, but that car was hundreds of miles away, waiting to be junked; it would be years before it came to anyone's attention.

Kearney police sent the skull to a forensic odontologist and anthropologist, who hoped the face had left an impression in the contours of the concrete. No such luck: the head had been covered with a stocking cap. They were able to determine the skull belonged to a forty- to sixty-year-old man with existing teeth in good condition and extensive dental work.

In his garage turned study in Gulfport, Chip took over pushing the power button on Ellen's recalcitrant computer. None of the web sleuths I'd met had gleaming, state-of-the-art MacBooks. Not the least bit wealthy, the volunteers all owned clunkers that needed to be wrestled into submission. Ellen's screen flickered. She was lucky, not only because her boyfriend supported her addiction, but also because Glass, a cable TV technician, knew his way around electronics. We watched him wedge his stocky frame underneath the desk. Ellen and I looked on the way the driver of a disabled car hovers helplessly while a mechanic pokes around under the hood. We heard muttering, something about "power distribution . . . source code . . . video card."

"Still won't come up?" Ellen asked after a few minutes.

"Negative," Chip responded.

"I knew something else was going to go wrong." Ellen turned to me despairingly. "I wanted your visit to be perfect."

I've known women like Ellen Leach. They worry. They plan ahead. They try to think of everything. Before I flew to Mississippi, Ellen had kindly helped me book a room in an ancient white-pillared former mansion on an isolated, rural side road just past what appeared to be defunct railroad tracks. At night, the motel-like strip of rooms in the rear of the antebellum-style main building was eerily silent, apparently hosting no other guests except some peacocks and ducks paddling around in a stream opposite my door. Writers need solitude, Ellen said. She didn't seem to know that former New Yorkers sleep better with the wail of sirens outside their windows. I passed a sleepless night thinking about ax murderers.

May moved between two worlds, a friend told the *Los Angeles Times*.

He had an eagle tattooed on one shoulder

340

and a clipper ship on the other. Although his collection of Civil War rifles, swords, uniforms, muskets, Western movie posters, photographs, and documents was valuable, he wasn't a flashy dresser, given instead to straw cowboy hats, denim jackets, and "gentleman's loafers," as Shannon put it. The *Times* reported that May strolled Bellevue's Riverview Street with Duke, also known as Moose, who was tattooed from arms to thighs. The two eventually found jobs in a tattoo parlor across the river in Illinois. They would shoot pool at night and swing by the Frontier Cafe for breakfast. Waitresses remembered May as quiet, friendly, but reserved. Duke was the boisterous one, always cracking jokes. They stayed pretty much to themselves.

After Duke's girlfriend, Julie Johnson, came to town and moved in with them, waitresses noticed a change in Duke: he would sit alone in a corner with Johnson, looking somber and quiet.

"My father did not mince words," Don May told me years later. "He described Julie as a sneaky bitch, and that's a lot coming from a man who did not use profanity." Don had, as a teenager, met Duke (or Moose) back in Kenosha and recalled him as a sketchy character who could turn from jovial to sharp-tongued without warning. Don suspected his father felt sorry for Duke. Greg May's son had long known about his father's trusting nature and occasionally misguided generosity.

Although Greg May grew up in Lake Forest, a swanky Chicago suburb, and moved easily among the largely conservative crowd of Civil War buffs who frequented antique shows and museums, his love of tattooing sucked in ex-cons like Duke. Many tattoo artists are secretive about their craft, but May taught Duke about shading and coloring, showed him the machines that drove tiny inked needles like pile drivers deep into the dermis; showed him how to sterilize the needles in an autoclave, how to push the foot pedal with just the right amount of pressure to pierce the skin with even, solid lines of color and no so-called holidays, or gaps, but not so deeply as to cause excessive pain and bleeding. Finally, May would have shown him how to gently dab away drops of blood or plasma and bandage the new, raw tattoo with clean gauze.

Besides the occasional game of pool and their shared love of tattooing, May and Duke sometimes went fishing together. They used a white plastic bucket to carry their bait.

■ ■ ■ ■

On January sixteenth, five days after Jan left May's house for the last time, one of Greg May's neighbors saw the woman Jan Buman knew as Julie Ann Johnson loading some of May's antiques into a yellow Ford Ryder moving truck. An acquaintance helped Duke carry a large replica of a clipper ship from the house. Into the truck went bayonets, canteens, 140-year-old newspapers, vintage and modern guns, medals, and engravings. Duke told the landlord he and May were breaking their lease and leaving town. He gave away May's furniture to neighbors. Then he and Julie drove off.

Crime in Bellevue, Iowa, in the late 1990s consisted primarily of smalltime thefts and traffic violations. With Dan and Shannon May insisting something bad had happened to their father, the local police chief called in the state Division of Criminal Investigation.

They found no record of a Julie and Doug Johnson, which was how Julie and Duke were known around town. The police had no plates to run on the Ford Ryder truck the neighbors had noticed outside May's house, but they did get a lead on Greg May's missing car. A 1996 red Chevy Blazer with Wisconsin plates had turned up abandoned in a parking lot 145 miles away, in a suburb of Chicago called Aurora, Illinois. Police found May's keys and wallet inside.

They tracked Duke through a part-time job he had held for a time in a Galena, Illinois, tattoo shop and learned his real name was Douglas DeBruin and he was on parole for weapons possession and domestic assault in Wisconsin.

At home in Santa Monica, a sharp-eyed friend of his father's showed Don May a brochure from an auction company in Illinois that specializes in antique firearms and military artifacts. Don was shocked to see more than seventy pieces from his dad's collection, historic items he had known since his childhood, listed for sale. He knew his father would never auction off such cherished artifacts.

The police questioned the auction house and learned a woman identifying herself as Julie Johnson had said her uncle had died, leaving her and her mother an impressive collection of Confederate swords and Civil War-era uniforms valued at more than seventy thousand dollars. The paperwork putting the items up for sale went to a Mary

Klar in Webster, Wisconsin. A little digging unearthed the fact that Mary Klar is the mother of Julie Johnson, whose real name, it turned out, is Julie Miller.

In April 2001, investigators drove seven hours to Wisconsin. They told Klar a man was missing and that her daughter's boyfriend was a person of interest in his disappearance. Julie, Klar told them, was with DeBruin, living in the back of a Ryder truck in a trailer park in Flagstaff, Arizona.

On April 10, 2001, Miller and DeBruin were arrested in Flagstaff. Their truck contained a notebook with an inventory of May's collection, Civil War antiques including a rifle worth ten thousand dollars, a Confederate sword valued at fifteen thousand, and other items the pair claimed Greg May had given them. They had "no idea" where May might be. Inside the truck investigators also found a green jacket belonging to DeBruin. There was a suspicious-looking stain on the lower part of the right sleeve.

Two days later, Gary Chilcote was in his office at the Patee House Museum in St. Joseph, Missouri. St. Joseph is around four hundred miles southwest of Bellevue, Iowa, but it's only an hour's drive from Kearney, where the head in the bucket showed up at the truck stop. The whole region is Jesse James country.

In an ironic parallel to May's own fate, in 1882 Jesse James, in what turned out to be a serious misjudgment of character, took in two boarders, brothers Robert and Charlie Ford, and concocted a plan with them to rob the Platte City Bank. Set on collecting a five-thousand-dollar bounty on James's head, the brothers shot him to death in his home.

Chilcote, a Wild West buff and a fan of James, was especially proud of the museum's acquisition of the house located a block away where Robert Ford fatally shot James behind the right ear in 1882. Chilcote founded the museum in 1963 and served as its unpaid director. That day in April, he saw that a package had arrived from an establishment called Pack N' More in Glendale, Arizona.

Inside was a yellowed letter, written in a flowing, handsome script and mounted in a wood frame. Chilcote recognized the letter. He'd seen it years earlier, hanging on the wall of his own museum. The owner, a collector from Illinois, had mounted an exhibition of his historic possessions. Written in 1883, the letter is from ex-soldier and alcoholic newspaper editor John Newman Edwards, who is credited with creating the myth that Jesse James was a kind of noble Southern Robin Hood.

The letter offered encouragement to Jesse James's older brother, Frank, on the eve of Frank's 1883 trial for murder and robbery. It was a prize worth at least a thousand dollars, one any Civil War–era historian would be proud to own, and particularly significant to Chilcote because of its local connections. In his day, Edwards had worked at the *St. Joseph Gazette,* the same newspaper where Chilcote had spent forty years as a court reporter, and the letter was written on stationery of the Pacific House, a rival hotel to the Patee House.

Chilcote reached into the package and pulled out what looked like a photocopy of a handwritten note. "I would like to donate this letter," the note stated. "I've read about them and now may contribute to their memory." The note was signed Greg May. Chilcote told me he didn't find this too surprising. Things sometimes just showed up at museums. But who was this Greg May? Curious, Chilcote phoned the Illinois collector, who confirmed that he had sold the letter to a Greg May around eighteen months earlier.

That same day, the James Farm Museum in Kearney received a similar package with the same photocopied note. This time the unexpected gift was a letter to Frank James written in 1885 concerning legal wranglings involving a Minnesota robbery. Museum director Elizabeth Beckett told a reporter from the *Dubuque Telegraph Herald* that although some might consider it odd to receive a valuable historic letter out of the blue, nothing to do with the James brothers surprised her anymore.

The messages within the letters themselves were curious; the one Chilcote received expressed hope that a murderer and robber would beat the charges against him. But the directors didn't seem to read too much into the letters' content. They were simply grateful that generous history buff Greg May thought their museums worthy recipients of these very interesting artifacts.

A crime lab in Des Moines confirmed that the stain on Duke's jacket sleeve was blood. Using samples from Don and Shannon May in a reverse paternity test that links parents and children, the blood was determined with 99 percent certainty to belong to Greg May.

■ ■ ■ ■

DeBruin was returned to Wisconsin to do time for his former parole violation. Investigators sat down in Arizona with Julie Miller. Chilcote, who later saw Miller in the courtroom, described her as a typical forty-four-year-old middle-aged person. She looked like a store employee with her hair pulled up on top of her head. She looked, he said, like someone you might meet in a bar.

Miller was charged with theft and interstate transport of stolen property. The notion that May was alive and well, donating Jesse James letters to museums, didn't fool investigators. As they pressed Miller on May's whereabouts, she confirmed what they suspected: May was dead. She told them she was in the basement that day in January. She heard a ruckus upstairs. It sounded like May and DeBruin arguing. She ran up to the kitchen to find May lying on the floor and DeBruin saying, "I killed him, it was an accident. I hit him too hard and I killed him." She and DeBruin wrapped the body in plastic bags and sealed them with duct tape. She helped DeBruin drag May to DeBruin's Volvo. She cleaned up the blood. He was gone for hours. He returned and told her, "Greg always liked the Mississippi River."

Soon after the Missouri museums received the letters and DeBruin and Miller were arrested, the Iowa Division of Criminal Investigation dredged the Mississippi and asked farmers and hunters to keep an eye out for anything wrapped in plastic that might be human remains. For Don and Shannon May, wishful thinking was over. They printed five hundred color posters offering a fifteen-thousand-dollar reward to anyone who came across the black trash bags wrapped in duct tape containing their father's remains. They drove grimly through two counties and a stretch of Illinois plastering gas stations, bars, grocery stores, post offices, parks, and churches with the flyers.

But despite Miller's confession, Iowa assistant attorney general James Kivi knew what he was up against. Before he could prove Doug DeBruin killed Greg May, he had to prove May was dead. Most of the evidence was circumstantial, Jackson County attorney John L. Kies pointed out later. It was true that Doug DeBruin had gotten caught with Greg May's goods; that no one had heard from Gregory May since he was last seen with DeBruin; and that May's car and wallet had been abandoned in Aurora. But all they had of Greg May himself was a spot of his blood on the sleeve of a jacket.

In December 2001, Julie Ann Miller, also known as Julie Johnson and Julie Ann Kern, pleaded guilty to stealing seventy thousand dollars' worth of May's antiques. It had been an eventful year for Miller and Doug DeBruin. Around a week after a neighbor had seen May's replica clipper ship loaded into a yellow moving van that January, the pair drove to Missouri, then to Corpus Christi, Texas, stopping along the way to sell May's possessions at flea markets. A photo taken around this time shows De-Bruin sitting like a peddler surrounded by his wares at a Texas flea market. Behind him are items Don May was sure belonged to his family.

Back in Kearney, Missouri, police had exhausted all leads on the identity of the man whose head was found in the bucket. Lieutenant Tom O'Leary had seen busts done by forensic sculptor Frank Bender profiled on *America's Most Wanted*. Bender, with a pointed goatee, shaved head, and hooded eyebrows, had over thirty-three years done more than forty busts for law enforcement, earning a reputation as eccentric but astoundingly effective at giving faces to the unidentified. Bender sometimes sat with a skull for days, as if trying to channel the spirit of its owner. What would the dead man's expression be like? How would he wear his hair? "I call myself the re-composer of the decomposed in the classical fashion," Bender reportedly once said. Law enforcement had come to rely on him for conjuring — with very little information — an incredibly accurate portrayal of what a person had looked like in life.

What did this particular skull tell him? That the individual was middle-aged. A little on the heavy side. Balding.

Using charts developed by anatomy experts that determined the thickness of tissue at various points over the skull, Bender molded clay directly on the skull, made a plaster cast, and sanded, filed, and painted the resulting bust. Early in his career Bender had used wigs, but ultimately decided he'd have more control if he sculpted the hair himself.

On September 26, 2002, Bender's bust arrived in Missouri. Lieutenant O'Leary was blown away. He had sent off a skull; what he got back was almost human.

The man in the bust had a wide mouth, receding hairline, jowly neck. His nose was straight and somewhat prominent, his eyes deep-set under bushy brows. He looked like a pleasant enough fellow, a man you'd exchange the time of day with at the post office.

The reconstruction sat on O'Leary's file cabinet. It stared at O'Leary when he walked in in the morning. It was the last thing he saw when he went home at night. O'Leary had faith that one day the right lead would come in — the lead that would result in an identification.

Around a year after Bender completed the bust, O'Leary posted photos of it on a site he had come across called the Doe Network.

Ellen Leach saw the photo of Bender's reconstruction and the details of the discovery at the truck stop. She was convinced the head in the bucket was Jimmy Hoffa's.

At first, this struck me as laughable. Ever since former Teamsters leader Hoffa vanished in 1975 on his way to meet two mafiosi, his name was on everybody's lips whenever a body turned up in the Hudson River or inside a cement bridge piling.

There's an Aimee Mann song about how Jimmy Hoffa jokes are passé, yet Hoffa could be the poster child for the whole cold case movement. He's missing. There's no body. He was almost certainly murdered.

The bust did look a little like pictures I'd seen of Hoffa. Ellen believed for a time that the head in the bucket had to be a mob hit, the MO reminding her of cement shoes. Thirty years too late, her theory didn't make a lot of sense to me, but I realized that a web sleuth's ability to brainstorm, to extrapolate, to make leaps of faith, might be correlated with her success rate.

The bust showed up under listings for the unidentified, but the Doe Network's parallel database for the missing did not include Greg May. Volunteers who scoured the media for missing-person cases simply hadn't come across him. Other national and international sites dedicated to missing persons didn't include May, either, so his name did not come up when Ellen tried to match characteristics of the middle-aged man Bender had depicted to men reported missing.

Not finding what she was looking for in all her usual haunts, Ellen started to scan sites posted by medical examiners and police departments in individual states.

Since Mike Murphy launched Las Vegas Unidentified in 2003, more states had been mounting sites devoted to the missing and unidentified, although by no means all states had them. So if, for instance, a body surfaced in Iowa, Ellen would check that state's missing first because, in her experience, the unidentified often turned up relatively close to home. If she didn't find anything, she would circle out geographically — Minnesota, Wisconsin, Illinois, Missouri, Kansas, Arkansas — and expand the time frame.

Iowa's Missing Person Information Clearinghouse posted a weekly list of the missing, arranged alphabetically by name, with age, gender, date of last contact, originating agency, and not much else. It could, with some effort, be searched for physical characteristics and date of disappearance. But it was painstaking, tedious, and potentially fruitless to search record after record for a male of a certain height and age, say, when the estimated height might be off by as much as five inches and the age by ten years.

One day in 2004, Ellen spotted a new listing. Iowa had just posted (reposted, but Leach didn't know that) a photograph of Gregory May, missing since 2001. The photo was of a man with shaggy hair, a mustache, and a warm smile.

In Kearney, Lieutenant O'Leary got an unrelated tip from a Colorado member of the Doe Network. It wasn't unusual for multiple volunteers to work on cases simultaneously. This can result in law enforcement being inundated with proposed matches, each one time-consuming to investigate. The Doe Network, trying to be sensitive to this, submits only its members' most promising tips.

One of the conundrums of web sleuthing is this: law enforcement welcomes a positive match and abhors a waste of time. Web sleuths provide both. The trick to minimizing the time wasters, a California death investigator believes, is education. He spends hours on the phone encouraging web sleuths to submit to him only potential matches that have dental records, fingerprints, or DNA on file. He cajoles police into entering those identifiers into missing-person and unidentified records whenever they have them. It's a sad fact that many unidentifieds will never be matched to a missing person because their dental records are languishing in a filing cabinet, inaccessible to investigators.

The Doe panel sent a tip — not Ellen's

— to O'Leary suggesting a missing Texas man could be a match for the head. The reported victim was last seen on or about September 1, 1998. O'Leary looked at pictures of the missing man. He thought they looked pretty damn close. A year after Bender fashioned the bust, O'Leary let himself hope. This tip felt like it was about to hit pay dirt.

On January 9, 2004, almost exactly three years after May was killed but still with no body in evidence, Iowa prosecutors charged Douglas DeBruin with his murder.

It wasn't easy to get DeBruin back to Iowa to stand trial. From federal custody in Arizona, he was sent to Wisconsin, where he'd violated parole on a firearms violation. DeBruin fought extradition to Iowa; requests and motions flew back and forth, with DeBruin steadfastly filing his own motions to dismiss because, he claimed, his right to a speedy trial had been violated.

DeBruin's trial was set for November 2004, then continued to January 2005. Just as jury selection was slated to begin and Don and Shannon May, bags packed, were about to board a plane to Iowa, DeBruin's public defender asked for a continuance. It was denied, then appealed to the Iowa

Supreme Court, which ordered a temporary stay. It would be three more months before the May siblings traveled to Iowa.

Prosecutors Kivi and Kies were frustrated by the delays but also worried about the challenge ahead of them. Prosecuting Douglas DeBruin would be a landmark case: Iowa's first murder trial without a body.

In 2003, dental charts had ruled out O'Leary's missing Texas man as a match for the Kearney truck stop victim. O'Leary looked at the bust, still sitting in his office. He imagined the eyes under the bushy brows glaring at him reproachfully.

After sending a few possible matches to the Doe Network area director for Missouri, Ellen heard nothing. This was not unusual; an area director, a volunteer like all other members, reviewed a possible match and then submitted it to an administrative group for a consensus on whether it was a convincing enough match to submit to law enforcement. Ellen got tired of waiting. (Eventually, what some web sleuths saw as the Doe Network's bureaucracy — the review by the potential match panel, the waiting for decisions to be handed down on whether a match is good enough, the rules prohibiting members from contacting law enforcement directly — caused a rift so serious that it temporarily shattered the organization.)

At the time, Ellen's proposed match went from the area director to O'Leary and then tumbled into a computer-glitch black hole. The area director sent it along again. Ellen got back in touch with her a couple of months later and learned that O'Leary had never received it.

There was some confusion, O'Leary recalled. The Doe Network was always sending him potential matches, sometimes two or three at a time. The batch that included Ellen's tip had apparently slipped through the cracks.

Leach was frustrated, to put it mildly. On March 17, 2005, O'Leary saw the Doe Network suggestion — Ellen Leach's suggestion — that Bender's reconstruction looked just like a photo of a Gregory John May missing from Bellevue, Iowa. It was four months after she had submitted it. The age estimate and time of discovery of the skull indicated a possible match.

O'Leary decided to call the Bellevue police department, but he wasn't holding out much hope. He had pursued leads on forty-two men over the years and, he told me, the funny thing was, he had thought the Texas man who was ultimately ruled out looked a lot more like the head in the bucket. He tried not to get too excited about leads. He had been let down too many times.

Ellen had just gotten home from her shift at Home Depot. The phone in the kitchen rang. The voice was a stranger's, but Ellen instantly recognized Doe Network area director Traycie Sherwood's name. She and Sherwood had been trading e-mails for months. Ellen hung up and fist-pumped, yelling, "Awwright!"

She was elated, she told me later. She was happy to help out the police, the family. And Greg May was her first solve. She'd been web sleuthing for six years. So, yeah, she said, after the thousands of possible matches she'd put in over the years, to finally get one was a good feeling.

In Iowa, prosecutors Kies and Kivi couldn't believe their luck. Days before the DeBruin trial was scheduled to begin, pieces of the puzzle were starting to fall into place. It looked like they might even have the body — or part of the body — they so desperately needed. Later, Kies told a TV crew, "I am not one to readily believe in karma, or perhaps the spirit of Greg May directing things. But wow, it certainly makes one think there may be forces out there working for justice other than us."

"If this doesn't make you believe in a higher being," the state's investigator said, "nothing will."

The skull had been sent from Missouri to Iowa, where Greg May's dentist identified the restorations he had completed on May's teeth — the bridgework the Kearney detective had seen emerging from the concrete. Soon afterward, police called Don May to tell him that, after four years of searching, they finally had some of his father's remains. Don was relieved; the family had yearned to be able to put Greg May to rest. Don asked what they had found. The investigator hesitated. "Are you sure you want to know?" he said.

Working on information that Julie Miller had recently divulged, Don and Shannon May spent a Friday in mid-April pursuing, as one Dubuque reporter put it, "a morbid treasure hunt" along a steep, densely wooded hillside along US 52. Don, grimly rummaging among deer carcasses and trash, came upon what looked like a human bone. State forensic experts confirmed it was a right femur, sliced through with what looked like the blade of a saw. The siblings couldn't imagine things getting any worse.

The state had granted Julie Miller immunity in 2002. In exchange, she agreed to testify against DeBruin. Just before the trial in 2005, Kies and Kivi decided to talk to Miller one last time, expecting a routine pretrial interview between prosecutors and witness. To their surprise, Miller changed her story yet again. The scene she described shocked and horrified them.

In a crowded courtroom a few days later, Miller, wearing a prim blouse and her oversized glasses, said that in January 2001, DeBruin covered the basement laundry room with plastic sheets. Later, up in the kitchen, he asked May to check out a tattoo of a wolf DeBruin was doing on Miller's back. As May sat, bent over Julie, DeBruin snuck up behind him, slipped a yellow cord around his neck, and pulled it tight. Moose — six-four, 250 pounds — and Miller — five-three, 110 pounds — staggered down the stairs with May's six-foot frame supported between them. (The slamming Jan heard may have been May's corpse thudding down the stairs.) The pair dragged May's body to the basement.

DeBruin's version was somewhat different. In the courtroom, he was barely recognizable as the burly ex-con who used to be
seen around town with Greg May. Clean-
shaven, his graying hair combed back neatly,
he wore glasses and a suit that made him
look like a kindly fifty-something businessman. He testified that on January 11, 2001,
he was smoking in the basement. He heard
odd sounds coming from upstairs. "Then
[Miller] came downstairs mad, slobbering,
mumbling and making no sense," said De-
Bruin. After climbing the stairs to the
kitchen, he noticed a large kitchen knife and
rag, and saw May slumped over the table.
He had blood on his chest. DeBruin felt his
neck for a pulse, he sobbed from the witness stand. Miller had stabbed May in the
chest as he sat at the kitchen table, DeBruin
said. He laid May on the floor, went back
downstairs, and vomited. "He's my best
friend," he said. "I didn't want to do what
she said."

Nevertheless, Miller and DeBruin both
testified that the next morning they drove
together to a Lowe's in Dubuque and
bought concrete and an electric chain saw.

When they arrived back at the house, they
went to work.

After placing May's body on a washing

machine, they sawed off his head over a utility sink. Blood flowed down the drain. DeBruin used the chain saw to dismember the rest of the body. Miller used a kitchen knife. They sliced off the feet and hands, severed the legs above and below the knees. They tucked the pieces in black plastic bags and secured the bags with tape.

They mixed cement and water in one of the five-gallon plastic buckets that the friends had used when they had gone fishing together. DeBruin encased May's severed head in a stocking cap and plunged it into the bucket. They piled the body parts into DeBruin's Volvo and drove toward Dubuque, pitching sections of limbs over the edge of US 52 into a steep ravine south of the city across from a housing development. They wrapped May's torso in plastic and tied weights to it before dropping it off the Mississippi River bridge between Sabula, Iowa, and Savanna, Illinois.

DeBruin and Miller left the chain saw and some of May's clothes at a Goodwill collection site in Dubuque. They ditched the Volvo at a Bellevue auto body shop. Miller testified that she drove May's car from Bellevue to Dubuque and finally abandoned it in Aurora, Illinois, where investigators found it with May's wallet and keys on the front seat.

A few days after packing May's collection and the bucket containing his head into the truck, they drove north to Missouri and pulled into a truck stop in Kearney to spend the night.

The truck stop was on the west side of the interstate. Under the highway and across a set of railroad tracks you can find the Mount Olivet Cemetery, where Jesse James is buried. From where the bucket sat, you could practically see the outlaw's grave, Jesse James fan Gary Chilcote told me.

Was it a coincidence that the pair stopped in Kearney? Investigators found a weigh-station receipt in the Ryder truck. The bucket may have been ditched in Kearney only to lighten the truck, which was laden down with May's Civil War collection. Others believed the location was deliberate. Chilcote told me that at the trial Julie Miller insinuated that leaving May's head there was the ultimate insult: the pair decided that Greg May loved Jesse James so much, they'd leave May's head where he could "keep an eye" on James's grave.

On April 21, 2005, the jury took an hour to declare DeBruin guilty of the murder of Greg May.

Contradictions between Miller's testimony

at DeBruin's trial and her prior testimony in the stolen property case led the state to indict her for perjury. Miller pleaded guilty, and the district court judge sentenced her to a maximum term of sixty months.

Miller's former pastor testified that she was a person of good character who deserved a break because she had been abused as a child. A divorced mother of three, "Julie has never had a traffic ticket," Julie's mother, Mary Klar, told the *Inter-County Leader*. "She's a gentle and good person."

More than a decade after Jan Buman saw Greg May for the last time and kissed him good-bye outside his Bellevue home, she remembered him as "the best boyfriend" she had ever had. A tattoo of an eagle that May had started for her remains unfinished. Greg himself never got more tattoos than the two on his shoulders because he couldn't take the pain, Don May ruefully explained to me.

"Greg May ruled!!!" a Chicago aficionado who had bought an antique tattoo machine from May in 1994 posted as part of an online tribute to May. Another tattoo buff uploaded a flash design May had designed and inked years ago on a friend's bicep. Hand-drawn on paper, flash is displayed on the walls of tattoo parlors and in binders to show walk-in customers. Artists painstakingly draw and hand-paint the flash of their original designs using unforgiving watercolors. It can take months of work to paint enough flash to fill an average tattoo shop, and Don May recalled, when he was a small child, his father painting his flash long into the night after working all day in his shop. "He was a very hard worker, my dad."

The tattoo posted on the forum was of the head of a panther, fangs bared, nostrils and tongue bloodred, eyes orange and fierce, black fur slick and shiny. The lines are clean and bold; the head looks vaguely classical, as though May had been influenced by the ancient Greeks. Below the design are the words "by Greg." The cursive capital *G* is finished with a fanciful curlicue; the *e* mimics a curvy number three. Out of deference to his father, a successful businessman who wasn't thrilled with his son's choice of profession, May never signed his creations with his last name. The finely wrought details of the panther are proof enough of his skill, recognizable as May's work by those in the know.

DeBruin was sentenced to life without parole. He claimed to spend sleepless nights wishing that someone would shoot him and put him out of his misery, gazing at the tattoos on his body, tattoos the man he had described as his best and only friend had once meticulously inked.

The sparse remains of Greg May were buried in a tiny casket in Des Plaines, Illinois. Don May didn't buy Miller and DeBruin's story about dropping the torso off a bridge. Checking meteorological records, Don saw there was a layer of ice up to eight inches thick on the Mississippi that January.

Don's theory is that his father was shot, not strangled, and that the torso would have provided evidence of a bullet, potentially traceable to both DeBruin and Miller. But May's torso has never been recovered. Perhaps a case for the web sleuths, I suggested. "That's true," Don mused. "It could be out there listed on a website somewhere."

Miller completed a five-year sentence for perjury and was released from federal prison in Pekin, Illinois, in 2011. She has never been charged in connection with May's murder, a fact that Don May finds unconscionable. He has vowed to find a way to put Julie Miller back behind bars. Inspired by the case, the Iowa legislature passed a law that makes it a felony to "mutilate, disfigure, dismember, hide, or bury a hu-

colored woven baskets and bowls, some voluminous enough to hold a pheasant and others that would accommodate no more than a few marbles. The gullah, whose hands never stopped whipping tender stalks back and forth as if she were fighting off the devil with short swords, grinned toothlessly when Halleck admired the dozens of baskets encircling the woman's skirts. I later learned that in the 1800s African slaves fashioned such baskets out of indigenous low-country sweetgrass to carry food and such in homes and fields. The art, handed down from generation to generation, survives only in Charleston.

Halleck told me later that she was a huge fan of Roberto Clemente, who'd played for her hometown Pittsburgh Pirates in the 1960s. One of her most treasured possessions was a fielding mitt she claimed he had given her when she was a girl. Clemente was known for his formidable skills on the field and also for helping underprivileged children from his native Puerto Rico improve their lives through baseball. Each of Lauran's web posts ended with a Clemente quote: "If you have a chance to accomplish something that will make things better for people coming behind you, and you don't do that, you are wasting your time on this earth."

Lauran struck me as a born romantic, a child of the sixties. "Are you a former hippie?" I asked as we eyed a display of tie-dyed T-shirts.

"Still am!" she said, grinning.

Given Halleck's countercultural streak, it didn't surprise me that her nemesis was a ramrod-spined Texas lawman.

In December 2007, a trim, silver-haired man who looked like Edward Woodward in the 1980s crime series *The Equalizer* stood next to an attractive blonde some years his junior on unpaved County Road 101 where it dead-ended at Route 288 in the oil town of Manvel, Texas. The pair, busy photographing what looked like a patch of bare earth, didn't notice the cars flying by — north toward Houston and south toward the Gulf Coast — or the figure in a baseball cap and tennis shoes striding toward them.

"What are you doing here?" Baseball Cap demanded.

"Why do you want to know?" Silver Fox countered. "This is a public road."

Baseball Cap identified himself as a Manvel police officer. He was suspicious of the couple's presence at the very spot where, in

1990, a motorist getting out of his car to take a leak nearly stumbled on a pile of bones that turned out to belong to a young woman. Between seventeen and twenty-one years old, petite — around five feet — she was found wearing six rings, among them a silver Robert E. Lee High School ring with a deep-blue sapphire. Princess Blue, as she had come to be known, was not identified; her attacker had not been caught.

For nearly thirty years, as the young cop and almost everyone else in the region knew, multiple killers had abducted, raped, and murdered dozens of women and dumped their bodies in isolated spots along what became known as the Highway from Hell — the Interstate 45 corridor from Galveston to Dallas, which, with Route 288, created a pie-shaped wedge encompassing rural Brazoria and Galveston counties. A single vacant lot in League City, just inside the wedge, had come to be known as "the killing fields" after four girls' bodies were found there on four separate occasions between 1983 and 1991.

What the young cop didn't know was that he was in the presence of none other than thirty-five-year law enforcement veteran and private investigator Matt Wingo — former investigator with the Brazoria County district attorney's office and son of the late "man hunter" Cecil Wingo, FBI criminal profiler, two-time police chief of nearby Angleton, Texas, and longtime chief investigator for the Harris County medical examiner.

The Manvel cop surely couldn't have guessed that the man before him and his lady friend had sought out Princess Blue's death scene the way some people embarked on a pilgrimage to Lourdes. It was their first date.

Matt Wingo's companion, Kristy Gault, ran a website dedicated to unidentified and missing persons. Gault had traveled to Texas from Ohio partly to document the eerily deserted locations where the remains of Princess Blue and other possible victims of the notorious serial killer or killers had been found (she would later post on her site one of the photos she took that day) and partly to meet Wingo, who was as haunted by the deaths as she was.

Investigators never agreed on how many killers were involved in the Texas slayings, the subject of several books and movies. Murders committed in the 1980s appeared to copycat the original 1970s crimes; one FBI profiler believed that as many as five or more murderers may have taken advantage of this boggy, desolate region of oil refineries within easy reach of megacities Dallas and Houston. There were so many Jane Does among the victims that police took to mounting their pictures on I-45 billboards.

In his heyday as a detective, Matt Wingo had worked as many as three such homicides in one night. Now retired, he had never given up hope that Princess Blue and the other unidentified serial-killer victims would be identified and their murderers prosecuted.

The baseball-cap cop looked at the pair, considering. He acknowledged that Wingo's name rang a bell. Still, he told them he needed to run checks on both of them, and on Gault's car. The Manvel police chief would later demand that Wingo stay out of his town for good. Wingo never for a moment considered halting his expeditions to the dumping grounds.

Kristy Gault, aka Miss Killjoy and Starless, avid gardener and reputed onetime exotic dancer, enlivened her daily posts to the bare-bones bulletin board she had founded, Cold Case Investigations (also called OCCI, for Official Cold Case Investigations, and later Cold Case Examiner), with a dizzying array of animated icons: twirling blue stars, dancing pink milk cartons with legs, leaping exclamation points, frenetic lightning strikes, buzzing bees trapped in jars. When I told her why I was calling, Gault revealed she was working on her own book, each chapter describing an unidentified body — some I had heard of, many I hadn't. Gault had an uncanny memory for the unidentified. When I mentioned the Lady of the Dunes, she rattled off the particulars as though she'd just seen the police report. She seemed happy to chat with a like-minded caller; she confided that the uninitiated often found her pursuit a bit off-putting.

Gault told me that while she was growing up in Barberton, Ohio, her mother, a true-crime buff, had dragged her to see serial murderers on TV the way some kids might be plopped in front of the Disney Channel. "See that man?" her mother would say, pointing to a handsome face on the screen with wavy dark hair and intense eyes. "That's Ted Bundy."

Gault first encountered Wingo on Web-sleuths.com. Users weren't allowed to contact other users directly, and Gault felt constricted by the site's rules. She also wasn't permitted to contact people in connection with investigating crimes, which is what she most liked to do. Still, she continued to post on Websleuths until Wingo — in one of their very first interactions — publicly took her to task for an error he perceived in one of her posts. He also used her screen name to "yell at" everyone on the site, she recalled. The site administrator banned them both. But Gault and Wingo stayed in touch, and Gault went to Texas in 2007 to meet him. She ended up moving in with him while she continued to beef up OCCI.

Gault and Wingo were anomalies in the world of web sleuthing, equally involved in real-life investigations as in posting details of cold cases online. Gault claimed to "officially" solve one case and help close the books on six others by unearthing and passing along tips to police.

For a time, Gault was obsessed with the bizarre case of Florida death row inmate Franklin Delano Floyd, who allegedly kidnapped a four-year-old girl, raised her as his daughter, and later married her. The young woman died in 1990 in a hit-and-run accident that may have been tied to Floyd, who was convicted in 2002 of murdering another woman. Gault corresponded with Floyd for four years and contacted members of his family in an attempt to uncover details about his victims, finally giving up when Floyd started asking her for money.

Besides looking into whether a Galveston prostitute named Brenda Diamonte might be a possible match for Princess Blue, Gault hoped to unearth evidence that would support the theory, which both she and Wingo adhered to, that Roy Alan Stuart, a suspect in four murders and nine sexual assaults since 1964, was involved in the Princess Blue murder. That day, the pair photographed deserted roadside sites where Stuart, imprisoned for aggravated kidnapping, was suspected to have dumped other victims.

Matt Wingo's association with OCCI likely boosted the forum's credibility in the web-sleuthing world, particularly in Houston, where Wingo's father, Cecil, was a local legend. At age twenty-three, Cecil Wingo became the first and youngest police chief of Angleton, Texas, and spent part of his ensuing decades-long career in law enforcement with ViCAP, the Violent Criminal Apprehension Program, where he helped profile serial killers Ted Bundy and Carl Eugene Watts, aka the Sunday Morning Slasher. Cecil Wingo also served as chief investigator under the famed Joseph "Dr. Joe" Jachimczyk. Houston's first and longest-serving chief medical examiner, Dr. Joe, who studied both law and theology before pursuing a medical degree, spent thirty-five years "sorting out the grim results of the city's violence," as his obituary put it, before he retired in 1995.

Cecil Wingo and Dr. Joe may have ignited Matt Wingo's compassion for the unidentified in 1984 when they hosted a funeral service for a headless, legless, and handless torso twenty years after it was found in Fort Bend County. Dr. Joe had held on to the remains in the unfulfilled hope that the victim would one day get back a name.

So for Cecil Wingo's only son to be detained by a wet-behind-the-ears cop at the Princess Blue dump site was humiliating and infuriating. Despite being retired from the county sheriff and district attorney offices, Wingo was still following up on leads for some of the bodies he helped recover in the 1980s, when he scoured the county's dark, lonely roads for the bodies of girls and women abducted from Houston.

Wingo told me that, unlike websites that harbored idle speculation (a faintly veiled dig at Porchlight and Websleuths), Gault's Official Cold Case Investigations was the only web-sleuthing crime forum that did any "real work." By 2007, OCCI had gained a reputation as a serious forum, devoid of the drama that plagued some other sites. But shortly afterward it experienced its own brouhaha.

One day, Gault and Wingo logged on and saw the word "PORCHLIGHT" swallow up their screen. Someone calling himself or herself luvmycat had infiltrated the inner workings of OCCI and doctored Gault's and Wingo's passwords, effectively locking them out of their own site. Wingo fumed about "all the fruitcakes out there" sabotaging the self-respecting web sleuths like Gault and himself, but he had no immediate recourse except to patch up the damage to the site and to his ego.

Wingo was certain he knew who was behind the hack.

I had arrived at Lauran Halleck's house in the middle of nowhere, South Carolina, with dusk approaching.

Halleck shooed aside the two yippy dogs and opened the door, an apple in her hand. One of the cats followed us to the fenced-in field where she fed the pony. She had taken in the lame creature, and an old mare, and the dogs, and some of the cats, when their owners could find no other homes for them.

Inside the house, a nineteenth-century

hand-carved carousel horse, a beautiful antique in faded burgundy and forest green, stood alongside open sacks of dog food and general dust-covered clutter. There was more of Halleck's painted glassware: she presented me with a round Christmas ornament covered in pansies. A disheveled kitten mewed feebly from a box on the kitchen table. "Come on," Halleck said, poking a bit of shredded meat at its mouth. "Take it." The kitten didn't respond to the food; its head lolled alarmingly to the side. In an adjacent room an open jar of peanut butter sat on a shelf, knife protruding, and a cup of tea had grown cold next to the keyboard of an ancient desktop PC. A hard drive as big as a milk crate sat next to it. I figured the hard drive was up on the desk instead of the floor because of Ozzie.

Halleck had seemed hesitant to invite me into this room. With the door shut behind us, I saw why. A lanky, coyote-like creature — a feral dog, she informed me — crouched under the desk, looking antsy. Next to the bed, a chestnut-brown mastiff staggered to its dinner-plate-sized paws.

Ozzie leaned against me affectionately, all 220 pounds of him pinning my midsection between his rib cage and the frame of a water bed jacked high off the floor to prevent him from leaping on it and collapsing it. He stood patiently, one enormous paw on my left foot, wheezing asthmatically through pendulous jowls. Ozzie was someone's castoff, the most recent in Halleck's long succession of mastiffs. She said that at one time she owned six of the giants. One was Monkalup, Halleck's most-used screen moniker.

We sat in front of the computer. Ozzie, seeking an ear rub, lugubriously swiped a paw at me, a habit he had picked up from his former owner's pit bulls. It was like being hit with a barbell. Halleck, raspy-voiced from years of smoking, reprimanded him in baby talk. He settled his toaster-sized muzzle on my lap, gazing up at me with one rheumy brown eye while a puddle of drool spread on my thigh. The objects on the desk shook and rattled with his breathing, as though experiencing a minor earthquake.

With a few clicks Halleck raised Porchlight on the screen. Besides her search for Jean Marie, the main reason she joined the Doe Network in 2000 soon after its creation and then founded her own public database for the missing and unidentified was because so much information was vanishing from the Web.

Halleck viewed the Internet as an ideal

communication and information-gathering tool. Except it wasn't reliable. Articles, data, entire sites emerged and then disappeared in a poof of ether. So Halleck started Porchlight, initially, as a repository. Some used it to try to make matches between the missing and unidentified, aided by message boards and forums consisting of every article, every mention, every bit of information users could dig out about a given case. Others stuck to bolstering the growing database. Members of law enforcement had been known to call and write Halleck, she said, thanking her for background case material more comprehensive than what they had in their own files.

With the help of a computer whiz named Carl, Halleck said she aimed to make Porchlight the most searchable, sortable, and intuitive database on the Web. But Porchlight might never have existed if Halleck hadn't been banned from the Doe Network in the first place.

At the base of Halleck's differences with the Doe Network was a philosophical rift in the web sleuth world between two camps I'll call the mavericks and the trust builders. The mavericks want to contact law enforcement directly. They want to take their gold nugget of a possible match directly to the cops. They want recognition — glory, as it were — for finding the Holy Grail: a positive identification.

The trust builders are more team-oriented. They hope to build a reputation as responsible, behind-the-scenes helpmates to law enforcement. In the mid-2000s, a handful of cops, detectives, and coroners did begin to recognize that the web sleuths could be useful, especially for very cold cases. They started to share bits of information. The web sleuths, for the most part, took this responsibility seriously. They believed that if they didn't violate trust, they'd get more tidbits — autopsy details or a picture of a piece of jewelry discovered with a body — that could facilitate matches. Law enforcement had supplied some of this information confidentially; if they learned of breaches, Doe administrators contended, the Doe Network and others like them would lose credibility.

For this reason, the Doe Network administrative board started to require members to submit all matches to the potential match (PM) panel, an elite committee that determined which matches looked promising enough to forward to law enforcement. The board felt this protected law enforcement from the type of pushy, time-sucking web sleuths whom certain cops had dubbed the Doe Nuts. (Yet, even rule-abiding web sleuths have at times considered the PM panel stifling and needlessly bureaucratic. Some have become incensed when, on occasion, the panel refused to forward matches that later turned out to be accurate. Others told me "gut instincts" convinced them of certain matches despite lack of definitive evidence.)

In 2006, Lauran Halleck was an administrator for the Doe Network, having worked her way up the ranks over the previous six years. Doe Network members claimed the real reason that Halleck was ousted that year was because she was a maverick. She reportedly gave another member — also subsequently banned — access to behind-the-scenes, "privileged" information from law enforcement. She insisted to me that this never happened. Still peeved six years after her banishment, Halleck maintained that the Doe Network kicked her out for contacting law enforcement outside her designated geographic area. (A Doe administrator confirmed that Halleck was guilty of that too.)

Soon after she was ousted, Halleck created a site she called Usedtobedoe. Halleck promised that Usedtobedoe would never prevent its members from getting directly in touch with law enforcement.

The name infuriated the old guard, but the site attracted like-minded users. Ellen Leach in Mississippi recalled how hard it had been to get the Doe Network to present her proposed matches for Greg May to law enforcement. She was among the Doe members who followed Halleck to the new site, eventually renamed Porchlight International for the Missing and Unidentified.

During all this, Halleck contended that her primary mission was the search for her foster sister, Jean Marie Stewart, who had disappeared in Miami Lakes in 1980. Those who use the sites to search for a missing relative have always had a certain cachet in the web sleuth world, and Halleck became known for posting on multiple sites, including Kristy Gault and Matt Wingo's OCCI, about her angst over Jean Marie's unknown fate. Halleck became an online ally of an OCCI member called Suzannec4444, who described herself as the half sister of child beauty queen, model, and actress Tammy Lynn Leppert, who, like Jean Marie Stewart, had vanished from Florida as a teenager. Leppert was last seen at age eighteen in Cocoa Beach in July 1983, three years after

Jean Marie disappeared.

Controversy over Suzannec4444 swirled from around 2005, when Leppert was featured on *Unsolved Mysteries,* through at least 2008. The boards exploded with questions and accusations from a dozen posters, including crystaldawn, NEWYORKEX, and unsolvedmysteriesfan. Was Suzanne, as she claimed, really Tammy's biological half sister, adopted out of the family at birth? Was she an attention seeker who happened to see Tammy featured on *Unsolved Mysteries* and was now tying herself to Tammy's celebrity persona? Was Tammy even dead? (Rumor had it that she dropped out of the limelight to pursue a nursing career or was in the witness protection program because she once witnessed a mob money-laundering scheme.) Creepiest of all, some wondered whether Suzannec4444 and Tammy Lynn Leppert were the same person.

Lauran Halleck, using the screen name Porchlight, always defended Suzanne: a hero, Halleck insisted, for her selfless devotion. To Halleck, the fact that Suzanne had never actually met Tammy made her dedication to finding her all the more impressive.

Gault, Wingo, and others on OCCI belonged to the Suzannec4444-is-a-fraud camp. Through OCCI, Wingo launched an "investigation" of Suzanne in which he and others posted doubts, accusations, and random nastiness, leading to a mini-firefight between him, Gault, Halleck, and Suzanne, who demanded OCCI remove Tammy's entire thread from the site. Well, we ain't gonna do that, Wingo wrote. You could almost hear his Texas drawl.

That was when the hack occurred. Besides locking Gault and Wingo out of the site, their passwords were changed to "TAMI," Leppert's nickname, convincing Wingo that Halleck had spearheaded the attack in revenge for OCCI's insinuations about Suzanne.

Insults and recriminations flew through cyberspace. Wingo labeled Halleck a strange duck, a nasty old woman full of drama and harassment. Wingo was incensed when Halleck allegedly e-mailed Kristy Gault: "Tell abcman [Wingo's screen name] he is history."

Ironically, Halleck and Wingo were both mavericks who supported web sleuths' "right" to directly contact law enforcement. They both were deeply immersed in their separate quests to identify the nameless. Their mutual animosity stemmed more from a clash of cultures (Wingo once taunted, "Resurrect your 1960s civil rights heroes and go live in San Francisco, or Kenya. You are an absolute waste of time and bandwidth." Halleck came from a family of liberals — her mother was a Democrat New Jersey councilwoman and self-described community activist) than any fundamental differences in their dedication to the cause.

Buried within Porchlight, in a section labeled "off topic" accessible only to herself, Halleck maintained a selection of the vitriolic barbs Wingo and others had aimed at her between 2007 and 2009. The accusations range from the unfathomable — questioning whether Halleck was present at a murder — to the farcical — someone took her to task for pocketing money from the sale of her painted glass instead of donating it to a missing-person group.

There was an element within the web sleuthing subculture that was all about power and control. Some individuals created mother lodes of information and then lorded it over anyone who came along to mine them. Others incited dissension, then peeked from behind a veil of anonymity at freak shows of their own creation. When emotional or physical limitations prevented some from navigating the real world, they seemed to delight in igniting online dramas and watching them blow up.

After the "luvmycat" hack, Gault banned Halleck from Cold Case Investigations. If Halleck showed up on the site, Gault wrote, she would prosecute Halleck for trespassing. (Exactly how that charge would play out is hard to picture.) "I just try to keep a sense of humor," Halleck told me, but it seemed that Halleck, eccentric and stubborn, had a bring-it-on attitude that didn't square with her self-proclaimed innocence and grandmotherly appearance. She never admitted to me that she could give as good as she got, but her online exchanges proved her as feisty as the Jack Russell terrier and the Chihuahua in her kitchen.

In 2007, Ellen Leach was still energized from her successful identification of Greg May, the murder victim whose head had been encased in a bucket of concrete. The coldest of cold cases still called to her. One such case was that of Jean Marie Stewart.

Halleck recalled that in 1980 the Florida police believed Jean Marie had run away, although that never made much sense to the family. Why wouldn't she have taken her money with her?

Two years would go by before law enforcement changed her status to "endangered."

At various times, there was incremental movement on the case. Pittsburgh police sent Stewart's dental records to Florida authorities. Halleck told me that *True Detective* magazine featured a NCMEC projection of what the curly-haired teen might look like as an adult. A Florida volunteer who sought to raise awareness about missing children succeeded in spurring Miami-Dade to reopen the case in 2004. Around the same time, as part of a routine look at cold cases, the Florida Department of Law Enforcement asked Miami-Dade police to track down Jean Marie's parents and obtain DNA samples.

Twenty-seven years after Stewart went missing, Ellen Leach spotted a posting on the Doe Network about unidentified remains that had been located years earlier in Florida. Digging deeper, she pored over a report that had surfaced on the Florida Unidentified Decedents Database, known as FLUIDDB.com. Created in 2002, the site followed closely on the heels of coroner Mike Murphy's Las Vegas Unidentified, but it was taking years for the Florida medical examiner to populate it with the department's backlog of cases.

Case number 1981-01253 described the

unidentified remains of a young woman found April 20, 1981, in a remote field in Hialeah. No reconstruction provided a face for the skeleton. Many web sleuths relied on such images, but Ellen had other tactics. When I had met her in Gulfport, Ellen told me, "I go by distance a lot of times. Distance is your key, believe it or not. The closer they are from where they went missing, the more likely it's them." Ellen checked a map. The field off West Twenty-Eighth Avenue in Hialeah was around five miles from where Jean Marie Stewart was last seen in Miami Lakes. Then Ellen noted that the remains, like the missing teen, had an overbite.

Ellen posted on Porchlight on November sixteenth that she had sent faxes to detectives in Dade County and Hialeah indicating her belief that the Hialeah remains belonged to Jean Marie Stewart.

Only forty-five minutes after Ellen's faxes went through, she received a phone call from a Detective Robert, who told Ellen she had been unaware of the remains and was excited about Leach's proposed match. She said she'd let Ellen know if they found out anything.

Robert did find something: Jean Marie's dental records. She sent them along to the Miami–Dade County medical examiner for comparison with the Hialeah remains. Two weeks later, on December 5, 2007, Jean Marie Stewart was positively identified.

Accolades and congratulations from fellow web sleuths immediately poured in. One posted, "Good catch, Ell . . . again :)"

In 2008, Jean Marie was buried in Pennsylvania. The *Pittsburgh Post-Gazette* tracked down Jean Marie's parents, both in their seventies. Her mother had always suspected that something horrific had happened to her daughter. Robert Stewart was glad to finally know where Jean Marie was. Jean Marie's brother held out the hope that his sister's killer would be caught and brought to justice.

A Pittsburgh TV station reported that her death had been ruled a homicide and her former boyfriend, David Nolle, was considered a suspect. A newspaper article said Jean Marie's father had learned from Nolle's mother that on the night Jean Marie disappeared, Nolle and Jean Marie had argued, and she ran out of the car when he stopped to buy cigarettes. Jean Marie's father had heard that the relationship between the two had soured; during a phone call the day she disappeared, Robert Stewart later relayed to a reporter, David Nolle had made it clear he wanted Jean Marie to move back to Pittsburgh.

Other reports referred to a gunshot wound. Dinorah Perry, the missing-person advocate who claimed to have helped keep Jean Marie's case active, told a reporter that the teen's family received a "box of bones" with a "bullet in the skull."

The Florida police never explained why it took twenty-seven years to identify the body.

After working what he claimed were hundreds of homicides, Matt Wingo said he, like other veteran investigators, had developed a feel — a sixth sense — for perpetrators and the circumstances of crimes. He was curious about Stewart's murder and wondered about Halleck's radio silence after the discovery of Jean as a homicide victim. Where were the outraged posts about the insipid investigation, the impassioned call for the killer's capture? He never got an answer, but, like others, he aired his suspicions publicly and, at times, vindictively.

Halleck told me her brother had been cleared as a suspect and suggested that Jean Marie was a victim of "Beauty Queen Killer" Christopher Wilder. In the 1970s and '80s, Wilder was living in Boynton Beach, not far from Miami Lakes. Wilder's eight known victims were killed in Florida in early 1984. His suspected victims included young women whose remains were found around Florida in areas he was known to frequent. His modus operandi was to lure young women, sometimes from shopping centers and parking lots, into his truck on the pretense of photographing them for a modeling contract. Wilder killed himself during a scuffle with police in 1984, and his ties to other possible victims disappeared with him.

When I met Halleck five years after she had learned Jean Marie's fate, she still seemed to grieve. She felt she owed Ellen Leach an enormous debt of gratitude for revealing that Jean Marie was, as she put it, at peace. As we sat together, tears welled in Halleck's eyes and spilled down her wizened apple cheeks. It wasn't lost on Halleck that Ellen's identification of Jean Marie was Porchlight's first official solve. Halleck had founded Porchlight in Jean's honor and she intended to work on it as long as her failing health allowed, she vowed, so that Jean's life, although tragically short, would continue to make a difference to others. Halleck looked beaten and tired that day, an old woman who'd faced perhaps more than her share of struggles. She looked like a soft touch for a misfit mastiff, a lame pony, a doomed kitten — or a wayward teen who'd ended up dead in a field.

# 14
# THE OLDEST UNSOLVED CASE IN MASSACHUSETTS

In Quincy, Massachusetts, in 2012, Bobby Lingoes, retired from web sleuthing, was counting down the months — around forty-eight — before he could retire with a pension from his job as a dispatcher. He fielded 911 calls most nights at the Quincy police station, played his sax during the day, and spent time with his wife, Debbie, a blond bartender with a quick smile, and their black-and-white Kitty Cat, so cute he needed two names. ("I stole that joke off of George Carlin," Bobby admitted.)

After thirty-plus tumultuous years in the projects, the horror of his nephew's murder, and his sister's premature demise, Bobby finally seemed to have found peace of mind.

I thought his respite from delving into death through the Internet well deserved. Bobby was one of the Doe Network's first and most successful web sleuths, as well as a former regional area administrator for the organization. I got it when Bobby told me he was burned-out on unidentified bodies. But I needed him to come out of retirement.

I reached Bobby close to midnight, just as he arrived for his shift. He sounded only mildly surprised by my request: Would he help me search for the Lady of the Dunes's identity?

I didn't remind him that the case was thirty-eight years old and there had never been a match found for the victim's DNA or for her elaborate dental work. I didn't point out that no one had ever found her severed hands, or recognized her enigmatic, manufactured smile. Like many web sleuths, he was easy to entice. "I'm sure it can be done," he rasped, sounding as street-tough Boston as I remembered. I figured he meant he was sure we could look; surely he couldn't be foolish enough to think we had any chance of success.

Bobby said he'd have to clear my visit with the Quincy top brass again, but sure, I could come in to the station. Did I want to meet him at the beginning of his all-night shift or closer to the end, near dawn? I chose six a.m. I figured there wouldn't be much traffic.

■ ■ ■ ■

In the months following the murder in 1974, media coverage of the Lady of the Dunes exploded. The *Provincetown Banner,* the *Cape Cod Times, The Boston Globe,* and the *Boston Herald* ran story after story. These dwindled over time to an annual wrap-up written by reporters who hadn't been born when the Lady of the Dunes died.

Like other cold cases, hers would be reincarnated on the Web. In 2005 the first posts about the Lady of the Dunes started popping up.

On Websleuths — the same board that featured the thread about missing California teen Liz Ernstein, who for a time was thought to be Tent Girl — Richard, mysteriew, upallnite, PonderingThings, and maima speculated about the Provincetown murder.

"What I find most intriguing is the removal of the hands. Conventional thought is that was done to 'conceal the identity of the victim,' but to what end? Most likely that translates into concealing the identity of the murderer since he/she is most likely to be a friend or family member," one user wrote.

Onetime Provincetown resident Andy Towle posted on his blog an early sketch, more crudely drawn than later versions, of the wide-eyed, ponytailed victim. Towle noted that a rookie on the Provincetown police force once described P-town as wild in the 1970s. "Lots of drugs, lots of bikers."

The web sleuths, picking up on that comment, focused on a woman missing from Florida since March 1974 who was last seen riding off on the back of a motorcycle. "I took a look at Amy Billig's picture and that is an uncanny resemblance," mysteriew agreed.

Others suggested the Lady of the Dunes could be a British woman, Elizabeth Swann, who was last seen in the UK in early 1974.

Some marked the thirty-seventh anniversary of the day the girl — who would now be in her fifties — and her dog found the corpse. There had been more than seven thousand murders in Massachusetts since 1974, but being the oldest unsolved case gave the Lady of the Dunes notoriety. The fact that she was unidentified fueled people's imaginations. A web sleuth named Shecky wrote, "This is a Jane Doe case that has always haunted me."

■ ■ ■ ■

Over the years, Provincetown investigators chased down lead after lead. Chief Jimmy Meads checked with contacts in Rhode Island to see if the murder might have been a mob hit. In Providence, he quizzed prostitutes about whether they knew her. Authorities contacted every dentist in Massachusetts and published photos of her crowns in two dental journals. Investigators enlisted the help of Interpol.

Reporters interviewed Meads about the case so many times, fellow cops ribbed him that he got more publicity out of an unsolved murder than others did from apprehending suspects. When TV news crews traveled to P-town to gather footage of the spot where she was found deep in the dunes, a beleaguered Meads started escorting them to a more accessible pine grove. "This is it," he told Dan Rather, among others, but apparently none of the reporters suspected they weren't viewing the real crime scene.

Meads kept scouring the case files to see if he had missed anything. The notion that an important, unseen clue lurked in that massive heap of paperwork haunted him. If the case were ever solved, he swore, he'd dig back through all the files and if the clue had been there all the time, he'd cry from sheer frustration.

One of the most promising leads involved a young woman named Rory Gene Kesinger. A runaway at fifteen, she robbed banks under five aliases. In 1974, at age twenty-five, Kesinger attempted to shoot a police officer during a drug bust. She escaped from jail and was never heard from again. The body on the dunes, between five-six and five-eight, matched Kesinger's height. She looked like the sketches. Meads and the Provincetown sergeant who took over the investigation were sure for a time that Kesinger was their victim, but a DNA sample from the body did not match a sample taken from Kesinger's mother.

Serial killer Hadden Clark told Alec Wilkinson, a journalist and onetime Wellfleet police officer, that he was vacationing on Cape Cod in 1974 at his grandfather's place in Wellfleet and came across a beautiful girl that he lured into the dunes and smacked on the head with a surf-casting pole. After she was dead, he removed her clothes, folded them neatly, and put them under her body.

He claimed he then went back to his truck

for a saw, cut off her hands, and stuffed her arms into the sand as if she were doing push-ups. "Then I took her hands and put them in her purse, like a beach bag. I cut off a couple of her fingers and used them for fishing bait. I buried her hands in a different place. I didn't bury her because I was making a statement. I don't know why I was doing it; maybe if you were a trained psychologist you could tell me." But Clark could have read the details about the folded clothing and the severed hands in the newspaper, and his confessions to other murders hadn't panned out.

The body was exhumed in 1980, in 2000, and again, in cloak-and-dagger style, on May 6, 2013. I had spent that morning talking to locals and then drove down Winslow Street, planning to seek out the small granite marker carved with the words "Unidentified Female Body Found Race Point Dunes."

The cemetery was not as deserted as I had anticipated.

"You're okay on the road. You can't get any closer," a Provincetown cop said as he waved me off the grounds to the far side of yellow crime scene tape. Across a stretch of lawn, Department of Public Works employees clad in T-shirts, white face masks, and stretchy blue gloves leaned on shovels. A Provincetown cruiser blocked a narrow paved path leading to the site at the bottom of a bluff where a row of headstones were lined up below a small, gray-shingled chapel bearing a simple verdigris cross. The sky was a brilliant blue; it was a picture-perfect, bucolic New England scene, except for the coffin-sized hole in the ground.

A woman in street clothes and purple latex gloves handed, like a surgeon's assistant, a vial and other items to a tall, solid figure in a hooded blue paper suit. The blue-suited figure climbed out of the hole and deposited things I couldn't make out into the purple-gloved lady's clear plastic bins, which were about the type and size you'd use to stow a pair of shoes or carry cupcakes. They were apparently collecting fragments of the Lady of the Dunes's weathered bones.

At the grave, a white pickup and a blue sedan blocked the view from where I sat on the grass, around the length of a soccer field from the action. Leaning against a cement post that had long since lost its wooden struts, I clicked away on my laptop, aware I was the sole uninvited spectator to a bit of local history. In 2000, TV cameras and reporters had thronged the site where I now sat. Except for the occasional rumble of a car on the street behind me and the squawk of the cops' walkie-talkies, it was a quiet day at the St. Peter the Apostle cemetery. The silence and relative calm didn't jibe with the urgency of the situation; I realized this exhumation might be investigators' last remaining maneuver to gain some traction on a case that had managed to slip away from so many.

NCMEC, based in Alexandria, Virginia, staffed with retired police officers and FBI agents, doesn't normally investigate cases in which the victim is older than twenty-one, but in 2010, Provincetown police chief Jeff Jaran convinced the organization to try. Using a three-dimensional CAT scan of the victim's skull, long perched on former Provincetown police chief Jimmy Meads's desk and then moved to the state medical examiner's office in Boston, Smithsonian Institution anthropologists worked with NCMEC to create a computer rendition of what the young woman would have looked like at the time of her death. It was those images, in *The Boston Globe,* that had induced me to go on the Web the day I first came across the Doe Network.

Around a year and a half after I had sat with Jimmy Meads at a maple dining table in his wood-paneled dining room with its brick fireplace, the dim, cool room soaking up the day's bright sunlight, talking about the case that had consumed him for most of his professional life, Meads died suddenly on Christmas 2011, surrounded by his family. After thirty-two years with the Provincetown police, ten as a cop and twenty-two as chief, he had never stopped hoping that the Lady of the Dunes would be identified in his lifetime. Now his successors had taken over his pet case, and they seemed to be starting from scratch.

At the Lady of the Dunes's gravesite, the purple-gloved lady tucked the plastic bins into a canvas tote and spirited them away. Blue Suit dropped a black trash bag into the sedan's open trunk, shed the gloves, and peeled back the suit to reveal a sweatshirt stretched over a chest bump and khakis with a holster strapped across the hip. She — I could see now that Blue Suit was a she — had short, wavy salt-and-pepper hair and a police officer's splayfooted strut. Donning a vest and sunglasses to complete the *Cool Hand Luke* look, she tossed a clipboard inside the car and climbed into the driver's seat. Uniformed cops slid in and slammed the doors. Three of the men in the face masks started hoisting shovelfuls of grass-

412

studded dirt into the hole. One blew away excess earth with a leaf blower and another neatened up with a broom; within minutes, nothing indicated that a grave had ever been gaping open at their feet.

The cruisers and other cars — I figured those belonged to the purple-gloved lady and state medical examiner's staff — pulled out in single file like a funeral procession, leaving the yellow police tape fluttering in the breeze. I, too, got in my car and wound my way through Provincetown's narrow streets, past the granite Pilgrim Monument tower, Commercial Street's touristy shops, and the entrance to Race Point Beach, where the victim had been discovered all those years ago. I had just pulled onto Route 6, flanked by the windswept dunes, and was settling in for the two-hour drive back to Boston when an unfamiliar number with a local area code popped up on my car's Bluetooth phone display. I tapped the "yes" button.

A voice, low and gruff but decidedly female, growled, "If I'd known you were going to show up, I would have brought you snacks."

I drove, speechless, staring stupidly at the phone number. I didn't recognize the voice. The caller apparently felt she needed no introduction. Then it clicked: the famed Detective Meredith Lobur, voice of the Provincetown police on all things Lady of the Dunes. I'd been following her comments to the media with interest: "The official cause of death was listed at the time in 1974 as blunt-force trauma to the head with signs of strangulation, sexual assault, and amputation of both hands," she'd told reporters in March 2012. I hadn't heard anything about a sexual assault before. And she mentioned photographs of an estimated size-10 footprint in the sand "that belonged to someone heavy and running." Could that be related to park ranger Jim Hankins's mysterious sand imprints?

My caller was the one-and-same Detective Lobur who'd blown me off for the past eight months every time I'd sought an interview with the chief. She must have been the Blue Suit conducting the exhumation. Of course, the diligent detective wouldn't entrust the Lady of the Dunes's precious remains — what was left of them after two previous exhumations — to anyone else.

And now she'd dialed my cell, not bothering to ask for me by name. She clearly knew who I was. But we'd never met. How did she recognize me, slouched minutes ago on the damp grass in jeans, Chuck Taylors, and a black jacket, laptop propped on my knees, as the writer who'd e-mailed and called all those times? Then I remembered the blue sedan, its occupants' faces masked by tinted windows, pulling away from the grave, creeping out onto the street past my car parked directly behind the fence post I was using as a backrest. Creeping slowly enough to scrawl down a license plate number.

"I wasn't sure I'd be there myself," I said finally.

"How long were you camped out there — days?"

"Not that long."

"Okay. You were tipped off."

I didn't bother to set her straight. "So what next?"

"How much do you know?" she demanded in turn. She sounded angry. "Are you going to write about it?" Then the classic police-to-media gripe: "You could compromise the investigation."

I couldn't promise anything, I said vaguely. I had wanted to go over the history of the case, I told her, talk to Chief Jaran and former acting chief Warren Tobias, who'd headed the investigation as staff sergeant after Jimmy Meads retired. I knew about the DNA test that had been done in

2001. I'd heard tales about the office of the Boston medical examiner — tales of incompetence, lost evidence, botched autopsies. In any case, I asked Lobur, why would news of the latest exhumation compromise the investigation? And why should I keep quiet about it? After all — what with the hazmat suits and the gravediggers and the patrol cars and the police tape — anyone who'd happened by the cemetery where the Lady of the Dunes was interred could have figured out what was going on.

"We were doing this on the QT," she sighed. (Were we in a Raymond Chandler novel?) "That's why I wasn't responding. I'd hoped to have something to tell you." So I was supposed to wait patiently and obediently until they decided to return my calls, or until they procured a new DNA profile, maybe even an ID, for the most notorious cold case in Massachusetts history? Now I was getting mad. Was it even legal to run a law-abiding citizen's plates without probable cause? And I was dubious about her proposed deal. "I'm not going to be the first person to find out what you learn," I shot back.

No, the detective admitted. But she hoped to have some news in a few weeks.

Six months later, I still hadn't heard from her.

Bobby ushered me to the station's communications center, an open room lined with workstations, three TV screens mounted on the ceiling, a table holding soda bottles and condiments, and a few potted plants. Bobby's desktop was crowded with monitors. Amid boxy hard drives on the floor, a foot pedal controlled a microphone through which Bobby spoke to the officers on patrol.

On an ancient Dell monitor, Bobby pointed out the locations of units 777, 778, and 784 among the twenty or so patrol cars at that moment cruising Quincy's streets. Bobby showed me his nifty devices: a direct phone line to every police department in the state, a teletype through which the deaf could type Bobby a message and he could choose an automated response: "Do not hang up" or "Help is on the way."

I asked him if, in his web sleuthing days, he would have considered adopting the Lady of the Dunes.

He would have, he said quickly, if it had ever crossed his radar. (He wasn't sure why it hadn't.) It was local, and it was perplexing that she hadn't been identified after all these years. "It would be a challenge, you know."

Bobby pulled up on one of his screens the home page of the Doe Network, where the Lady of the Dunes was case file 119UFMA.

If Bobby chose to adopt the case, he said that he'd study it, memorize every detail. Height, weight, hair color. "And this, see this? She's got very expensive 'New York–style' dental work. That gives you a little hint. Maybe she's from the New York area."

He pointed to a photo on the screen. It was the image I remembered from *The Boston Globe.* I was struck all over again by the knowing look in her eyes, the neatly swept-back hair, the Mona Lisa smile.

"See this NCIC number?" Bobby said, pronouncing it "nick." He grabbed a pen and scratched out U-615805149 on a scrap of paper, muttering each digit under his breath. Bobby led me to one of the other workstations and plopped onto a rolling desk chair. Here was where his special access gave him an advantage over the civilian community: Unlike your average web sleuth, he could enter a query into the national crime database. He typed the Lady of the Dunes's case number and hit a key. The teletype sputtered to life, jittering out an incomprehensible string of uppercase letters and numbers onto blank sheets from a perforated stack.

Running one finger over the text, he translated: "It says it's an unidentified person, entered by the Provincetown police department." He pointed to a row of *R*'s interspersed with two *N*'s, like something a child playing on a keyboard would produce. "These signify body parts. See, this is strange. They got an *N* next to hands, meaning they were not recovered. Everything else is recovered.

"Estimated year of birth — they're narrowing it down to 1939 to 1949. Estimated date of death — they're listing that as July 12, 1974, a couple of weeks before the body was found. Obviously, they didn't find the hands, so they didn't have fingerprints." He peered at the sheet. "You know, not a lot of people got red hair; that could cut it down."

He rattled off the rest: eye color could not be determined; eyes and ears may have been removed; extensive gold dental work.

Back online on the Doe Network site, Bobby clicked through to the "missing" side and chose "female" and "Massachusetts" from a drop-down menu. Around a dozen names appeared. Next to each was the date each individual was last seen. I scanned the dates over Bobby's shoulder. There was one woman from 1974. Even though that was the year we were searching for, I was taken aback that we had come across another woman who had been missing for as long as the Lady of the Dunes had been dead. I thought about her family, waiting and wondering, maybe even hoping. Or perhaps whoever had reported her missing had given up or was no longer alive. For each person listed — Bobby moved on to another screen full of names — there was a story, almost guaranteed to be a sad one. It was a lot of sorrow and regret for one computer screen to contain.

"Right here, this girl here, she went missing in August," Bobby was saying. The body in Provincetown was found in July. Not a possible match. Bobby clicked through to the next page. More names, more stories we didn't know and didn't have time to investigate.

Bobby hunted and pecked the letters of "gold dental" into the page's search box. The Lady of the Dunes's gold and porcelain crowns, root canals, and gum treatments would have cost ten thousand dollars, the equivalent of tens of thousands today. Even the Tufts University forensic dentist who analyzed her teeth soon after she was found declared her rather fastidious, commenting that most people wouldn't go to that much trouble about their teeth.

Bobby predicted our search terms would generate all manner of gold-related clues, not only those related to teeth, and he was right: one missing woman was wearing a gold chain necklace when she disappeared. Another woman had a gold key chain holding fifteen keys.

Sitting side by side, our heads almost touching, we scanned the pages for "gold" and "dental," which showed up in bold within the list of cases. We eliminated name after name. I thought I was getting faster but Bobby had me beat, whipping through page after page like a speed demon. We read for a while in silence, Bobby clicking the right-pointing arrow as he reached the bottom of each page.

Persistence, patience, and attention to detail might seem like basic requirements for web sleuthing, but I had never fully absorbed the extent to which that was true. Bobby had more patience than I did. "We got this New York clue," he said after a time, referring to the note in the case file about her dental work being "New York–style." He suggested that if we struck out with women reported missing from Massachusetts, we could start looking at those from New York.

I had known that web sleuths faced a Herculean task. But at that moment, seeing all those faces struck me in a visceral way. There were so many missing people, so many unidentified bodies. And so few of us trying to connect the dots.

If all this wasn't daunting enough, we were on page eleven of twenty. My eyes started to glaze over. I couldn't tell which details might be pertinent; I no longer trusted my judgment, or whether I would recognize a possible match if I saw one. I remembered how much I used to identify with Agatha Christie's clueless Hastings instead of with Poirot. I took a deep breath. Bobby noticed my flagging attention. "You just got to keep looking," he urged. "It's a process of elimination. It's tedious, you know."

I couldn't say I was sorry when Bobby's shift was over. We took a grimy elevator back down to the station's cinder-block lobby, walked past a bulletproof-glass-enclosed front desk and bulletin boards plastered with mug shots of Class 3 sex offenders. The world outside was just coming to life. People filtered out onto the sidewalks holding Dunkin' Donuts cups, dressed for work. It was the start of a sunny late-spring day.

In my car, I tailed Bobby's Chevy Blazer with the two Red Sox bumper stickers to the clapboard rooming house where he lived nearby. Satellite dishes sprouted from the side of the triple-decker like toadstools on a tree trunk. Bobby inserted a key and wrapped both hands around the doorknob, wrestling with the sticky lock until it gave way. The place wasn't the Taj Mahal, Bobby had warned me.

I followed him inside, tugging the door closed behind me, and started climbing. It was so dark, I felt my way up the narrow, green-carpeted staircase. We emerged on a landing that could have used a fresh coat of paint, and there was a musty odor, but the communal kitchen was orderly, with utilitarian white-painted cabinets and bare counters. We continued down a hallway past identical plywood doors; Bobby opened one. The room on the other side held a double bed, a small desk and computer, a saxophone and clarinet propped on stands under a window, and an electric keyboard. He pointed to faded photos in dime-store frames on the wall over the desk. "My favorite singer, Billie Holiday," Bobby said. "Stan Getz. My parents. Me, from when I was a boxer."

The other boarders didn't mind his practicing, he said, as long as he didn't wake the cabdriver who worked nights and weekends.

Debbie, who joined us, said Bobby drew crowds when he played jazz on the porch of the clapboard house where she kept a room next door. I pictured him standing out there, coaxing moody notes from his sax for an impromptu concert, the audience leaning on the parked cars in the asphalt lot. Debbie said she was a country and western fan herself.

Back in the police station, I'd had to concede that Bobby and I were not about to achieve fame and fortune by solving the mystery of the Lady of the Dunes. I was ready to leave the case in the hands of law enforcement; in fact, in May 2012, Provincetown detective Lobur had told me she and Chief Jaran were working on a promising lead. I had a good idea what she was referring to.

A few months earlier, I was driving my teenage daughter, a figure skater, to the local rink for predawn ice time. I reached to turn down the radio that she had set to brainjarring rap when I caught a theatrically urgent voice saying something about New England's most infamous cold case. News at eleven.

What were the odds that the Lady of the Dunes, which had produced no news in

decades, would suddenly resurface?

At home that night, perched on the edge of the couch, I turned on the TV news and sat through coverage of fires, accidents, weather. Finally, the male voice-over breathed, ". . . a murder so gruesome . . . the woman has never been identified." "Nameless grave" and "thirty-eight years later" scrolled down the screen in designed-to-look-creepy letters. Something, again, about a footprint in the sand. Finally, her image appeared on the screen, the auburn ponytail and soulful eyes of the latest digital reconstruction. The reporter said notorious South Boston mobster James "Whitey" Bulger had been seen in Provincetown in the 1970s. With him was a woman who looked like the Lady of the Dunes.

Now, in his rooming house, sitting at his computer, Bobby leaned toward me confidentially. "Did you read" — he glanced around, his throaty voice low — "that she" — Bobby meant the Lady of the Dunes — "could be involved with Whitey Bulger? They say he was seen with a girl that looked just like her down in P-town. There could be something to that."

Bulger, the eighty-two-year-old former Boston mob boss and FBI informant, was arrested in California in 2011 after sixteen years on the lam. In spring 2012, as Bobby and I talked, Bulger was awaiting trial, charged with participating in nineteen murders. He was in jail, but his fabled history and reputation as one of the nation's most wanted fugitives was very much intact. Bulger, though usually associated with South Boston, and his girlfriend, Catherine Greig, had lived in Quincy for a time in the 1980s, sharing a condo around three miles from Bobby's rooming house.

And now Bulger's name had surfaced in connection with the Lady of the Dunes. It was, investigators thought, a killing eerily similar to those Bulger and his associates were accused of carrying out.

"Did you hear that?" Bobby asked Debbie, four gold hoops rimming the edge of her right ear. "She could have been another one of his victims."

"Who's to say?" She shrugged. "If he was involved, a witness might not want to come forward. They may think they'll end up the same way. It's never all come out, never ever." ("Nevah evah," in Debbie's Boston accent.)

Bobby said even in retirement he searched NCIC reports for any potential matches for that unidentified skeleton found decades ago in the Quincy woods — the case that had launched his web sleuthing career. That victim had been killed with a blow to the head and buried in a shallow grave. For all we knew, that John Doe could have been one of Bulger's victims, too, Bobby said. "Bulger still has his connections," Debbie insisted. "His people are still his people."

Even though Bulger had been named in connection with the Lady of the Dunes murder on the most public forum imaginable — the TV news — the topic clearly made Bobby nervous. Was he picturing some Bulger cohort coming after him — and after me? A law-abiding citizen worrying about becoming a possible mob target might strike some as melodramatic. Nevertheless, we were in Boston, the setting for *The Departed, The Fighter, Mystic River.* I wondered if Bobby's concerns were legit. I contacted Thomas J. Foley, a retired Massachusetts state police colonel who had investigated and helped convict a half dozen of Boston's most notorious thugs in the course of his decades-long career.

As Foley related in his 2012 book, *Most Wanted: Pursuing Whitey Bulger, the Murderous Mob Chief the FBI Secretly Protected,* it was word of Foley's investigation and imminent indictments of Bulger and others that spurred Bulger to flee Boston in the first place. In 1995, Foley led a team of investigators that uncovered the bodies of three of Bulger's alleged nineteen victims in shallow graves along the muddy banks of the sewage-fouled Neponset River, not far from where Bobby and I were sitting.

Former state police colonel Tom Foley turned out to be not as comforting as I'd hoped. "I would be hesitant to tell anyone they have nothing to worry about," Foley told me. Then he added, somewhat reassuringly, "Though I would say Bulger's influence is extremely diminished or nonexistent in this area." (As it turned out, Bulger's 2013 trial — in which a federal jury tied him to eleven murders and found him guilty of extortion, money laundering, drug dealing, and weapons possession — included many spine-chilling accounts of cold-blooded killings but no documented mention of the Lady of the Dunes.)

It was a testament to Boston's reputation as onetime home base for the Irish Mafia that even though Bobby Lingoes spent every working day surrounded by police officers — or maybe because he spent every day surrounded by police officers — he didn't think it wise to speculate publicly about a mobster and a victim, even though the mobster was geriatric and the victim had been nameless for almost four decades. I'd seen the movies, but Bobby lived the reality. I looked over at him slumped in his desk chair, arms crossed over his black Hawaiian shirt, his squinty eyes narrowed as he contemplated what might happen if the wrong person got wind of our conversation. "They're gonna find me dead," Bobby chuckled a tad nervously. "They'll find me in the Neponset River."

# 15
## RELIEF, SADNESS, SUCCESS

In May 2011, Todd Matthews had a conference to attend in Hot Springs, Arkansas; I tagged along to meet Bobbie Ann Hackmann's youngest sister, Rosemary Westbrook.

Todd and I arrived on separate flights and rented a car at the airport. We drove sixty miles from Little Rock to Hot Springs, which I envisioned as a quaint resort town. The hotel website promised a "spa in the park" and a view of the Ouachita Mountains.

The hotel turned out to be an enormous concrete-walled complex with a creaking elevator whose doors didn't close all the way. The lobby was painted an institutional peach and decorated with faux-wood chairs and couches upholstered in garish metallic fabrics. An enormous framed photo of a former Miss Arkansas hung behind the reception desk.

I was given a key to a room that contained a cigarette smoke-infused bed with scratchy sheets, a white plastic lawn chair, threadbare towels, peeling wallpaper, a single wall outlet, and carpet stains whose origins I couldn't identify. The "spa in the park," sporting a neon "Open" sign, turned out to be a fluorescent-lit row of fiberglass bathtubs.

After working up a sweat wheeling a heavy display booth to the convention hall in the next building, Todd returned looking a little ashen. He'd heard that a conference attendee never showed up for breakfast that morning. She'd been found dead in her room. Most likely a natural death, we told ourselves, but jarring nonetheless. I wasn't finding Todd's workday as cushy as some imagined.

After Todd deposited the NamUs booth in preparation for the next day's conference, we circled back to Benton, the quintessential Southern small town that served as the setting for Billy Bob Thornton's *Sling Blade.* It was the kind of place that once would have made me apprehensive in a "what-lies-beneath" kind of way.

Rosemary and Putt lived in a tidy ranchstyle house among others just like it. The neighborhood's generous lawns were studded with birdhouses and American flags on poles. RVs, horse trailers, and pickups sat in driveways. White aluminum siding covered the Westbrooks' house; an overhang shaded the striped porch swing and tinkling wind chimes. We pulled up behind an SUV. The car doors had barely slammed before Rosemary, petite and youthful-looking at fifty-four, with a silver-gray pixie cut, appeared in the driveway and wrapped her arms around Todd. I hung back as they embraced and made little happy noises.

Todd and I sat in the Westbrooks' living room next to a massive saltwater aquarium where brightly colored fish darted around stalks of coral. Rosemary pulled out a collection of photos and documents she called "the Bobbie book" and told me about meeting Todd and Lori in that emotional time just as it was dawning on Barbara Ann Hackmann's sisters that the young woman had likely been murdered — a fate none of them imagined for her when they were growing up.

In the middle of that January night in 1998, elated, anxious, and scared, Todd fired off an e-mail with "Missing sister" as the subject line. Exhausted and energized, he couldn't sleep, but even that felt different

from all the other insomniac nights. The nagging sense of guilt was gone. By the light of day, the previous night's exhilaration had turned to doubt.

He'd had harsh encounters in the past decade with people who had made it clear he and his opinions didn't matter. Sometimes the cops, sheriffs, and politicians he'd reached out to didn't bother to hide their impatience. They clearly thought he was crazy, or stupid. The case was too cold, too far removed from what they imagined as a Tennessee hillbilly's more likely passions: a night in a bar, working on his truck, a football game on TV.

Todd was a factory worker, a cog like one of the metal parts he used to pluck off the plant's assembly line. If he knew then what he knows now, he would have been even more anxious than he actually was, he told me on the phone, reliving that day in January for maybe the fiftieth time. He had had no idea how much of his future was riding on the accuracy of his hunch.

At the time, it took his eleven dollars an hour and every penny of Lori's income to cover the mortgage on the trailer, the family's food and credit card bills, dog and cat treats, car payments, and Dillan's *Star Wars* figures; but, post–Tent Girl, almost every facet of his life would change. "We wouldn't be here" — I could picture Todd waving a hand around the two-story brick house he and Lori built, with a designer kitchen; walls painted in shades of pumpkin, spice, and sage; French doors; a cathedral-ceilinged living room with a leather couch — "if not for Tent Girl."

At the time, he knew only that he had set something exciting — and terrifying — in motion.

Todd wanted to get on the phone with Rosemary and blurt, "Your sister isn't missing. She's an urban legend in Georgetown, Kentucky." He thought better of it. She might not believe there really was a Tent Girl, that it wasn't some story he had concocted. It suddenly seemed utterly impossible, even to him, that Rosemary Westbrook's sister was buried under a tombstone with a cop's pencil sketch engraved on it.

Todd's original e-mail — "Please contact me as soon as possible. We need to compare some info" — bounced. He sent it to another address, hoping it would be forwarded. When Rosemary finally responded, he gushed, "I was afraid I was never going to find you.

"I hope for your sake that the woman I

know of is not your sister . . . I feel myself hoping that I have found the identity of the Tent Girl, but at the same time I share your prayer that your sister is still alive. I have done a lot of research on the Tent Girl so I think together we can determine if she is your sister or not."

When Rosemary saw Todd's "Contact me" message, her first thought was that some joker, maybe a bogus private detective, was targeting her for some quick cash. She had heard all about Internet predators, she told me the day Todd and I visited her at home. "Oh, God, you scared the shit out of me." Rosemary turned to face Todd, sitting on the sofa. "I didn't know what to do, to be honest with you."

Looking back with more than a decade's worth of experience, Todd's horrified at his impulsiveness. He was operating on a hunch. What if he had been wrong? At the time, he didn't even know if DNA could be collected from thirty-year-old remains. If his claim about Bobbie Ann turned out to be impossible to prove, he would have sent a family into an emotional tailspin for no reason.

That realization would lead to the Doe Network's stringent rules prohibiting members from directly contacting families or law enforcement. Todd knows now that a potential match should be handled as cautiously as a stick of dynamite.

He did notice that Rosemary and her sisters, when he met them, seemed reserved and anxious. It puzzled him that they didn't seem to share his exhilaration. At the time, in his eagerness to nail down Tent Girl's identity, he didn't realize he was transforming a missing sister and mother into a murder victim — and a brother-in-law and father into a possible murderer.

Todd asked one of Lori's sisters who lived near Georgetown to make a phone call for him. The Riddle name still pulled weight in Scott County.

Bobby Hammons had long ago replaced Bobby Vance as sheriff. Jenny Riddle got through and Todd soon received a call back.

"So you think you know who this Tent Girl is?" Todd thought Hammons couldn't have sounded more condescending. It was happening all over again. Was Hammons going to hang up without hearing him out? Todd explained what he'd found on the Internet. It suddenly occurred to him that many equated the fledgling Internet with scams and hoaxes.

Lucky for Todd, Kentucky was the first state to hire a full-time forensic anthropologist: Emily Craig. She had, of course, heard the local legend of Tent Girl. During Craig's first days on the job, Scott County coroner Marvin Seay Yocum, who had donated Tent Girl's distinctive red tombstone in 1972, had approached her with a proposition.

Craig had once been an anatomical illustrator. Maybe she could do a new sketch to help the stalled investigation in the most baffling case in Kentucky's criminal history? Craig demurred; she felt the existing sketch created by the police artist in the 1960s — the one engraved on the gravestone — was accurate.

A few years later, Yocum reappeared in her office with Sheriff Hammons. They wanted her to look at a photograph.

In 2011, Emily Craig ushered me into her lakeside home not far from where Wilbur Riddle had come across Tent Girl. Sixtyish, with a stylish blond bob, Craig reminded me of Glenn Close in *Damages*. With her taste for tailored suits, you might easily take her for an attorney or a real estate broker instead of someone who routinely plunged her hands into corpses. After working as a medical illustrator, she sold her house to

437

pursue a PhD degree in forensic anthropology. She became the only full-time state forensic anthropologist in the country in Kentucky in 1994.

When she met Todd Matthews in 1998, neither Craig nor Todd knew where the Tent Girl case would lead. "He came out of central Tennessee like Sergeant York," she laughed, referring to a hillbilly who famously served in World War I. She thought Todd's innocence refreshing, but she was certain he had no idea what he was getting into by trying to identify Tent Girl. Neither, for that matter, did she.

Despite a bum knee, Craig seemed energetic and nimble enough, bustling around, preparing tea and cookies. We settled on comfy sofas in her tastefully decorated living room. It was all quite genteel. But to get an accurate reading of the challenges of identifying the unidentified, she told me, I needed to see the PowerPoint.

Every year, Craig gave the recruits at the Lexington, Kentucky, police academy a tutorial on how to properly collect corpses, or what's left of them after they've been out in the Kentucky woods for a while. "This is pretty disgusting," she said as she opened the computer in her study to an image of a body in such an advanced state of decomposition that I was hard-pressed to identify it as human. She used it as a stomach-churning example of why relying on a photo to identify remains wouldn't work. "That took ten days in May," she said. "Ten days."

Craig impressed upon me that the uninitiated often miss critical forensic clues: tiny bits of metal scattered on the forest floor could be staples from gallbladder surgery or orthopedic screws used to fix torn ligaments and shattered bones. She scolded the recruits who simply jumbled human bones into a body bag that gathering skeletal remains in the woods is a death investigation, not an Easter egg hunt.

In her opinion, physical descriptions of missing persons entered into law enforcement databases are largely useless. A missing woman's family members who always saw her in heels might have added two inches to her height. A mother called her daughter's hair strawberry blond and the investigator who found the body thought it was red. A father was unaware his son had a tattoo of a python on his lower back.

Ideas of what it means to look white, black, Native American, or Asian vary wildly and include misconceptions such as "Hispanic" being a race. "People don't understand we can't tell what languages dead people speak from their skeletons," Craig said. Forensic anthropologists also don't want to hear about eye color and hair color. They seek out dental records, descriptions of tattoos, old surgeries, bones that were once broken. "He had one great big nose" could be an enormously helpful clue.

Craig feels web sleuths should be encouraged, because, as she proved to me with the photo of the body that had been exposed to the elements for ten days in May, identifying the unidentified was really difficult — much too difficult to be left to software.

The web sleuths are essential, she says, because when it comes to identifying people, there will never be a computer as good as the one right between our ears.

Kentucky coroner Yocum and Sheriff Hammons showed up in Craig's office with a blurry, forty-year-old photograph Rosemary Westbrook had dug out of a family album. A Tennessee man, they told her, had come across a missing woman on the Internet. She might be a match for Tent Girl. What did Craig think?

Aspects of Barbara Ann Hackmann's life clearly matched up with the few facts investigators had gleaned about Tent Girl. Both women had slight builds and bobbed

hairstyles. Tent Girl had had an impeccable manicure; Bobbie Ann's sisters recalled that Bobbie Ann was vain and fastidious about her nails.

Now Craig looked from the sketch to the autopsy photos of Tent Girl's ruined, decomposing features to the picture of a pretty young woman with a small gap between her front teeth. She thought they just might be onto something. An exhumation was warranted. But, she pointed out, it was February of a very cold winter. The ground was frozen solid. Everyone was going to have to wait a few weeks longer.

By March 2, the weather broke long enough for a backhoe to exhume the grave. Craig herself climbed down into the hole with a trowel, sifting through the earth on her knees and handing up bones to a police deputy under a gray, sleeting sky.

In 1968, Tent Girl was said to be in her teens. Through scientific tools unavailable three decades earlier, Craig determined that Tent Girl was actually between twenty and thirty years old. Bobbie Ann was twenty-four when she disappeared. Tent Girl had had a white cloth draped on one shoulder. Bobbie Ann had recently given birth to baby Shelly.

Suddenly, all the media outlets that had

given Todd the cold shoulder about the unsolved Tent Girl case were knocking on his door. Todd and Lori took their first-ever plane trip, to appear on the Leeza Gibbons talk show in LA.

The producers at *48 Hours* reached Todd before *20/20,* so their cameras captured a hospital employee swabbing Rosemary for DNA in Arkansas. A sample of her blood and a bit of pulp from one of Tent Girl's teeth were sent to LabCorp in North Carolina, which tested for mitochondrial DNA — the same method the New York City medical examiner used to analyze the degraded DNA of 9/11 victims.

As she waited for the results, Rosemary paced a rut in the floor. She was torn about the exhumation. How did she dare disturb the dead, especially if it didn't turn out to be Bobbie? Oh, God, what had she done?

In the end, her father, levelheaded Charlie Rule, convinced her that even if the woman in that Kentucky grave wasn't her sister, she was somebody's sister. Rosemary would be opening a door for another family, providing an answer for somebody, somewhere. The answer might extinguish hope. But the wondering, the not knowing, was a torturous emotional roller coaster that Rosemary herself had lived with for decades. She knew she wouldn't wish that on anyone.

In late April 1998, Rosemary and Putt piled into the family's white van with Rule in the driver's seat for the nine-hour trip from Arkansas to Kentucky. Just before they left, Rosemary called Emily Craig one last time. "Do we need to turn this big ol' van around?" Craig hadn't divulged the results of the DNA test, but Rosemary figured she wouldn't let them make the trek from Arkansas for nothing. The Westbrooks, Shelly and Bonnie in Ohio, and Rosemary's sisters all had to take days off from work for the trip.

Craig told them to keep on driving.

Todd recalled that when he arrived at the courthouse, there were reporters everywhere, including the now-familiar faces of the *48 Hours* crew. While they set up, Craig drew aside a very nervous Todd. Afterward Todd stood quietly in the hallway, alone for what felt like the last time in his life. He walked inside the room at the Scott County courthouse where microphones lined the table and cameramen flanked the back wall and took a seat next to Rosemary Westbrook.

Although Todd knew what Craig was about to say, his heart still leapt as she announced, "The Tent Girl is indeed Barbara Taylor."

Todd heard Rosemary suck in a quick breath. He saw her eyes, searching out her sisters' faces across the room, well with tears. He felt like crying himself. "It was such an emotional moment for us all," Todd wrote later. "Relief, sadness, success."

Rosemary Westbrook's honey-smooth voice turned wistful, sitting with Putt, Todd, and me as she flipped the pages of the Bobbie book. Family snapshots showed Bobbie at a half dozen ages between five and fourteen, wearing jumpers, light-colored blouses with round collars, hair secured with a plastic clip above her right temple.

There was Bobbie standing soldier-straight among classmates in elementary school, Bobbie sitting at a kitchen table in front of a birthday cake. Her wavy dark hair was cut short, then worn longer, skimming the back of her neck and the tops of her thin shoulders.

In each photo the same shy smile played on her lips, always closed, perhaps to hide the slender gap between her front teeth. "All of us girls have splits in our teeth," Rosemary said. A 1956 photo showed a thirteen-year-old Bobbie, already a beauty with delicate features, high cheekbones, perfect eyebrows, and a wide, sensuous mouth. In later pictures, Bobbie posed with her son, Sonny, and stepdaughter, Bonnie. There was a photo of Bobbie from 1967, the year she went missing, looking more mature but still sweetly girlish. It wasn't hard to imagine how the initial autopsy declared her a teenager rather than a twenty-four-year-old woman.

As we turned the pages, Rosemary related the details of her sister's death as if she were narrating an episode of *CSI,* telling me, "They did find a blow to the back of her head and found broken fingernails, so she wasn't dead when they stuffed her in there. For five and a quarter months, she was inside that bag. She froze in the winter.

"They picked up my sister after being in that bag," Rosemary was saying matter-of-factly, leafing through the album as if looking for something.

"Surely you're not going to show it to her?" Putt exclaimed from his easy chair across the room. He must have guessed what she had arrived at.

"Sure, I'm going to show it to her," Rosemary said calmly. Turning to me, she said, "I'm going to show you what they did for me."

"She may be like me! You may ruin her supper!" Putt protested.

Rosemary ignored him. "This is what my sister looked like when they picked her up," she said, handing me the photo that made my stomach lurch and my throat tighten every time I saw it. It was the one taken at the autopsy, with half of Bobbie's face eaten away. Her eyeballs bulged, her teeth were bared in that gruesomely coy grin. Her scalp was stiff and blackened by decay. It was the image that materialized in Todd Matthews's nightmare years before a reporter pulled it out and showed it to him in his kitchen.

"And they still picked her up," Rosemary was saying. "They didn't know who she was. They did what they had to do for her. Not only for her, but for us, too."

"They" were the deputy coroner, the deputy sheriff, and others who had been called to the scene the day Wilbur Riddle had stumbled upon Bobbie Ann. "They" had cut open the green tarp. "They" had swatted away the swarming insects and brushed aside the wriggling maggots. "They" had uncurled the doubled-over figure of the young woman, laid her on a stretcher, and slid the stretcher into an ambulance. To Rosemary, these were acts of generosity and selflessness. Acts that she feels compelled to pay forward.

The discovery of her sister's body wrapped in a canvas tent eventually led Rosemary to what many might consider an unusual choice of volunteer work — as assistant coroner of Arkansas's Saline County.

Her first coroner call was to a wooded area where a small private plane containing a family of six had crashed after takeoff from Hot Springs.

Rosemary saw a little girl, age eleven or twelve, who looked like someone had laid her out on a log, her hands on her belly, her head missing. She found the pilot still in his seat, smoldering in the wreckage. It was a long, difficult night, but Rosemary stuck with it until they recovered every piece of every one of the bodies, and she continues to attend to victims whenever she's needed. It's her way of giving back.

The young man calling himself George Earl Taylor had left the U.S. Army under dubious circumstances. Early 1962 marked America's first combat missions against the Vietcong. Perhaps he didn't relish the idea of being shipped overseas. Around the time he went AWOL, a fire conveniently destroyed Army records containing the names of dozens of enlistees, Taylor's among them.

Taylor may not even have been legally free to marry in August 1963. It would come to light that in addition to Bonnie and the two children he had had with Bobbie Ann while they were married, Taylor had fathered at least ten more children with nine women between 1958 and his death in 1987. As an adult, Bonnie posted notices on Ancestry-.com message boards searching for half brothers and half sisters in the states Taylor frequented: Ohio, New York, Arkansas, Florida.

It was a pattern, Rosemary told me, that became apparent when pieces of the puzzle of Bobbie Ann's last four years started to fall into place. Earl would take one child with him — one time, he even took a boy who was not his biological son — and move to a new city. The child's mother had left them, he'd say. Run off with another man.

He played the single dad, alone with a kid, in need of the kind of help a young woman might provide, she said. A sympathy ploy if you ever saw one.

Why hadn't Bobbie Ann's husband reported her missing? Rosemary's guardians, the Rules — Bobbie's aunt and uncle — recalled Taylor as mean and impulsive, even violent. Wilbur Riddle had found the body not far from I-75, the highway leading from

Lexington, Kentucky, to Ohio, where Taylor's family lived. The canvas that Bobbie was wrapped in resembled the kind used to store a carnival's rolled-up tents.

If Bobbie had been identified soon after Riddle found her, Taylor would likely have been questioned. Three decades later, almost everyone who might have been able to shed light on the events of late 1967 and early 1968 is dead. In one of her works of fiction, mystery author Kate Atkinson described a missing girl as "an incorporeal mystery, a question without an answer. A puzzle that could tease you until you went mad." Even with a body and a name, Tent Girl and the story of her last moments are maddeningly unknowable.

Todd, in his outreach for NamUs, sometimes asks Rosemary Westbrook to place a phone call to a stranger, someone missing a family member. The stranger is often poised for an answer that will extinguish years of hope. Rosemary always relays that even though she was sad to learn her sister was dead, a lot of good came of it. The more she and Todd Matthews share their story, she tells the stranger, the greater the chance that they will give someone the strength to search for a missing loved one.

Rosemary's real purpose in becoming deputy coroner of Saline County is opportunities like these to talk to the living. Having been through her sister's death, she felt she knows what families are going through. She knows how much it meant to her that strangers had picked up her sister's body in its horrific state and treated it with respect. Rosemary figures that if those men could go out in a field and pick up her sister in an advanced state of decomposition, she could do the same for somebody else. She never hesitated to do it, she told me, "not one little iota at all."

Her words reminded me of Mike Murphy and Rick Jones in Vegas, who considered themselves privileged to talk to family members at what had to be the worst moments of their lives. They reminded me of Marcella Fierro, asking the unidentified dead on her autopsy tables for their stories. They reminded me of Clyde Gibbs, Bobby Lingoes, Ellen Leach, Betty Brown, and everyone else I had met whose words and actions demonstrated the formidable depth of their compassion.

I looked at Rosemary, fierce and plaintive, sitting on the couch, clutching the Bobbie book on her lap.

"Everybody needs to go home," she said doggedly. "Everybody needs to go home."

# EPILOGUE

The web sleuths are all around you. Your coworker with the bowl of saltwater taffy on her desk, the guy who swipes your card for a latte, the high school teacher who kept that ball python in the glass tank: any one of them and thousands of others might be one click away from solving a cold case in your hometown — or anywhere in the world. Anyone can join the skeleton crew. In fact, as soon as you put down this book, go straight to your computer, Google "NamUs," sign up as a public user for both the missing-and unidentified-persons databases, and start sleuthing. You'll be a cyber–Sherlock before you know it.

But beware.

As web sleuths and many of us know, communicating online is risky under the best of circumstances. Psychologist John Suler contends that computer-only dialogue can be rife with misinterpretation. Lacking auditory and visual cues, the tone of an e-mail, blog, or newsgroup post is often ambiguous. Those reading a message can project — sometimes unconsciously — their own expectations, wishes, anxieties, and fears onto the writer.

To make matters worse, web sleuths sometimes compete for recognition from law enforcement. That recognition is often slow in coming, or nonexistent, because of the unspoken implication that civilians are pointing out something law enforcement should have picked up on.

Forensic anthropologist Emily Craig once compared the search for matches to a gold rush. When people first sought to duplicate Todd's success with Tent Girl, the Internet was like an untapped mine of data. People found nuggets everywhere and staked out their own territories. It was — and still is — difficult for many prospectors to give that up.

The federal government's entrée into the online world of the missing and unidentified was another game changer.

In 2005, the National Institute of Justice, the research arm of the U.S. Department of Justice, convened a strategy session in Philadelphia of federal, state, and local law enforcement, medical examiners and coroners, forensic scientists, policy makers, victims' advocates, and families of the missing. This national task force determined what medical examiner Marcella Fierro had pointed out almost three decades earlier: agencies that worked on these cases needed a uniform means of information-sharing. NamUs, the National Missing and Unidentified Persons System, came online in 2007, the first system open not just to criminal justice professionals but also to the general public.

But many web sleuths were loath to share their hard-won information with NamUs. When NamUs hired Todd Matthews as an administrator, he traded his factory job for a government paycheck and his double-wide trailer decked out in nylon flowers and gold cherubs for a custom-built house with French doors and cathedral ceilings. Rare phone calls from small-town newspapers morphed into requests to appear on *Good Morning America* and to consult for TV shows.

To a contingent of web sleuths, Todd had become a sellout, a traitor.

Todd had bumped up against the widespread belief that doing good for financial gain was not as pure as doing good for its own sake. Todd himself could see how his new situation was jealousy making, how his good fortune seemed built on the backs of others' misfortunes.

In April 2011, the Doe Network voted to kick him out.

On the phone to me, Todd fretted about the charges against him — breach of confidentiality and failure to uphold administrative standards — that ostensibly stemmed from remarks he had made at a forensics workshop a year earlier. But he was convinced his real crime was working for NamUs.

After witnessing months of web sleuth feuding and backstabbing, I shouldn't have been surprised that Todd had become a target in a Doe Network firefight. Or was he the instigator? I don't get it, I told him. Wasn't he the celebrated solver of Tent Girl? Hadn't he been with the Doe Network since the beginning, helping it grow and gain national recognition? Hadn't he courted financial ruin and divorce through his dedication to the cause? Wasn't he the public face of the Doe Network?

"You never think people following you will turn around and crucify you," he told me ruefully. "But they will."

In April 2010, Todd was an invited speaker

at a meeting of law enforcement and forensic specialists in Fort Lauderdale. Wearing both his NamUs and Doe Network hats, he advised cops that volunteer organizations could help them investigate missing persons and unidentified cases — if the cops knew how to work with the volunteers.

The Doe Network tried to vet its members, Todd was saying to the cops, coroners, and medical examiners. "It's not easy. It's actually been called 'Doe nut-work' before, because I guarantee you, I've heard from every lunatic in the world. You have to sift through these people very carefully."

Months later, the North Carolina web sleuth with the uncanny visual memory — Daphne Owings, Doe's prolific matchmaker, who got involved partly to take her mind off her husband's tour of duty in Iraq — came across a recording posted online of Todd's talk.

At one point in his presentation Todd spotted conference attendee Clyde Gibbs, the zombie fan/death investigator from the North Carolina Office of the Chief Medical Examiner. Gibbs interacts with "quite a colorful volunteer," Todd said into the microphone. "I think she's the chief medical examiner there [in North Carolina], or she thinks she is . . ."

As a former Doe area director and administrative team member, Daphne Owings had been in touch with Clyde Gibbs on many occasions. Todd hadn't exactly named her, but if he tried to claim he wasn't talking about her, that was bullshit, Daphne told me later. To say she was irked by his remarks would be an understatement. To make matters worse, she believed she heard Todd refer to Doe volunteers as "lunatics" and urge cops to use NamUs instead of Doe.

Daphne wasn't swayed by Todd's conciliatory comment a few seconds later about how her "heart was in the right place" and how Doe Network volunteers were working to change things for the better. Daphne wanted to change things, all right. She wanted to see that pompous twerp Todd Matthews put in his place.

She filed a complaint with Doe administrators. The board, still led at that time by Helene Wahlstrom, advised Todd to resign quietly, citing his increased responsibilities with NamUs as his reason for bowing out. Todd refused. Armed with assurances from supporters that he hadn't in fact maligned the Doe Network at the workshop, Todd asked the board to let the matter drop.

As the Doe Network's Webmaster, Wahlstrom, though she lived in Sweden, had considered herself owner of the site since Jennifer "Stormy" Marra bequeathed it to her in 2001. For a decade Wahlstrom had worked almost constantly, she told me, entering cases into the Doe database, writing up case files, answering e-mails, forwarding tips to law enforcement. Fluency in ten languages enabled her to translate cases of European missing and unidentified individuals into English.

Wahlstrom called for a vote by the administrative board. It was four-to-two against Todd. Defeated, in April 2011 he resigned from the Doe Network.

A couple of months later, I met Todd in the Atlanta airport, where he was en route to a law enforcement conference. He flopped onto a plastic seat next to me in the Delta terminal. He had decided to take back the website, he announced.

It so happened — through an oversight or malevolence on Todd's part, depending on whom you ask — that the Doe Network domain was in Todd's name. (Wahlstrom acknowledged that Todd paid the annual fees but said she bought the domain name, doenetwork.org, in around 2000. The late Patrick Harkness, whose plea for help finding his missing cousin Sean Lewis Cutler led Carol Cielecki to the Doe Network, has also been credited with hosting the site during its early years.)

The next day, in between setting up a NamUs booth and driving with me to meet Tent Girl's sister near Little Rock, Todd called the service provider. As suspected, the board had blocked his access to the site in the wake of his resignation, but he convinced the domain provider he was the site's owner and received a new password — which was simultaneously routed to a second e-mail address belonging to a member of the board that had ousted him. Before Todd knew what was happening, the person had logged in and reset the password, shutting him out again.

Todd kicked himself. His enemies had beaten him at the game of revolving passwords, removed his name from the account, and put theirs on. But the domain provider again restored Todd's access, and this time he quickly orchestrated a complete change of guard. The new board, which includes Todd as head of media, public, and business relations, consists of his most loyal long-term supporters.

During a week in May 2011, behind the scenes at the Doe Network, computer-savvy members worked to restore data trashed by some members of the previous board. Users who happened to sign in during that time saw little evidence that the Doe Network had just undergone a major coup.

For Wahlstrom, the loss of the website was a terrible blow. She said she had founded and worked for the organization for more than twelve years. At one time, her ambition was to grow the group to "the size and fame" of human rights organization Amnesty International. The work gave her purpose and helped her grow as a person, she wrote to me in an e-mail. It gave her a feeling of contributing to the world. It helped her recognize her strengths.

Wahlstrom was blindsided by what she saw as Todd's perfidy. She had believed the group altruistic, yet one person — Todd — ruined everything with his struggle for power, or recognition, or something else she didn't understand.

A year after Todd laid claim to the Doe Network, Wahlstrom still didn't trust her emotions enough to speak to me on the phone. But she e-mailed me that she did want the truth to be known.

"This is very painful for me, and something I'm still trying to come to terms with . . . [A]t this time it is hard for me to take pride in [my work on the Doe Network] or even consider it a good thing. I hope I will again, one day. Right now," she wrote, "I am just sad."

In the fifteen years since Todd solved Tent Girl, web sleuthing has set in motion an ongoing coup of its own by transforming law enforcement's relationship with the public. As Robert McCrie, a police science professor at New York's John Jay College of Criminal Justice, put it, law enforcement's too important to be left to the police alone. The Internet age has extended the ability of the public to help out with investigations, which some — pointing to the aftermath of the social media and entertainment site Reddit's 2013 misindentification of Boston Marathon bombing suspects — would argue is a mixed bag.

Law enforcement in America has always been a highly structured, authoritarian bureaucracy, but before the invention of the automobile, telephone, and two-way radio, the old-fashioned beat cop was a neighborhood fixture. In the 1980s, so-called team policing and community policing initiatives sought to resurrect the foot cop to make police more visible, available, and accountable. Community policing was a dismal failure. No one could agree on what it meant, and no one came up with a consistent way to evaluate whether or not it was working. But it paved the way for a middle ground.

Ralph Taylor, a professor of criminal justice at Temple University, said Internet groups such as the Doe Network are "digital-age throwbacks" to community policing and neighborhood watches. Web sleuths and missing-person advocates, by broaching what was once police-only territory, helped the shift — still in progress — toward citizens and cops working together more cooperatively than defensively. "The advocate is a tide washing in onto the shore," says a San Bernardino County, California, coroner's office death investigator who has worked with cops for decades. "That tide changes the shape of the land. It doesn't do it one wave at a time. It does it over years."

One former cop is hopeful. George Adams, a Forth Worth police officer turned Center for Human Identification program manager, works with Todd Matthews, the volunteer community, and law enforcement to collect and analyze DNA for inclusion in NamUs databases. Proposed legislation such as Billy's Law, working its way through Congress, would secure long-term funding for NamUs, streamline the reporting process for law enforcement and medical examiners by connecting NamUs to NCIC, and provide incentive grants to help coroners, medical examiners, and law enforcement agencies train others to add missing persons and unidentified remains details to the federal databases. Adams envisions web sleuths in the not-too-distant future sitting side-by-side with law enforcement at local police stations, entering cold cases into NamUs, tracking down dental records and DNA, and paving the way for future matches.

A cop can't work missing and unidentified cases in a vacuum, Adams told me. Sharing knowledge would make law enforcement far more powerful in bringing the national glut of unidentified remains to an end.

After the coup, the new Doe Network administrative board of Todd's supporters, plus others who had resigned in disgust over the previous board's drama, mounted a prominent banner on the home page. It read: "Celebrating more than ten years of volunteer efforts."

"I'm not who I should be," Todd insisted the first time I called him, out of the blue, asking about the Doe Network. "I shouldn't be here." Even now, he is convinced he's living an alien life, one he would never have encountered if, as he put it, the cyber-universe hadn't crashed into him. Although I came to appreciate early on just how insightful, funny, and formidably intelligent Todd is, it took me more than two years to finally have an inkling of what he means by "who I should be."

Although he still doesn't have a college degree, Todd has broken free of the rock wall of Appalachians surrounding Livingston, Tennessee. No longer a factory worker or a trailer dweller, Todd is a different person these days, even though he still lives within a hundred yards of his childhood home and still sports the same hairdo he had in high school.

His white-collar profession requires him to travel around the country regularly (his mother is still terrified every time he gets on a plane); he owns the first two-story brick house with architectural details in a neighborhood of small clapboard ranches and trailer homes; and he is the subject of a TV show, a documentary, dozens of newspaper and magazine articles, and now, a book.

He's considered moving to somewhere more connected to the twenty-first century,

website http://www.vidocq.org/.

**Matthew J. Hickman's first cubicle:** The sequence of events of the Bureau of Justice Statistics investigation of unidentified remains from author interview with Matthew J. Hickman.

**"coroners would . . . be worried":** Kevin B. O'Reilly, "Elected Coroners Report Fewer Suicides Than Appointed Counterparts," admed.news.com, posted Sept. 6, 2011: http://www.amednews.com/article/20110906/profession/309069996/8/.

**partly because of a woman named Cheri Nolan:** Author interview with Cheri Nolan.

**As of 2013 . . . eighteen of those proven innocent:** The Innocence Project, http://www.innocenceproject.org/Content/DNA_Exonerations_Nationwide .php.

**Daniel M. Lewin . . . a former member of the Israel Defense Forces' Sayaret Matkal:** Richard Sisk & Monique el-Faizy, "Ex–Israeli Commando Tried to Halt Unfolding Hijacking," *New York Daily News,* July 24, 2004.

**maverick biotech entrepreneur J. Craig Venter:** Nicholas Wade, "In the Genome Race, the Sequel Is Personal," *The New York Times,* September 4, 2007.

**Dr. Randy Hanzlick, the outspoken chief medical examiner:** Dave Hansen, "ID'ing John Doe: There Are New Ways to Determine Identities of Unknown Dead Victims," July 6, 2007, http://project jason.org/forums/topic/683-federal-government-assistance-for-cases-of-missing-and-unidentified-persons/.

**The phrase "silent mass disaster":** Nancy Ritter, "Missing Persons and Unidentified Remains: The Nation's Silent Mass Disaster."

## Chapter 6
## Inside Reefer 2

**Murphy became the public face:** The history of Las Vegas Unidentified and Jane Arroyo Grande Doe gleaned from author interviews with P. Michael Murphy and Rick Jones, and newspaper coverage such as Steve Friess, "To Identify 'John Doe' Victims, Investigators Turn to the Web," *The Boston Globe,* Jan. 25, 2004, and Office of the Coroner CCCO: 80-1221, "Las Vegas Unidentified: Jane Arroyo Grande' Doe."

**through the Integrated Automated Fingerprint Identification:** Federal Bureau of Investigation Integrated Automated

Fingerprint Identification System, http://
www.fbi.gov/about-us/cjis/fingerprints_
biometrics/iafis/iafis.

**Abigail Goldman wrote in the *Las Vegas Sun:*** Abigail Goldman, "Cold Cases Go Online, with Respect for Victims," *Las Vegas Sun,* Feb. 10, 2008.

**Antietam photographs were exhibited in New York City:** McNamara, Robert, "Alexander Gardner's Photographs of Antietam," About.com 19th Century History, http://history1800s.about.com/od/civilwar/ig/Antietam-Photographs/Unburied-Confederate.htm.

**Reefer 2 was crowded in 2003:** Official City of Las Vegas website: http://www.lasvegasnevada.gov/factsstatistics/history.htm.

**Imagine standing at the finish line of the Boston Marathon:** Elizabeth A. Thomson, "MIT Team Reports New Insights in Visual Recognition," MIT News Office, April 1, 2004.

## Chapter 7
## The Perks of Being Ornery

**For Betty, it all started:** Author interview with Betty Dalton Brown.

**The couple had a son they named Seif:**

Paul Garber, "Gone, Not Forgotten," *Winston-Salem Journal,* Feb. 13, 2011.

**In 1998, a Phoenix man committed suicide:** Author interviews with Stuart Somershoe and Shannon Vita; case details archived on Websleuths, http://www.web sleuths.com/forums/archive/index.php/t-92478.html.

**Sanchez's sisters, in their seventies and eighties, never knew:** Joline Gutierrez Krueger, "Missing Brother Mystery Resolved After 42 Years," *Albuquerque Journal,* April 11, 2011, http://www.abqjournal .com/upfront/112254587695upfront04-11-11.htm.

## Chapter 8
## Seekers of Lost Souls

**I had worked with Liles:** Author interview with George Liles.

**a DNA test showed definitively she was not the victim in the dunes:** Kay Lazar, "Dune Slay Victim a Mystery Once More," *Boston Herald,* March 5, 2002.

**Daphne Owings, the most prolific:** Author interview with Daphne Owings.

**a twenty-five-year-old night shift worker:** Author interviews with Todd Matthews.

**Detective R. Allen Cheek hadn't divulged:** Author interview with R. Allen Cheek.

**Forensic sculptor Frank Bender:** Ted Botha, *The Girl with the Crooked Nose: A Tale of Murder, Obsession, and Forensic Artistry* (New York: Random House, 2008).

**Mark Christopher Poe, an ex-sailor:** Joseph Cosco, "Poe Guilty of Murder; He Could Get Life in Prison Without Parole," *Virginian-Pilot,* March 9, 1994, p. D1.

**the coroner identified Jasmine Fiore:** Brian Palmer, "What Can You Learn from a Fake Breast? The Secrets of a Silicone Serial Number." Slate, posted Aug. 24, 2009; Alfonsi, Sharyn, Cole Kazdin, and Lindsay Goldwert, "How Forensics Revealed Jasmine Fiore's Identity," ABC News, Aug. 25, 2009.

**Hold the skull in profile:** Dr. Bill Bass and Jon Jefferson, *Beyond the Body Farm: A Legendary Bone Detective Explores Murders, Mysteries, and the Revolution in Forensic Science* (New York: William Morrow, 2008).

**University of Wisconsin–Madison anthropologist John Hawks:** John Hawks

Weblog: "Paleoanthropology, Genetics and Evolution: Cranial Features and Race," Nov. 27, 2011, http://johnhawks .net/explainer/laboratory/race-cranium.

**One of three centers in the state:** Author interview with Clyde Gibbs Jr.

## Chapter 10
## Finding Bobbie Ann

**five hundred miles away, Rosemary Westbrook:** Author interviews with Rosemary and Mark Westbrook and Todd and Lori Matthews, and reporting by David Kohn for the CBS News show *48 Hours,* which aired a feature on the case April 30, 1998. Most of the material for this chapter was provided by http://www.cbsnews.com/ 8301-18559_162-8314.html.

**Almost fourteen inches of rain:** Teri Maddox, "Flood of 1957: Richland Creek Swallowed Downtown Belleville," *Belleville News-Democrat,* posted April 19, 2008.

**Since the 1920s, families:** Dramatic film footage of the fire can be found on the St. Louis County, Missouri, Parks and Recreation Web site, http://www.stlouisco.com/ ParksandRecreation/ChildrensFun/ StLouisCarouselat-FaustPark.

**Taylor returned and piled the sleepy children:** C. S. Murphy, "Long Time Gone: Modern Tools, Hope for Old Cases," *Arkansas Online*, Oct. 26, 2009.

## Chapter 11
## Quackie Is Dead

**Bobby Lingoes sat typing at a computer terminal:** Author interviews with Bobby Lingoes.

**AAU national finals alongside eighteen-year-old, 158-pound Marvin Hagler:** William Plummer, "Marvin Hagler Is Out to Prove Just How 'Marvelous' He Is in His Bout with Roberto Duran," *People* magazine archive, vol. 20, no. 20, Nov. 14, 1983, http://www.people.com/people/archive/article/0,,20086386,00.html.

**"The best kid anyone could ever lose":** Dennis Tatz, "Stabbing Death Shocks Teen's Friends," *Quincy Patriot Ledger,* Aug. 1, 1988.

**For weeks, G-town mourned Quackie Lingoes:** Among the newspaper accounts that contributed to this section are "Germantown Remembers 'Quackie,'" *Quincy Patriot Ledger,* Aug. 2, 1988, p. 1; and Robert Sears, "Robert Lingoes Praised as a Giving Person," *Quincy Patriot Ledger,*

Aug. 4, 1988.

**The FBI's Criminal Justice Information Services Division's:** The FBI's website describes the Criminal Justice Information Services Division on http://www.fbi.gov/about-us/cjis.

**According to a 2009 National Research Council committee report:** *Strengthening Forensic Science in the United States: A Path Forward* (Washington, D.C.: National Academies Press, 2009).

**"The NCIC protocol was lovely":** Author interview with Marcella Fierro.

**Police didn't always give families:** "Missing Person File: Data Collection Entry Guide," U.S. Department of Justice, Federal Bureau of Investigation, National Crime Information Center, revised Nov. 2008.

**Harry E. Carlile Jr., who had taught:** Presentation by Harry E. Carlile Jr. at the Missing and Unidentified Persons Workshop, Virginia Beach, Virginia, Sept. 30, 2010.

**churns through gigabytes of data seeking to match:** "What Is a $.M. Notification?" Federal Bureau of Investigation, National Crime Information Center (NCIC) Cross-Match Reference Card.

**Gary L. Bell, one of the trained foren-**

**sic:** G. L. Bell, "Testing of the National Crime Information Center Missing/ Unidentified Persons Computer Comparison Routine," *Journal of Forensic Sciences,* JFSCA, vol. 38, no. 1, Jan. 1993, pp. 13–22.

**the family of a Richmond, Virginia, runaway:** Author interview with Daphne Owings.

**if medical examiners could even get access:** W. D. Haglund, "The National Crime Information Center (NCIC) Missing and Unidentified Persons System Revisited," *Journal of Forensic Sciences,* JFSCA, vol. 38, no. 2, March 1993, pp. 365–78.

**in the aftermath of the 1995 Oklahoma City bombing:** "When Off-Line Is Better: Another Way to Search Crime Records," Federal Bureau of Investigation news stories, Jan. 4, 2010, http://www .fbi.gov/news/stories/2010/january/ ncic_010410.

**a Jane Doe who had turned up near Waco:** Helen O'Neill, " 'Doe Network' Restores Names to the Missing Dead," Associated Press, April 13, 2008.

**unidentified skeletal remains that had been discovered:** Author interviews with Sheree Greenwood, Bobby Lingoes, and

Vicki Siedow provided the timeline and details of the Brenda Wright case.

**A 2008 TV show featured the case:** Female Legal and Investigative Professionals (FLIP) founder Vicki Siedow appears in the premier episode of Women's Entertainment Network's program "F.L.I.P. Mysteries: Women on the Case," air date Aug. 6, 2008.

**the body was that of Peter Kokinakis:** Associated Press, "Amateur Detectives Help Solve Hard to Crack Cases," Feb. 2004.

**In 2003, a ten-year-old boy rounding up cattle:** Afsha Bawany, "Computer Sleuths Solve Vegas Man's Mystery," *Las Vegas Sun,* Sept. 11, 2003.

**This John Doe was a big guy:** The Doe Network Case File 799UMON, "Unidentified male, discovered June 28, 1991, in the Niagara River, Niagara Falls, Ontario, Canada."

**a statuesque blonde:** The Doe Network Case File 81UFAR, "Unidentified white female located July 10, 1991, in El Dorado, Union County, Arkansas."

**earned him the nickname "Bones Man":** Noah Shachtman, "Face on a Milk Carton? Amateur Sleuths Dig

Deeper," *The New York Times,* Jan. 1, 2004.

**gone missing from his home in northern Italy:** Robert Sears, "Dot-cop: Civilian Uses Internet to Investigate Missing Persons Cases," *Quincy Patriot Ledger,* March 26, 2002.

## Chapter 12
## The Head in the Bucket

**retired trucker Ronald Telfer:** Dozens of comprehensive news reports from 2001 to 2006 by Mary Nevans-Pederson, Becky Sisco, Emily Klein, M. D. Kittle, and other unnamed staff writers for the *Dubuque Telegraph Herald* and the Associated Press provided the details on the discovery of the remains, the arrest and trial of Douglas DeBruin, and the prosecution for perjury of Julie Ann Miller.

**Jan Buman and her boyfriend, Gregory May:** Author interview with Jan Buman.

**Ellen planned to show me around:** Author interviews with Ellen Leach and Keith Glass, as well as Kathie Farnell's "Gulfport Sleuth Helps Identify Missing," in *DeSoto* magazine, April 2008, provided background for this chapter.

**a skull found at a Missouri truck stop:**

Among the sources for this chapter are Frank Bender and Paul Plevakas, "The Head in the Bucket: The Murder of Greg May," *Vidocq Society Journal,* vol. 18, no. 1, Winter 2007, pp. 1, 4, 5; Daniel Schorn, "The Girl Next Door: Will Forensic Reconstruction Help ID Nameless Murder Victim?" *48 Hours/Mystery,* CBS News, air date Jan. 7, 2006; *Investigation Discovery: Extreme Forensics,* Season 2, Episode 6, "Road Trip Killers," original air date May 24, 2010; Ted Botha, *The Girl with the Crooked Nose: A Tale of Murder, Obsession, and Forensic Artistry* (New York: Random House, 2008); as well as author interviews with Gary Chilcote, Tom O'Leary, and Don May.

**May moved between two worlds:** Stephanie Simon, "In Small Town of Bellevue, Iowa, a Stranger Isn't Missed," *Los Angeles Times,* July 17, 2001.

**Kies wrote to her:** Letter from John L. Kies to Ellen Leach, dated Oct. 25, 2005, courtesy of Ellen Leach.

## Chapter 13
## The Hippie and the Lawman

**remembered her as an out-of-control teenager:** Jonathan Silver, "After 27

Years, Girl's Cold Case Becomes a Homicide," *Pittsburgh Post-Gazette,* Dec. 13, 2007.

**son of the late "man hunter" Cecil Wingo:** Breck Porter, "Houston Loses Cecil Wingo, Dr. Joe's Longtime Running Mate," *Badge & Gun,* Houston Police Officers Union, Feb. 2009, http://www.hpou .org/badgeandgun/index.cfm?fuseaction= view_news&NewsID=519.

**Gault had traveled to Texas from Ohio:** Author interview with Kristy Gault.

**In his heyday as a detective:** Matt Wingo, as told to "Serial Killers, Drug Lords, Murder . . . Bodies: The Memoirs of a Cop," *Police News,* Gulf Coast Edition, vol. 4, no. 8, Aug. 2007.

**Gault revealed she was working:** Gault's e-book, *Unsolved in America,* became available on Amazon.com in Feb. 2013.

**the bizarre case of Florida death row inmate:** Matt Birkbeck, *A Beautiful Child: A True Story of Hope, Horror and an Enduring Human Spirit* (New York: Berkley, 2004).

**hosted a funeral service for a headless:** S. K. Bardwell, "Chief ME, 'Dr. Joe,' Known for Patience, Dies," *Houston Chronicle,* Dec. 8, 2004, http://www.chron .com/news/houston-texas/article/Deaths-

Chief-ME-Dr-Joe-known-forpatience-1512992.php.

**the only web-sleuthing crime:** Author phone call with Matt Wingo.

**an OCCI member called Suzannec4444:** Much of the discussion can be found on the Websleuths thread on Tammy Lynn Leppert (started in July 2004 and by late 2012 comprised of twenty-one pages of posts) by user "Ms Suzanne," who identifies herself as "Sister of missing Tammy Lynn Leppert": http://www.websleuths.com/forums/showthread.php?t=34183. Lauran Halleck also posts on this thread as "monkalup"; plus a separate, archived portion of a contentious Suzanne-Tammy thread can be found on derkeiler.com, a newsgroup and mailing list archive: http://newsgroups.derkeiler.com/Archive/Alt/alt.true-crime/2008-06/msg01620.html.

**Their mutual animosity:** 07020 Edgewater (New Jersey) website, "Jean Marie Stewart," forums, Of Interest, General Discussion; "Jean Marie, updates and thoughts," July 2008: http://www.07020.com/forums/index.php.

**A Florida volunteer who sought:** Dinorah Perry, then head of the Pembroke Pines–based Missing Children International Ministries.

**Jean Marie's brother held out the hope:** Jonathan Silver, "Victim's Funeral Is Closure for Family: Brookline Girl, 16, Vanished in 1980," *Pittsburgh Post-Gazette,* March 25, 2008.

**A Pittsburgh TV station reported that her death:** "Family Bids Farewell 28 Years After Teen's Death," Pittsburgh TV station KDKA, July 10, 2008.

**A newspaper article said Jean Marie's father:** Ibid.

**Other reports referred to a gunshot:** Dinorah Perry, Florida missing-persons advocate, wrote on a forum that Jean Marie's skull had bullet holes: http://www.topix.com/forum/city/cooper-city-fl/T8AAKDQ4TU0VRJTFF.

**a "bullet in the skull":** Jerome Burdi, "Unidentified Bodies in South Florida to Be Exhumed for DNA Testing," *Sun Sentinel,* Feb. 11, 2010: http://articles.sun-sentinel.com/2010-02-11/news/fl-missing-bodies-exhume-20100211_1_dna-testing-gregory-vondell-andrews-national-dna-database.

**He was curious about Stewart's murder:** See this contentious 2008–2009 thread on the 07020 forum "Jean Marie, Updates and Thoughts . . ." in which Matt Wingo (as abcman) describes Lauran

Halleck's alleged hack of OCCI; Kristy Gault's 2008 banishment of Halleck and his reactions to Jean-Marie Stewart identification and homicide case, with copies of posts he had made as texasx on OCCI; and Halleck's possibly responding as "barney5" and "mquizical": http://www.07020.com/forums/archive/index.php/t-5712.html.

**a victim of "Beauty Queen Killer" Christopher Wilder:** Michael Newton, *The Encyclopedia of Serial Killers* (New York: Checkmark, 2000).

## Chapter 14
## The Oldest Unsolved Case in Massachusetts

**Serial killer Hadden Clark:** Alec Wilkinson, "A Hole in the Ground: Was There a Cape Cod Serial Killer?" *The New Yorker,* Sept. 4, 2000.

**Meads died suddenly on Christmas 2011:** "Former Provincetown Police Chief James Meads Dies at 78," *Provincetown Banner,* Dec. 2011.

**his fabled history and reputation:** Thomas J. Foley, *Most Wanted: Pursuing Whitey Bulger, the Murderous Mob Chief the*

*FBI Secretly Protected* (New York: Touchstone, 2012).

## Chapter 15
## Relief, Sadness, Success

**neither Craig nor Todd knew:** Author interviews with Emily Craig.

**Craig herself climbed down into the hole:** Emily Craig, PhD, *Teasing Secrets from the Dead: My Investigations at America's Most Infamous Crime Scenes* (New York: Broadway Books, 2005).

**"The Tent Girl is indeed Barbara Taylor":** Charles Wolfe, " 'Tent Girl' Homicide Victim Identified Through DNA test," AP Online, April 23, 1998.

**described a missing girl as "an incorporeal mystery":** Kate Atkinson, *Case Histories* (New York: Little, Brown and Co., 2004) p. 116.

## Epilogue

**computer-only dialogue can be rife with misinterpretation:** John Suler, "The Basic Psychological Features of Cyberspace," *The Psychology of Cyberspace,* www.rider.edu/suler/psycyber/basicfeat .html (article originally published 1996).

**convened a strategy session in Philadel-phia:** For the history of NamUs, see http://www.namus.gov/about.htm.

**remarks he had made at a forensics workshop:** University of North Texas Center for Human Identification Forensic Science Training Workshop, "Utilization of Volunteer Organizations in the Investigation of Missing Persons and Unidentified Remains Cases," audio recording, April 19, 2010, http://www.cedata.org/cd/HID2010FL/index.html.

**For a decade Wahlstrom had worked almost constantly:** Author e-mail exchanges with Helene Wahlstrom.

**her ambition was to grow the group:** Angela Ellis, "Doe Network Member Profiles: Helene Wahlstrom," December 5, 2003 http://www.doenetwork.bravepages.com/profiles/HWalstrom.html.

**law enforcement's too important to be left to the police:** Noah Shachtman, "Face on a Milk Carton? Amateur Sleuths Dig Deeper," *The New York Times,* Jan. 1, 2004.

**Internet groups such as the Doe Network are "digital-age throwbacks":** K. Carlson, "Cyber Sleuths: Shelley Denman's Sister Was the Private Investigator, Not Her," *National Post,* June 9, 2012,

http://www.canada.com/story.html?id=
cefc5c3c-be1a-4ea9-bc09-79c1e55d4b7f.

**"The advocate is a tide washing":** Author interview with David Van Norman, San Bernardino County Sheriff's Department, Coroner Division.

**Adams envisions web sleuths:** Author interview with George Adams.

# ABOUT THE AUTHOR

**Deborah Halber** is a Boston-based journalist whose work has appeared in *The Boston Globe; MIT Technology Review;* the interactive graphic magazine *Symbolia;* and many university publications. A native New Yorker, she received her BA from Brandeis University and an MA in journalism from New York University. After working as a general assignment reporter for weeklies and dailies in New York, Massachusetts, and New Hampshire, she became editor of Tufts University's alumni magazine and then a science writer for MIT, chronicling everything from quantum weirdness (that's the technical term) to dark matter, neuroscience, worm longevity, cell undertakers, and the properties of snail slime. A member of the American Society of Journalists and Authors, Mystery Writers of America, and the National Association of Science Writers, she lives with her family in a house in the suburbs with a lot of former pets buried out back.

The employees of Thorndike Press hope you have enjoyed this Large Print book. All our Thorndike, Wheeler, and Kennebec Large Print titles are designed for easy reading, and all our books are made to last. Other Thorndike Press Large Print books are available at your library, through selected bookstores, or directly from us.

For information about titles, please call:
  (800) 223-1244

or visit our Web site at:
  http://gale.cengage.com/thorndike

To share your comments, please write:
  Publisher
  Thorndike Press
  10 Water St., Suite 310
  Waterville, ME 04901